When Freedom Speaks

When Freedom Speaks

THE BOUNDARIES AND
BOUNDLESSNESS OF OUR
FIRST AMENDMENT
RIGHT

LYNN GREENKY

BRANDEIS UNIVERSITY PRESS

Waltham, Massachusetts

Brandeis University Press
© 2022 by Lynn Levine Greenky
All rights reserved

Manufactured in the United States of America
Designed by Richard Hendel
Typeset in Arnhem by Passumpsic Publishing

For permission to reproduce any of the material
in this book, contact Brandeis University Press,
415 South Street, Waltham MA 02453, or visit
brandeisuniversitypress.com

Library of Congress Cataloging-in-Publication Data
available upon request

ISBN 978-1-68458-092-7 (cloth)
ISBN 978-1-68458-093-4 (paper)
ISBN 978-1-68458-094-1 (ebook)

5 4 3 2 1

CONTENTS

ACKNOWLEDGMENTS

I am a living, breathing example of the cliché that success in life requires the stamina of a long-distance runner and not the fast-twitch muscle power of a sprinter. This book was a long time in coming. Over the years I have had the great fortune to be supported by incredible friends and family. Each of you, whether or not mentioned by name in these pages, has my profound gratitude for your embrace during every stage of my life, the celebratory and the solemn. Most particularly thank you to my children (and their children) and their spouses Zach, Brooke (Chase and Hallie), Ryan, Elizabet, Samantha, and Scott for bringing me so much joy. A very special thank you to Samantha, who spent long hours reviewing and commenting on the manuscript and employing her remarkable skills correcting and recorrecting my citations.

The journey of this book began during my days as an undergraduate at Northwestern University and then as a law student at Emory University School of Law; it culminated as a professor at Syracuse University. My deepest appreciation to the faculty and staff at Syracuse for all that they do. A singular shout-out to Dr. Amos Kiewe, who has mentored me throughout my career at the Communication and Rhetorical Studies Department.

Editors are angels draped in the fabric of grammar and words. Thank you to Evelyn Duffy, Ben Gambuzza, and Anna Fiorino at Open Boat Editing for your expert advice and guidance. Thank you also to Sue Ramin, director of the Brandeis University Press, for her belief that this book has value and for holding my nervous hand through the publication process. To the peer reviewers who helped me make these pages more interesting and more accurate, thank you. And of course, thank you to Sarah Russo and the staff at Sarah Russo Public Relations (SRPR) and their invaluable assistance with all things related to marketing and publicity.

In the theater, the starring characters are generally awarded the final bow in the performance. There is no question that honor belongs to my husband, Dr. Brett Greenky, MD. We were lucky enough to meet and fall in love during our sophomore year at college. I could not imagine a better, more encouraging partner. Thank you. I love you.

When Freedom Speaks

THE FIRST AMENDMENT

Congress shall make no law respecting an establishment of religion, or prohibiting the free exercise thereof; or abridging the freedom of speech, or of the press; or the right of the people peaceably to assemble, and to petition the government for a redress of grievances.

The freedom to speak belongs to the wealthy and influential, who celebrate their power and use their amplified voices to persuade the reluctant to follow their lead. It also belongs to the poor, the weak, the vulnerable, and the despised to buttress their protests and ensure they, too, will be heard. The constitutionally protected freedom to speak belongs to the president, to politicians, to corporate CEOs, to factory workers, and to the homeless. All of us, all of them, enjoy the embrace of the First Amendment.

First Amendment constitutional history is about real people with real lives and real families speaking their minds. Each of their experiences is described in case law. David O'Brien burned his draft card to protest the Vietnam War. Taunted and beaten, he landed in jail. His case became a preeminent story about symbolic speech—and whether all conduct intended to communicate should be sheltered by the First Amendment. Each decision by the Supreme Court about the people, the characters in the story, builds on the narrative of the First Amendment. And each narrative builds on the one before it by **constitutional** precedent (prior decisions).

The First Amendment provides protection to five freedoms. It protects the freedom of speech as well as the freedom of religion, the freedom of press, the freedom of assembly, and the right to petition the government for a redress of grievances. Each of the five freedoms deserves singular attention that can fill the pages of another book. This book's focus is on only one: the freedom of speech.

Ideas and beliefs can be verbalized, written, performed, or crafted using visual media. Expressive activities can take the form of debate, gossip, parody, entertainment, celebration, or sacrament. Whether or not ideas and their expression are granted First Amendment protection will often depend on context:

> As ugly and painful as it is, hate speech is protected by the First Amendment. But assaultive speech, often laced with hate, and intended to elicit fear or provoke a response from the target, cannot use the First Amendment as a shield.

> Contrary to popular belief, politicians and celebrities cannot easily sue and collect damages for falsehoods published about them.

> Pornography and obscenity are not the same. One is protected, the other is not.

> Undoubtedly, money speaks.

> While money may speak, sometimes people choose to remain silent, and their silence often speaks volumes. The conflict between the right to speak through silence, refusing to bake a wedding cake for a gay couple for instance, represents a new a battleground in the culture wars.

Despite the confusion and conflict, it is essential to understand that the preface to the story of the First Amendment is grounded in the steadfast belief that democracy cannot flourish without the freedom to speak; democracy cannot flourish when debate is restricted; democracy cannot flourish when the only opinions given voice are those of the prominent and the strong. And democracy cannot succeed when ideas of the weak or even the offensive are silenced. Democracy requires, and the First Amendment insists, that we tolerate speech we find vexing or disturbing and either engage in the debate or turn a deaf ear.

Liberty has never come from the government.

Liberty has always come from the subjects of the government.

The history of liberty is a history of resistance. The history of

liberty is a history of the limitation of governmental power,

not the increase of it. — Woodrow Wilson[1]

George Mason arrived at the Pennsylvania State House in Philadelphia, now known as Independence Hall, on May 17, 1787. He was sixty-two. He had traversed over 200 miles of densely forested lands and raging rivers on horseback. The weather was just beginning to forecast the oppressive heat that was to come. Like many of the men attending the Constitutional Convention, he was part of the landed gentry class.[2] Somewhat of a curmudgeon,[3] and a stickler for detail,[4] Mason was a man who showed little emotion. However, he understood the enormity of the task before him. In a letter to his son, he wrote, "The expectations and hopes of all the Union centre [*sic*] in this Convention. God grant that we may be able to concert effectual means of preserving our country from the evils which threaten us."[5]

Mason's enthusiasm was matched by his fellow Virginia delegate, James Madison, later elected as the United States' fourth president. The thirty-six-year-old Madison was the first to arrive, having reached the destination two weeks before anyone else. At five feet, three inches tall, Madison was small in physical stature. He was a scholarly sort, with an easygoing temperament, and widely reputed to be knowledgeable and creative.[6] He was heard to proclaim that the Constitutional Convention was at the precipice of deciding "forever the fate of Republican government."[7] As the convention wore on, Madison's passion grew, but Mason's diminished, and they found themselves at odds regarding the breadth and scope of the national government's power and responsibilities.

Ultimately, twelve of the thirteen newly created United States of

America were represented at the Constitutional Convention. (Rhode Island was the single state that refused to send a delegate. Fifty-five men represented the interests of the participating states.[8]) Benjamin Franklin, at eighty-one, was the oldest man to attend the convention. Jonathan Dayton of New Jersey, at twenty-seven, was the youngest.[9] The task facing the delegates was overwhelming; the stakes were enormous. As described by constitutional scholar Jeffrey Rosen: "This [was] the most radical body of democratic deliberation ever assembled."[10]

The Constitution replaced the Articles of Confederation, which had been ratified on March 1, 1781. The Articles represented a loose agreement between the states. They provided for little coordination and did little to ease friction between the states. There was no common currency, no national defense, and no secure state borders. States taxed one another for imports and transport on state-owned roads. Local insurrections were threatening an approaching anarchy. It was an untenable situation. None other than George Washington, watching events unfold from his Mount Vernon estate, called the circumstances facing the nation "an impending storm."[11]

Initially, Washington was reluctant to participate in the convention, concerned that it would be a failed effort and tarnish his legendary reputation.[12] He was ultimately convinced that his reputation would suffer more significant harm if he remained absent. He also understood that his attendance provided the convention with needed legitimacy. He arrived in Philadelphia on May 13, 1787, and was greeted by a ringing of the city's bells.[13]

The Constitutional Convention was called to order on May 25, 1787. It was a wet and windy day.[14] The first order of business was to elect George Washington as presiding officer of the convention. The decision was unanimous.[15] He took his seat in a carved wooden chair placed in the front of the room. The carving included the sun peeking over the horizon. Later, James Madison is reported to have heard Benjamin Franklin saying, "I have often looked at that picture behind the president without being able to tell whether it was rising or setting. But now at length I . . . know that it is a rising . . . sun."[16]

News that the convention was in session was well publicized; however, the debates within the walls of Independence Hall were held in secret so that the men could express themselves without fear of their deliberations being prematurely reported. The meetings were held on the upper floor of the steepled, sweltering building while flies swarmed outside. The Liberty Bell hung in the tower, a reminder of the importance of the moment. The doors and windows were closed and guarded.[17] That we are now privy to the conversations that took place in the room where it happened is due to the copious notes taken by James Madison.

Madison had spent years studying and preparing for the event, assured of its need and certain that lessons could be learned from history. He was convinced that the newly born nation needed a strong central government to hold the states subordinate. Without it, the country would continue to face confusion and instability, which he was sure would cause the American experiment to fail.[18] Madison has been alternately described as the father of the Constitution[19] and its midwife.[20] Madison's leadership and skill in crafting the body of the Constitution and then the Bill of Rights was pivotal to the ratification of both.

As the days wore on, and the heat became more oppressive, tempers flared. Looming over the debate was the singularly divisive issue of slavery. More than thirty delegates to the Constitutional Convention were slaveowners.[21] The delegates were not blind to the moral duplicity of a country born out of a quest for life and liberty, and the treatment of some human beings as property. Debates about the future of slavery in the United States would almost shut down the convention. In the face of failure, the delegates left the issue for future generations to grapple with. The delegates who had hopes of ending the practice of slavery and codifying abolition into our Constitution were left despondent. Samuel Hopkins, a delegate from Connecticut, lamented: "How does it appear . . . that these States, who have been fighting for liberty and consider themselves as the highest and most noble example of zeal for it, cannot agree in any political Constitution, unless it indulge and authorize them to enslave their fellow men . . . Ah! these unclean spirits, like frogs, they, like the Furies of the poets are spreading discord, and exciting men to contention and war."[22]

The convention was adjourned on September 17, 1787. Thirty-nine of the original fifty-five delegates signed the six-page document.[23] Some delegates had left the convention early. Three, including George Mason, who had arrived at the convention beaming with excitement and hope, refused to sign. Mason was unnerved by the overwhelming centralized control provided to the federal government by the Constitution.[24] He was convinced such powerful authority would decimate the individual liberties that were central to the fight for independence. (It must be noted that while Mason was a strong proponent of people's natural rights to control and determine their own fate, he remained a slaveowner all his life and did not free the people he enslaved upon his death.)[25]

As the convention was nearing its end, George Mason argued that the Constitution was incomplete. He insisted the Constitution required a bill of rights outlining individuals' freedoms and privileges, thereby constraining uncontrolled government power. His proposal was unceremoniously rejected.[26] Without a bill of rights, Mason felt the document was fatally flawed. He would not support it.

Mason represented the views of the Anti-Federalists, who feared an overreaching government. Many Anti-Federalists were suspicious of a document drafted by the educated and wealthy, presumably operating in their own self-interest. Anti-Federalists sought to have individual states retain the bulk of power and keep the federal government relatively weak. As had George Mason at the Constitutional Convention, the Anti-Federalists contended that the Constitution required a bill of rights.

In contrast, the Federalists feared that a weakened government could not assure the strong and continued economic growth necessary to improve relations between the states and with foreign nations. That same dynamic continues today. Frequent complaints are heard that the federal government is wielding too much power over the states and its citizens. At other times, people complain that laws are inconsistent across states, and a national solution is necessary to reduce the confusion.

The Federalists posited that a bill of rights was at most unnecessary and at worst dangerous. They argued that the newly proposed government structure was anchored upon the concept of limited government. A limited government could exert only the enumerated powers assigned to it by the Constitution. They argued that the rights of individuals were already woven into the fabric of the document. More importantly, the Federalists were concerned that a bill of rights effectively created a list, and lists are necessarily incomplete. What of the rights that were not included in the list? Would those rights fail to enjoy constitutional protection? Might that endanger the rights and liberties for which the American people fought in the Revolutionary War?

Alexander Hamilton was vociferous in his argument that a bill of rights created more problems than it solved:

> I go further, and affirm that bills of rights, in the sense and to the extent in which they are contended for, are not only unnecessary in the proposed Constitution, but would even be dangerous. They would contain various exceptions to powers not granted; and, on this very account, would afford a colorable pretext to claim more than were granted. For why declare that things shall not be done which there is no power to do? Why, for instance, should it be said that the liberty of the press shall not be restrained, when no power is given by which restrictions may be imposed?[27]

The contrasting positions between the Federalists and the Anti-Federalists were repeated across the thirteen states in the ratification debates. In defense of the Constitution, Alexander Hamilton, James Madison, and John Jay wrote eighty-five essays between them supporting the Federalist position. Thomas Jefferson praised the essays, later labeled the Federalist Papers, as the "best commentary on the principles of government ever written."[28] But even Jefferson expressed surprise and disappointment that the document did not include a bill of rights.[29]

The Constitution was ratified in 1788. However, this was achieved only after the Federalists compromised with the Anti-Federalists and agreed to take up the matter of the Bill of Rights during the first session of Congress. Madison himself agreed to support such amendments. He was a man of his word. On July 8, 1789, as a duly elected member of Congress representing one of the districts in Virginia, Madison proposed seventeen amendments to the Constitution. Interestingly, the amendment guaranteeing the freedom to speak was third, not first.[30] The proposed amendments were carefully crafted based upon similar declarations in various state constitutions, most notably the Virginia Declaration of Rights, which had been drafted by none other than George Mason, Madison's erstwhile foe.[31] The Congress adopted twelve of the seventeen amendments Madison drafted, and only two years later, by 1791, the ten amendments we now know as the Bill of Rights were ratified by the states.

First Amendment: Congress shall make no law respecting an establishment of religion, or prohibiting the free exercise thereof; or abridging the freedom of speech, or of the press; or the right of the people peaceably to assemble, and to petition the Government for a redress of grievances.

Second Amendment: A well regulated Militia, being necessary to the security of a free State, the right of the people to keep and bear Arms shall not be infringed.

Third Amendment: No soldier shall, in time of peace be quartered in any house, without the consent of the Owner, nor in time of war, but in a manner to be prescribed by law.

Fourth Amendment: The right of the people to be secure in their persons, houses, papers, and effects, against unreasonable searches and seizures, shall not be violated, and no Warrants shall issue, but upon probable cause, supported by Oath or affirmation, and particularly describing the place to be searched, and the persons or things to be seized.

Fifth Amendment: No person shall be held to answer for a capital, or otherwise infamous crime, unless on a presentment or indictment of a Grand Jury, except in cases arising in the land or naval forces, or in the Militia, when in actual service in time of War or public danger; nor shall any person be subject for the same offence to be twice put in jeopardy of life or limb; nor shall be compelled in any criminal case to be a witness against himself, nor be deprived of life, liberty, or property without due process of law; nor shall private property be taken for public use, without just compensation.

Sixth Amendment: In all criminal prosecutions, the accused shall enjoy the right to a speedy and public trial, by an impartial jury of the State and district wherein the crime shall have been committed, which district shall have been previously ascertained by law, and to be informed of the nature and cause of the

accusation; to be confronted with the witnesses against him; to
have compulsory process for obtaining witnesses in his favor, and
to have the Assistance of Counsel for his defense.

Seventh Amendment: In Suits at common law, where the value in
controversy shall exceed twenty dollars, the right of trial by jury
shall be preserved, and no fact tried by a jury, shall be otherwise
re-examined in any Court of the United States, than according to
the rules of the common law.

Eighth Amendment: Excessive bail shall not be required, nor
excessive fines imposed, nor cruel and unusual punishments
inflicted.

Ninth Amendment: The enumeration in the Constitution, of certain
rights, shall not be construed to deny or disparage others retained
by the people.

Tenth Amendment: The powers not delegated to the United States by
the Constitution, nor prohibited by it to the States, are reserved to
the States respectively, or to the people.[32]

While each of the amendments delineate rights essential to democratic governing, the First Amendment serves as the cornerstone to the
Constitution. A cornerstone is the first stone placed in the foundation
of a building; it is important because it provides the reference point for
all other stones upon which the building is constructed. The materials
with which our Constitution's cornerstone is constructed are fundamental values and philosophies that ground democratic thought and
are predicated on self-government, individual autonomy, and a diversity
of views.[33] Those philosophies continue to guide the courts as they forge
meaning into the words "Congress shall make no law . . . abridging the
freedom of speech."

2 : FOUNDATIONS AND BUILDING BLOCKS

The past is what provides us with the building blocks.
Our job today is to create new buildings out of them.
— Theodore Zeldin, historian

Judge Robert Heron Bork was seeking a promotion. His final interview lasted eleven long days in front of a panel of friends and foes.[1] It was summer in Washington, DC, and it was hot. He was sweating from the heat and from frustration. He believed he had earned the job and was eminently qualified for it. Not a man known for his empathy, rather than acknowledge the effect his decisions would have upon millions of lives, he at one point exclaimed that the job would provide for him "an intellectual feast."[2]

During the previous five years, he had served as a judge on the Court of Appeals for the District of Columbia. On July 1, 1987, President Ronald Reagan nominated Judge Bork to the Supreme Court to fill the vacancy left by retiring Justice Lewis Powell. Judge Bork had worked hard and written distinguished opinions. He was smart; he knew it, and so did the senators questioning him who were fulfilling their constitutional responsibilities of advice and consent to the president. The problem was that Judge Bork had a past. Fifteen years earlier, as acting attorney general for President Richard Nixon, he had taken on the infamous role of axman in what came to be known as the Saturday Night Massacre.

The Nixon administration was in the throes of the Watergate scandal. Archibald Cox was serving as a special prosecutor investigating Nixon's reelection campaign. The campaign—which ironically used the acronym CRP (Committee to Reelect the President), derisively referred to as CREEP—had been accused of engaging in dirty tricks and subsequent cover-ups. As part of the investigation, Cox demanded Nixon release White House tapes, which would later reveal Nixon's role in the cover-ups.[3] On October 20, 1973, in an apparent effort to stonewall the investigation, Nixon directed Alexander M. Haig Jr., White House chief of staff, to fire Cox. Haig then turned to Attorney General Elliot L. Richardson to do the job. Richardson refused and resigned. The task was then assigned to Deputy Attorney General William D. Ruckelshaus, who also refused but was sacked before he could tender his resignation. Bork was next in line. He was immediately promoted to acting attorney general. Described in the *New York Times* as "a bear of a man with a scraggly red beard and untamed frizz on a balding pate who had an outsize love of food and drink,"[4] he agreed to the demand and fired Cox.[5]

Bork's acquiescence to Nixon and Haig's demand was consistent with his view of the expansiveness of executive power, which it turned out was a corollary to his restrictive view of the First Amendment. In a published and edited version of his lecture notes from the University of Chicago Law School, Judge Bork asserted that the First Amendment only protects political speech. Bork relied on a narrow definition of political speech: "speech concerned with governmental behavior, policy or personnel."[6] Explicitly political speech, Bork argued, is speech about governing. The category includes a "wide range of evaluation, criticism, electioneering and propaganda"[7]; however, it excluded "scientific, educational, commercial or literary expressions."[8] That is not to say Bork believed all speech other than political speech could or ought to be silenced. He simply believed that only political speech was constitutionally protected by the First Amendment. Congress could certainly draft legislation that could otherwise protect nonpolitical speech, but without an amendment, the Constitution was silent on the matter. Bork's interpretation of the breadth and scope of First Amendment protection is the most limited interpretation supported by justices and jurists. As we will see in later chapters, political speech enjoys the most robust protection offered by the First Amendment, and most First Amendment scholars and jurists extend its protection beyond Bork's restrictive interpretation.

A little less than four months after Bork was nominated, and after only two days of Senate floor debate, the Senate voted not to confirm him. He had been subject to unprecedented attacks, including demonstrations, television ads, and even a mock funeral attended by more than 1,200 people in Philadelphia.[9] He was defeated by a vote of 58–42,[10] one of the largest margins to date.[11] Since his defeat, Bork's name has been transformed into an action verb. *Borking* has entered the lexicon to describe an attack or defeat of a nominee or candidate for public office "unfairly through an organized campaign of harsh public criticism or vilification."[12]

Judge Bork's constrained view of First Amendment protections is in stark contrast to that supported by the renowned Supreme Court Justice Louis Brandeis, who served on the bench years earlier, from 1916 to 1939. While Judge Bork was defiant and caustic, Justice Brandeis sported a soft smile matched by a soft-spoken voice.[13] He was the brilliant son of Jewish immigrants who had come to America to escape persecution in Europe. He completed high school at fifteen and enrolled in Harvard Law School at the age of eighteen.[14] Justice Brandeis was a fierce defender of social justice. He believed the First Amendment was an essential tool in the fight, and that free speech was fundamental to human growth.

The right to freedom of speech, Brandeis argued, was an essential characteristic enshrined in the declarations of liberty in the Constitution. The principle that the First Amendment should serve and support the loftier goals of humanity was given voice in his concurring opinion in *Whitney v. California*:

> Those who won our independence believed that the final end of the state was to make men free to develop their faculties and that in its government the deliberative forces should prevail over the arbitrary. . . . They believed liberty to be the secret of happiness and courage to be the secret of liberty.[15]

In other words, the right to speak freely was an end in and of itself. As later articulated by Professor Thomas I. Emerson of Yale Law School, the position that freedom of speech is an essential element of our individualism and humanity is based on the philosophy that "expression is an integral part of the development of ideas, of mental exploration and of the affirmation of self."[16] Brandeis also believed that a corollary to the right to speak was the audience's **right to know**. So, too, did Justice Hugo Black, who served with Justice Brandeis at the end of Brandeis's tenure. They each asserted that speaking freely and hearing uncensored views are inseparable elements of the whole and, as such, must be protected in all but the most extreme circumstances.[17]

The philosophies espoused by Bork and Brandeis represent two ends of the spectrum. Some argue that the First Amendment is both less expansive than Brandeis claimed and more expansive than Bork claimed. One such view is grounded upon the belief that the First Amendment's purpose is to reveal truth. The means to discover the truth is a robust exchange of ideas through debate and deliberation. This position analogizes the exchange to a marketplace of ideas.[18] Just as an open marketplace for commerce provides the competition necessary to ensure superior products and services for the consuming public, an open marketplace of ideas provides the competition essential to encourage debate among the polity and animate policies that support individualism and cooperative citizenship. In the marketplace for commerce, inferior products often fail to weather the competition. In the marketplace of ideas, flawed opinions should fail to withstand the competition provided by vigorous debate. It is a Darwinian theory: Only the best will endure the assault.

The importance of the search for truth in the marketplace of ideas was eloquently expressed in a dissent in *Abrams v. United States* by Justice Oliver Wendell Holmes Jr., a Supreme Court colleague of Justice Brandeis, who himself concurred in the dissent:

> [T]he best test of truth is the power of the thought to get itself accepted in the competition of the market, and that truth is the only ground upon which their wishes safely can be carried out. That at any rate is the theory of our Constitution. It is an experiment, as all life is an experiment. Every year if not every day we have to wager our salvation upon some prophecy based upon imperfect knowledge.[19]

Of course, even in the marketplace of commodities, sometimes market forces are corrupted, and harmful products survive. In those situations, governmental intervention is necessary to protect competition by creating regulations that prevent harm to the public, sometimes by removing the offending article from commerce. Similarly, many who support speech restrictions insist the marketplace of ideas also requires government intervention to protect against forms of speech that are believed to be harmful. Some also argue that there is inequitable access to the marketplace of ideas; those with money and power have greater access, so the government should intervene to provide admission for those with less strength who seek to express opposing views.

As is evident from the foregoing, not all Supreme Court justices subscribe to the same philosophies. That leads to conflicting opinions between cases and sometimes even within cases. Additionally, constitutional analysis can vary. The most unyielding analysis of the First Amendment is the absolutist approach, which views the First Amendment proscriptions as inflexible: Congress shall make no law, period. Another method of analysis categorizes some speech as having greater value than other speech and, therefore, being more worthy of the First Amendment's superpower protection. And still another method of analysis takes what some might call a more practical approach. It recognizes that the rights embodied in the Constitution are sometimes in conflict. In those situations, the legislatures and the courts weigh and balance rights, all based on context. Sometimes the First Amendment comes out on top, and sometimes it doesn't. Nonetheless, these decisions provide a roadmap to our history and guideposts for our future reliance on the First Amendment to protect the right to speak our minds.

3 : THE ROAD TO THE SUPREME COURT

[F]reedom of thought, and speech . . . is the matrix,
the indispensable condition, of nearly every other
form of freedom. —Justice Benjamin N. Cardozo[1]

Civil rights and abortion rights have played an outsized role in First Amendment jurisprudence, and provide an important window into the continued conflict between the power of individual states to respond to the politics within their borders and the need for clear and consistent national policy.

In 1971, a woman's right to terminate a pregnancy was utterly dependent on her zip code. All fifty states had regulations on the books, which ranged from prohibiting abortion in all cases to providing legal abortion services up to and including the first twenty-four weeks of pregnancy. In 1973 that changed. In 1973, the Supreme Court decided *Roe v. Wade*, which nationalized the right to abortion.[2] After *Roe*, neither a state nor the federal government could prohibit a woman from terminating a pregnancy during the first trimester. After the first trimester and until the point that a fetus can survive outside the womb, which most experts agree occurs at twenty-four weeks of pregnancy, the government could impose regulations only if they were reasonably related to the mother's health and safety. Once there is fetal viability, a state can regulate abortion including banning the procedure.

In the years since *Roe*, many state legislatures have tested the boundaries of the decision, significantly limiting its protections for pregnant women, and we might find ourselves back to the future if the current Supreme Court decides to overturn *Roe*, and the right to choose reverts back to state borders.

The intense abortion debate is ongoing, and the freedom to engage in that debate places the First Amendment directly in the middle of the melee. On February 8, 1971, the debate was somewhat more temperate. On that day, the front pages of newspapers across the nation were awash in stories of the South Vietnamese invasion of Laos, the newest expansion of the Vietnam War. Below the fold were stories of the successful Apollo 14 mission, which was coming to a close. The abortion issue was not headline news. Somewhere in the interior pages of the *Virginia Weekly*, the Women's Pavilion of New York City ran this ad:

UNWANTED PREGNANCY
LET US HELP YOU
Abortions are now legal in New York.
There are no residency requirements.
FOR IMMEDIATE PLACEMENT IN ACCREDITED
HOSPITALS AND CLINICS AT LOW COST
Contact
WOMEN'S PAVILION
515 Madison Avenue
New York, NY 10022
or call any time
(212) 371-6670 or (212) 371-6650
AVAILABLE 7 DAYS A WEEK
STRICTLY CONFIDENTIAL.
We will make all arrangements for you and
help you with information and counseling.

A woman in Virginia reading that ad could legally abort a pregnancy in her home state only if the pregnancy resulted from rape or incest or if the pregnancy was a threat to her life or health. There were similar laws on the books in Arkansas, Colorado, Hawaii, Illinois, Iowa, Kentucky, Louisiana, Maryland, Minnesota, Mississippi, Missouri, New Jersey, Nevada, Ohio, Pennsylvania, Vermont, and Wisconsin. In many of those states, including Virginia, advertising for abortion services was illegal. On the other hand, in New York a woman could choose to terminate a pregnancy up to and including the twenty-fourth week for any reason. After that, she could terminate the pregnancy only if her life was in danger. There was no residency requirement for a woman to seek care in New York. It was the most liberal abortion law in the nation, passed by the New York State legislature only the year before. Pro-choice groups saw the opportunity to help women across the United States and, like the Women's Pavilion, purchased ads in newspapers across the country. The ads were effective; from 1970 to 1971, 60 percent of the abortions performed in New York were for out-of-state residents.[3]

Jeffrey C. Bigelow was the director and the managing editor of the *Virginia Weekly*. He was tried and convicted of a criminal misdemeanor under the Virginia statute that prohibited the ad placed in the newspaper by the Women's Pavilion of New York City.

Almost forty years later, after the protections in *Roe* had become the law of the land, Eleanor McCullen, a seventy-six-year-old grandmother, wanted the opportunity to counsel women as they approached abortion clinics in Massachusetts. She aimed to advise the women against having the procedure, even if it was legal. She was opposed to the angry and violent methods often employed by others. She insisted it was her desire to surround pregnant women with love. She matched her interests with action and worked with a group, Pregnancy Help, that provides women with financial help. The group will often pay for lapsed insurance policies, host baby showers, and provide babysitting services once the child is born.[4] However, Mrs. McCullen was warned that, while she certainly had a right to assert her beliefs, her ability to do so in and around facilities that performed abortions in her state was severely restricted. A newly enacted Massachusetts law created a buffer zone around patients entering and leaving a facility that provided abortions. If Mrs. McCullen chose to counsel the women on a public way or sidewalk within thirty-five feet of an entrance or driveway to any reproductive health care facility, she would be arrested and charged with a crime.[5] Mrs. McCullen and others sued the Massachusetts government seeking to **enjoin** (stop) the law's enforcement.

Both cases ultimately made their way onto the Supreme Court docket, and there, the litigants' right to free speech was upheld. Mr. Bigelow could run the ad. Mrs. McCullen could counsel women on the sidewalk of an abortion clinic. Neither of them would face criminal prosecution, thanks to the protections afforded by the First Amendment.

Currently, legal arguments about the viability of *Roe v. Wade* largely turn on whether the court misread the Constitution and whether the power to regulate abortions properly belongs within the purview of the states. The debates between the Federalists and the Anti-Federalists about the balance of power between the federal and state governments at the Constitutional Convention forecasted the present day's federalism debates. The constitutional tug-of-war between the pro-life and pro-choice movements and whether the right to restrict abortion belongs to the state or the national government is at the heart of federalism. Anti-abortion advocates insist that federalism requires that the state, as the more responsive geography to the will of its citizens, should have the power to legislate abortion.

While the debate rages on about where the power center should lie regarding abortion laws, where the power center should lie regarding regulating speech or protest about abortion, or any other issue, has been largely determined. Since the 1920s, the court has expanded the definition of "liberty" to embrace more and more of the protections in the Bill of Rights. The vehicle for that expansion is the Fourteenth Amendment, and the manner of its application is known as the "incorporation doctrine."[6] The incorporation doctrine is grounded on the proposition that the Bill of Rights represents "fundamental principles of liberty and justice which lie at the base of all our civil and political institutions."[7] In other words, state laws that are subject to the incorporation doctrine, like federal laws, can be examined under the US Constitution.

Both Mr. Bigelow and Mrs. McCullen were engaged, at least in part, in political speech. Their arguments differed, but the nature of their communication was the same. Punishment turned on the content of their expression. By safeguarding speech on both sides of this controversial issue, the First Amendment, as applied to the states via the incorporation doctrine, provides consistency and confidence that our right of expression will not vary depending on the state in which it is exercised.

Constitutional issues pertaining to state laws take a bit of a circuitous route to the Supreme Court. If a federal constitutional question is raised by the application of a state law, it will generally have to be examined by state courts first, working its way through the state appeal process. After the state's highest court renders a decision, the **litigants** (parties to a lawsuit) can appeal to the US Supreme Court via a petition. The petition asks the court to issue what is called a **writ of certiorari**. Both Mr. Bigelow's case and Mrs. McCullen's case took this route.

The Supreme Court has the discretion to issue the writ of certiorari and hear the case. If the Supreme Court grants the writ, the case will be placed for argument on the Supreme Court docket. In reality, though, this result is exceedingly rare; in fact on average, the Supreme Court grants the writ and hears less than 4 percent of the cases that seek an appeal to it in any given year. The Supreme Court granted the writ for both Mr. Bigelow and Mrs. McCullen. Their cases were presented, and the Supreme Court's justices held that both Mr. Bigelow's and Mrs. McCullen's right to speak freely was protected.

If a federal law is being questioned for its constitutionality, it will go through the lower federal courts first before the litigants seek an appeal to the Supreme Court via the same writ of certiorari. (There are exceptions to this process, but they don't apply here.)

A Supreme Court decision need not be unanimous; only a majority is necessary. Nine justices are appointed to the Supreme Court: a chief justice and eight associate justices. They are appointed for life. As seats on the Supreme Court become vacant, a justice is nominated by the president and confirmed with the Senate's advice and consent. No one justice has more votes than another; the chief justice has one vote, and the eight associate justices each have one vote apiece. To that end, the chief justice's vote has no greater weight in the final decision by the Court than those of any of the associate justices.

The chief justice is responsible for some administrative duties, including assigning responsibilities to write the majority decision in a particular case. Even if a justice is not assigned the responsibility to write the majority decision, they may still write an opinion. If a justice agrees with the majority and nonetheless chooses to write an opinion clarifying an issue or discussing a related issue, they will write a concurring opinion. If a justice disagrees with the majority, they may write a dissenting opinion.

The Supreme Court could not have made any decision about the Virginia or the Massachusetts laws on its own initiative. Unlike the legislature, and in some cases the executive, no court can draft a regulation or otherwise create a law. The courts are limited to making decisions based upon issues brought to them by litigants. Litigants can be citizens or noncitizens, governmental entities or officers, corporations or nonincorporated groups.

While the legislature cannot explicitly overrule the Supreme Court, the legislature may have the power to reverse the effect of a Supreme Court decision. Congress, or a state legislature, may accomplish this simply by amending the law to bring it in line with the court's restrictions. You will see several examples of this in later chapters.

The Constitution can also be amended to overturn a Supreme Court decision, but usually this is not a realistic option. Amending the Constitution is a very complicated process requiring approval by two-thirds of both houses of Congress and three-quarters of the states. In our politically divided country, achieving such a broad national consensus is unlikely. Although thousands of amendments have been discussed or proposed, the Constitution has only been successfully amended twenty-seven times, and not at all since 1992. The Twenty-Seventh Amendment, ratified in 1992, required that if Congress voted to alter compensation for its members, the change could not take effect until after a subsequent election in the House of Representatives.

Finally, the Supreme Court's membership changes, and although the court places a great deal of value on precedent, it does sometimes reverse precedent. Today, abortion remains constitutionally protected; however, as the court grows more conservative, that protection might disappear. Regardless of any future decisions about the medical procedure, our right to speak, counsel, and shout will remain steadfastly within the embrace of the First Amendment.

4 : SYMBOLICALLY SPEAKING

[I]t is nevertheless often true that one man's vulgarity
is another's lyric. —Justice John Marshall Harlan[1]

The 1960s was a time of social and political upheaval, due mainly to the civil rights movement, the protests against the war in Vietnam, the availability of contraceptives on demand, and the legalization of abortion. People, particularly young people, embraced the power of protest and expressed dissatisfaction with the way things were, insisting on the need for rapid, sweeping change.

DRAFT CARD BURNING

In 1966, David Paul O'Brien was nineteen years old. He had been required to register for the draft the year before. Even today, all eligible men between eighteen and twenty-five must register with the Selective Service. Failure to do so is a violation of the Military Selective Service Act. If a man is convicted of the violation, he might face jail time as well as a fine.[2] Currently, the United States operates a volunteer army, but in 1966, once registered with the Selective Service a man became eligible for the draft and was issued a draft card. If not exempted or deferred, he was called to service.

O'Brien was a pacifist, and as a member of the Committee for Non-Violent Action, he objected to the draft and the Vietnam War. He did not look the part of the hippie protester of the times. He sported short hair and horn-rimmed glasses. He had not yet been called up for duty, but he had no intention of serving. On March 31, 1966, a bitterly cold day in Boston, O'Brien arrived at the South Boston District Courthouse, intent on making his point. Dressed in a suit and tie, he resolutely climbed the stairs. Ten other young men and women joined him. In front of a gathering crowd, O'Brien and three of the men who had joined him on those steps quietly lit their draft cards on fire.[3]

As the cards burned, O'Brien and the others were accosted by a large number of local high school students. One of the protesters suffered a broken nose and was transferred to a hospital. O'Brien was saved from a beating by FBI agent Thomas McInerney, who pushed O'Brien into the janitor's closet.[4] Afterwards, O'Brien was escorted from the courthouse and arrested. Two weeks later, a grand jury seated in the US District Court in Boston indicted O'Brien and three of the other protesters for violating the Universal Military Training and Service Act of 1951 (USMTSA). None of the teens who had participated in the violence were arrested or charged with any crimes.[5] Although the local newspaper accounts reported the violence, there was little sympathy for the injuries suffered by O'Brien and his companions; most of the editorials voiced criticism only of the draft card burners.

That lack of sympathy was mirrored in Congress and by the Johnson Administration. They were incensed by the draft card burning and interpreted it as an open defiance of governmental authority. Indeed, it was open defiance. O'Brien admitted that he "did not recognize the legitimacy" of the government's demands. He would not "play their game" or submit to the draft and fight in their war.[6] Protesters argued that the war was both immoral and unwinnable. They asserted that Americans and Vietnamese were dying in increasing numbers for a military action that supported an authoritarian and corrupt regime in South Vietnam. It was also becoming more apparent that the draft was disproportionately burdening the poor and people of color.

The USMTSA under which O'Brien was charged had recently been amended to make it a crime to intentionally mutilate or destroy a draft card. Prior to the amendment, any such action might have been viewed as frustrating but not criminal. The amendment was a response to increasing protests where draft card burning was the chosen means of messaging.

O'Brien's trial began on June 6, 1966, and lasted only one day. He was convicted under the USMTSA and sentenced to six months in prison. At his sentencing, he read this statement:

> I feel that the draft card burning symbolizes my choice to work for the betterment of our society in a very radical way, radical in that all our motivations, all our actions, all our beliefs must be reexamined

and those that are incompatible with the well-being of the individual and those that deny love must be changed.[7]

He appealed his conviction and was released on bail while awaiting appeal after having served two months in jail.[8] In the appeal, he argued that by burning his draft card, he was engaging in political speech. His message: The government lacked the moral authority to engage in the undeclared war in Southeast Asia. Further, he argued that the recent amendment to the USMTSA was specifically aimed at restricting speech. It was, he insisted, unconstitutional and unenforceable. He concluded that he should not be jailed for engaging in behavior that functioned as speech and communicated a clear political message.

A short two years later, the case was placed on the Supreme Court docket. Only eight justices participated in the decision. Justice Thurgood Marshall sat it out. The justices are not required to give reasons for their recusal, so we rarely know why they do so. The justices, eight men ranging in age from fifty-one (Justice Byron White) to eighty-two (Justice Hugo Black), were not removed from the vagaries of everyday life. They understood that a thought or an idea could be communicated by means other than speech or written word. The Supreme Court acknowledged that sometimes conduct serves as the medium for a message. Expressive intent can be found in many nonverbal forms. Dance communicates. Art communicates. The burning draft card also conveyed a message. The message of defiance was carefully crafted and framed; the audience at the courthouse clearly understood the message — and responded to it with threats and violence. To be sure, both before and after O'Brien's messaging tactics, the court recognized the value of expression through action. In addition to art and dance, messages can be communicated with tattoos, clothing, even silence. In constitutional parlance, such nonverbal efforts to communicate are considered **symbolic speech**. Symbolic speech often includes elements of conduct:

· Wearing black armbands to protest American military involvement in Vietnam[9]
· Participating in a sit-in protesting segregation[10]
· Picketing as a means of protest[11]

- Boycotting as a means of securing compliance by both civic and business leaders for equality and racial justice[12]

But, the court added, simply because conduct is intended to convey sentiment does not automatically invoke First Amendment protection. The court accepted O'Brien's claim that he intended to communicate his anger and resentment regarding the government's role in the Vietnam War. They further acknowledged that the burning draft card was symbolic of his fury. However, the court rejected O'Brien's assertion that the torched card, as a medium for the message, transformed his behavior into protected speech. The court stated:

> We cannot accept the view that an apparently limitless variety of conduct can be labeled "speech" whenever the person engaging in the conduct intends thereby to express an idea. However, even on the assumption that the alleged communicative element in O'Brien's conduct is sufficient to bring into play the First Amendment, it does not necessarily follow that the destruction of a registration certificate is constitutionally protected activity.[13]

The court held that when conduct is infused with messaging, both the message and the action must be examined to determine whether and how the First Amendment is implicated. The court accepted the government's argument that the amendment to the USMTSA was not aimed at restricting the speech of war protesters; instead, it aimed to preserve the integrity of the government's ability to raise an army. The fact that O'Brien sought to transform the action of burning a draft card into a message did not magically call the First Amendment into play and thereby shield him from criminal liability. According to the court, O'Brien was not punished for his message; he was punished for his behavior.[14]

The court explained that the government's responsibility to raise and support an army was an essential element of its obligation to the citizenry. The effect of the statute on O'Brien's ability to communicate discontent was inconsequential. The court made it clear that even though O'Brien was limited in the methods he could use to convey his politics, his right to speak his mind and protest government policies, as long as he did not otherwise break any laws, remained unscathed. There were multiple avenues still available for O'Brien to communicate his opposition to the war; had he burned a copy of the draft card, he could have communicated his message without running afoul of the law. Upon losing his appeal in the Supreme Court, O'Brien's sentence was reduced to three years' probation and community service at a hospital in lieu of military service.[15]

Since O'Brien was being punished for his conduct, not his message, the First Amendment was not pressed into service. But, as is evident in the next two stories, when the government targets the message enmeshed in the conduct, the First Amendment will often be deployed.

PROTECTING THE LANGUAGE OF THE STREETS

It was a chilly morning in Los Angeles on April 26, 1968. The final Supreme Court decision on the O'Brien case was still a month away. On his way out the door, Paul Robert Cohen grabbed his jacket to keep warm. It was a jean jacket typical of the time. The night before, Cohen had been to a party and a friend added decoration to it by painting "Fuck the Draft" on the back. In fact, that particular epithet did not stand out among the graffiti that adorned the jacket. Several other messages were written and painted on the panels and sleeves, including peace symbols and the statement, "Stop the War."[16]

Cohen was scheduled to testify as a witness in court that day. Shortly after entering the courthouse, he removed the jacket and folded it across his arm so that the back of the jacket was no longer visible. He was not wearing the jacket when he entered the courtroom, prepared to testify. Apparently, he did not remove it fast enough. Two police officers saw Cohen enter the building and saw the decorated jacket. They were angered by it. Remember: It was the late 1960s. While the word "fuck" is somewhat commonplace now, at that time it was considered the height of vulgarity. Having those words painted on the back of a jacket and wearing it into court was, at least to those officers, crude and discomfiting. The police officers followed Cohen into the courtroom and requested the judge find him in contempt of court, subjecting Cohen to immediate arrest. The judge, however, refused the request. So the police waited for the hearing to end and promptly arrested Cohen when he left the courtroom.[17]

Cohen was thereafter charged and convicted of violating the California Penal Code, which criminalized offensive conduct that "maliciously and willfully disturb[ed] the peace or quiet of any neighborhood or person."[18] He was sentenced to thirty days in prison. At the time, this case garnered little interest. Even when it reached the Supreme Court, the justices and clerks were dismissive. The newspapers, too, mostly ignored this case. Only upon further analysis did minds change.[19] Over the decades, its contribution to First Amendment jurisprudence has grown.

In Cohen's appeal to the Supreme Court, the government argued that Cohen was punished for his conduct. A bare majority of the justices, 5–4, disagreed. In direct contrast to its decision in *O'Brien*, the Supreme Court agreed with Cohen and held he had been punished for his message, not his behavior.

The court noted that reprehensible language to some was poetry to others; our language cannot and should not be cleansed into bland platitudes. Language is rich with meaning, and one set of words can express a thought with a greater depth of feeling than other words targeted at the same subject. Words can perform as symbols. They have connotative or emotive effect. The word "fuck" is actually a slang or derogatory term for sexual intercourse, but it has a more impassioned meaning depending on the context in which it is used. Certainly, "The Draft is Terrible" or "I Hate the Draft" conveys something different, less impactful than "Fuck the Draft." The court explained that the First Amendment is broad enough to embrace the affective content of language.

The court held that a speaker has the right to use language that most accurately reflects their intent, even if the speaker intends to be crude. To allow the government to censor words might ultimately lead to a dystopian situation in which certain viewpoints are banned from the marketplace of ideas. The court noted:

> [W]e cannot indulge the facile assumption that one can forbid particular words without also running a substantial risk of suppressing ideas in the process. Indeed, governments might soon seize upon the censorship of particular words as a convenient guise for banning the expression of unpopular views.[20]

Claims that an unsuspecting public might be offended by the jacket did not justify punishing the message, particularly when the viewer could avoid the offense by simply looking away. To allow an audience to shut down speech the audience did not like would empower it in a manner contrary to the very foundations of the First Amendment.[21] Cohen's conviction was overturned. While the jacket, which was used as evidence in his trial, was never returned to him, he did not have to spend any time in jail.[22]

Northwestern University Professor Franklyn Haiman praised the *Cohen* decision for extending First Amendment protection to the language of the streets. And by extension, it protects the protesters of the streets, the grassroots movements whose language is often gritty and harsh.[23] The *Cohen* court emphasized that the cacophony that exists in conjunction with our freedom to disagree and speak our minds is a necessary part of the functioning of a healthy democracy. To allow the government to reduce the noise of speech in all its beauty and ugliness is to reduce the power of democracy, because it gives the government the ability to control debate.[24]

FLAG BURNING

Twenty or so years later, David Paul O'Brien had earned his PhD in psychology from Temple University[25] and Robert Paul Cohen had slipped into obscurity, choosing to be identified by a different, undisclosed surname.[26] It was Gregory Lee Johnson's turn to add his character profile into the First Amendment parable.

In 1984, President Reagan's renomination by the Republican Party to serve a second term with George H. W. Bush as his vice president was more like a coronation than a political contest. The Republican National Convention was held in Dallas that year at the height of the summer, August 20 to August 24. Despite the brutal heat, approximately 30,000 people poured into the city to celebrate the president and, at every opportunity, chant, "Four more years!" There were 2,235 delegates, 2,235 alternates, and 1,700 journalists in attendance at the convention. The rest were visitors who had come to witness and participate in the spectacle.[27]

Reagan and Bush ran virtually unopposed for the nomination. Reagan won a unanimous roll call vote, and Bush was only two votes shy of unanimity.[28] The Democratic ticket was headlined by former Vice President Walter Mondale, a nice guy from Minnesota who simply could not match the former actor-president's charisma and showmanship. Geraldine Ferraro was the Democratic vice presidential candidate. Ferraro's nomination garnered intense interest. She was a former teacher, a New York City native, the daughter of immigrants, the first woman to run on a major party ticket for national office in the United States, and a pro-choice Catholic.[29] None of that really mattered; it rarely does in the vice presidential race. Ultimately, the Republican candidates won the election in a rout. Reagan and Bush won 59 percent of the popular vote and forty-nine out of fifty states in the electoral college.[30] However, even in an atmosphere of celebration, as was the case in Dallas during the Republican convention, discontent about several administration policies was evident.

Prior to the start of the convention, the city processed 28,000 permits for demonstrations.[31] One of those permits went to the Youth International Party, or "Yippies." Yippies were a countercultural group of the political left founded by Jerry Rubin, Abby and Anita Hoffman, and other superstar radicals of the 1960s. The Yippies were known to engage in political theater, and on August 22, 1984, they marched through Dallas as part of a larger protest: the American War Chest Tour.[32] They chanted slogans and engaged in die-ins in the middle of the street to dramatize the consequences of a nuclear attack. They disrupted shoppers, spray-painted obscenities on buildings, and scattered deposit slips on the floor of a bank after spattering it with red paint. Almost a hundred protesters were arrested and charged with disorderly conduct.[33]

Gregory Lee Johnson traveled from Atlanta to participate in the protest.[34] He apparently was not part of the mayhem described above, but when the group reached City Hall, Johnson "unfurled the American flag, doused it with kerosene, and set it on fire."[35] While the flag burned, the Yippies chanted: "America, the red, white, and blue, we spit on you."[36] No one was injured, but several people were offended. One patriotic citizen collected the remains of the flag and buried them, consistent with the United States Flag Code, which provides direction for respectful disposal of flags not appropriate for display.[37]

Johnson was arrested for his performance, and on December 13, 1984, he was convicted by a six-member jury of violating a provision of the Texas Criminal Code: Desecration of a Venerated Object (Texas Desecration Statute), which provided for criminal prosecution if a person "intentionally desecrated, defaced or damaged a public monument, a place of worship or burial, or a state or national flag and thereby seriously offended a person who observed or discovered the desecration."[38] Johnson testified at his trial and explained his motivation for burning the flag:

> The American Flag was burned as Ronald Reagan was being renominated as president. And a more powerful statement of symbolic speech, whether you agree with it or not, couldn't have been made at that time. It's quite a just position [juxtaposition]. We had new patriotism and no patriotism.[39]

Johnson was convicted, fined $2,000, and sentenced to a year in jail, the maximum sentence allowable for the offense.[40] He appealed his conviction. One of the Texas appellate courts affirmed his conviction, but the other reversed it, and the State of Texas sought and was granted a writ of certiorari to the US Supreme Court.[41] The entire appeal process took four years. After hearing arguments, Justice William J. Brennan Jr. delivered the decision for the five-justice Supreme Court majority. He went through a very systematic analysis of the issues presented to the court. First, the court had to determine if Johnson was engaged in expressive conduct. Both parties, Johnson and the State of Texas, agreed that he was. Only after that determination was made could the court move on to the next question, which was whether the Texas Desecration Statute was targeted at suppressing free expression. This was an essential turning point in the analysis. Was the Texas Desecration Statute, like the USMTSA, targeted at conduct within the purview of government responsibilities and unrelated to messaging? If so, then the court only needed to determine that the statute was sufficiently **narrowly tailored** to the government interest in controlling conduct and had a minimal impact on speech. On the other hand, if the Texas Desecration Statute was targeted at messaging, then the court would subject the statute to a much more rigorous analysis. Texas would have to prove it had a **compelling**

interest in criminalizing flag burning. Texas would also have to prove that criminalizing flag burning was narrowly tailored to support its government interest and not so broad as to stifle a First Amendment right to speak and to protest.[42]

Texas argued that it had a responsibility, and therefore a compelling government interest, to prevent a breach of the peace. Burning a flag, it argued, had the potential to induce such a breach. Texas also claimed it had a compelling interest to preserve "the flag as a symbol of national unity."[43] The court quickly disposed of the first offered justification. While the antics of some of the Yippies indeed caused a disturbance, there was no record of Johnson's action having done so. And while there was evidence that some people were offended by the flag burning, as was true in the *Cohen* case, the state could not criminalize speech to protect the audience's sensibilities. The court reiterated that "a function of free speech under our system of government is to invite dispute."[44] As we will see later, had there been a breach of the peace, or had a breach of the peace been imminent, law enforcement would not have had its hands tied by the First Amendment.[45]

The second justification offered by the State of Texas gave the court pause. The court recognized the laudable intent of the legislature in passing the statute: to preserve the flag as a venerated object and a symbol of national unity. Moreover, the desire to discourage any action that would show disrespect to the flag was commendable. However, the majority held that protecting the flag's reputation is not the function of government. And while the government's interest in maintaining civility and protecting parts of the population from being offended is admirable, it is not compelling. The majority found that, unlike the USMTSA under which O'Brien had been convicted, the Texas Desecration Statute was specifically targeted at messaging and, as such, was inconsistent with Johnson's First Amendment right of free speech.[46]

The four dissenting justices vociferously disagreed with the majority. They argued that the flag was different. It was more than merely a symbol; it was imbued with "mystical reverence."[47] They insisted that "the American flag has occupied a unique position as the symbol of our Nation, a uniqueness that justifies a governmental prohibition against flag burning in the way . . . Johnson did."[48] Chief Justice William Rehnquist postulated that the flag itself is a symbol suffused with patriotic messages. For many, the flag represents unity and democratic ideals. The chief justice emphasized the special value of the flag as a singular representation of America's greatness by quoting, in full, our national anthem and a classic Civil War poem by John Greenleaf Whittier. He described Johnson's actions as an "inarticulate grunt or roar"[49] purposefully uttered to antagonize others and not worthy of First Amendment protection. The statute, he insisted, was not aimed at messaging; it was neutrally aimed at conduct, and Johnson deserved to be incarcerated. Nonetheless, the majority rules even at the Supreme Court, so Johnson's conviction was overturned, and he remained a free man. Unlike David O'Brien, Gregory Johnson was not going to jail.

CONTENT-NEUTRAL AND
CONTENT-BASED STATUTES

Why were Johnson's symbolic speech actions protected by the First Amendment when O'Brien's were not? The answer: because the USMTSA, the statute under which O'Brien was convicted, was aimed at protecting the viability of the armed forces in a time of (undeclared) war. It was not aimed at speech. O'Brien converted the draft card into a medium of communication by lighting it on fire, but his action did not also reconstruct the statute's intent. The statute in O'Brien's case was clear: A person could not burn a draft card for any reason. O'Brien could not manufacture an exception to that prohibition by burning a draft card as a form of messaging.

In First Amendment jurisprudence, statutes enacted at non-speech related activities are called content neutral. A First Amendment content-neutral analysis proceeds along three lines of inquiry: (1) Is the statute directed at behavior that is important to a government function and unrelated to the suppression of speech? (2) Is the statute calibrated to that government interest so that it is not overly broad? and (3) Even if the statute has a collateral effect on speech, are other means of communicating the message still available?

The statute in the *O'Brien* case was content neutral. It was drafted to protect an important function of government. Obviously, it affected messaging: Young draftees could not burn their draft card as a means of protest; however, that was merely a minimal collateral effect of the statute. Laws that prohibit jaywalking are, from a free speech perspective, also content neutral. So that if people began jaywalking to protest the proliferation of sidewalk scooters, they could still be fined for jaywalking: The limitations on speech as applied to the protesters are a minimal collateral effect of the jaywalking prohibition. In jurisprudential language, both the draft card burning statute and the jaywalking statute are not overbroad. Protesters and their supporters still have available many other means of communicating their messages, and the marketplace of ideas remains robust.

On the other hand, the Texas Desecration Statute was directed at speech. The Texas statute prohibited burning the flag because of the message implicit in the action. It was not designed simply to protect the physical integrity of the flag; it was designed to protect the flag from being burned as a means of protest. If Johnson had burned the flag as a means of honorably disposing of a damaged flag, consistent with federal protocol, no one would have been offended, and Johnson would not have been arrested and prosecuted under the statute.

A statute that is targeted at messaging is considered **content based**. In order for a content-based statute to withstand the withering glare of the First Amendment, it must satisfy the "strict scrutiny" test. The **strict scrutiny test** requires that the statute must be designed to protect a compelling government interest. Further, the statute must be so narrowly tailored that it employs the least intrusive means of restricting speech to achieve the government objective.

In the Texas case, the government's interest in maintaining civility norms was not enough to criminalize conduct. The majority stressed that the First Amendment was not designed to promote good manners and kind words; it was designed to protect debate and disagreement. The court reiterated:

> If there is a bedrock principle underlying the First Amendment,
> it is that the government may not prohibit the expression of an idea
> simply because society finds the idea itself offensive or disagreeable.
> ... the constitutionally guaranteed freedom to be intellectually ...
> diverse or even contrary, and the right to differ as to things that

touch the heart of the existing order, encompass the freedom to express publicly one's opinions about our flag, including those opinions which are defiant or contemptuous.[50]

Shortly after it was rendered, Congress tried to overturn the *Texas v. Johnson* decision, and passed the Flag Protection Act of 1989. That act criminalized mutilating, defacing, or physically defiling the American flag. Not surprisingly, shortly after the legislation was passed and signed into law by President George H. W. Bush, Gregory Johnson was back at it again. On the day before Halloween, October 30, 1989, he and three others burned a flag on the Capitol Building's steps, shouting, "Burn baby burn." Once more, Johnson was arrested.[51] Others across the nation also burned the flag, specifically to protest the statute that prohibited it.[52] In record time, the Supreme Court was addressing the issue again in *United States v. Eichman*.[53] The justices and the attorneys representing both the protesters and the government engaged in a spirited debate at the Supreme Court hearing. Solicitor General Kenneth W. Starr, later to gain notoriety as independent counsel in the Whitewater investigation, which ultimately led to President Bill Clinton's impeachment trial, represented the government. He argued that flag burning unaccompanied by words communicated nothing. The late Justice Antonin Scalia, hailed as a great protector of conservative views, was incredulous at Starr's argument and said so. He pointed out that it should be self-evident that flag burning is saturated with a message. Well known for his candor and abrupt manner, he shot down Starr's argument, insisting that flag burners are obviously saying, "We hate the United States."[54] Again, Johnson avoided jail time. (In 2016 Johnson's antics finally earned him some cash. That summer he burned a flag outside of the Republican National Convention—this time in Cleveland, Ohio—in protest of Donald Trump's nomination. He was arrested but the charges were dropped, and he sued the city for violating his constitutional rights. The city of Cleveland settled with Johnson, paying him $225,000.)[55]

The court held that, like the Texas Desecration Statute, the Flag Protection Act was unconstitutional.[56] Also similar to *Texas v. Johnson*, *United States v. Eichman* was determined by a bare majority of the justices, 5–4. Efforts continue to criminalize flag burning,[57] so if the current conservative court again takes up the issue, the dissenting opinions of the past might hold sway.

O'Brien, Cohen, and *Johnson* each stand for the proposition that communicative intent is imbued in many activities and not constrained to that which is purely verbal or written. Of course, as was apparent in *Johnson* and *Cohen*'s slim majorities, the line between speech, which is protected by the First Amendment, and conduct, which is not, is not easily drawn. It is an issue of definition and perspective that, in the future, may largely turn on the composition of the court.

5 : THE TROUBLING SOUND OF SILENCE

Censorship reflects a society's lack of confidence
in itself. It is a hallmark of an authoritarian regime.
—Justice Potter Stewart[1]

In or around November 1955, the United States entered the civil war between North Vietnam and South Vietnam.[2] North Vietnam was allied with the communist government of the Soviet Union; however, many in South Vietnam sought to maintain economic and cultural ties to the United States and other Western nations. Throughout the conflict, the United States supplied South Vietnam with weaponry, intelligence, and troops on the ground. The United States government defended its role in the conflict by asserting the need to thwart the rise of communism in that part of the world. As such, some have argued it was essentially a proxy war between the former Soviet Union and the United States. It was in protest of this war that David Paul O'Brien burned his draft card and Paul Robert Cohen decorated his jacket. The war would continue until the fall of Saigon in April 1975, leaving almost 60,000 Americans dead and over 300,000 Americans wounded. The total number of casualties by citizens of all countries is by some estimates over one million.[3] The war ended with the United States' withdrawal, followed by communist takeover and control of the country under a unified government.

By the mid-1960s, some in the United States government began to question the wisdom of continuing to engage in the conflict. Among them was Secretary of Defense Robert McNamara. McNamara had served as secretary of defense from 1961 through 1968 under presidents Kennedy and Johnson. During that time, he served as a primary architect of the Vietnam strategy.[4] Many derisively referred to the conflict as "McNamara's War," a burden he carried with him to his grave.[5]

In 1967, McNamara instructed the Pentagon to research and draft a report that detailed the history of US engagement in the Vietnam War.[6] It took thirty-six scholars over eighteen months to complete, by which time McNamara had resigned the office and was replaced by Clark M. Clifford.[7] It was delivered to Clifford on January 15, 1969, in the very last days of the Johnson Administration.[8] The official title of the finished document was "Report of the Office of the Secretary of Defense Vietnam Task Force"; however, its popular title is the Pentagon Papers. The conclusions to be drawn from the Pentagon Papers were not ambiguous. There were no tactical opportunities for the United States to win the military conflict and, given the death and destruction occurring in their homeland, scarce ability to win the hearts and minds of the Vietnamese or their neighbors. Americans, Vietnamese, Laotians, and Cambodians lost their lives based on lies and deliberate misinformation promoted by the United States government. The proof lay in documents researched and drafted by government staffers and appointees.

The report, classified as Top Secret, included over 7,000 pages of government documents and analysis about US operations and decision making during the decades of US involvement in the region.[9] Only fifteen official copies of the Pentagon Papers were printed, assuring its conclusions would never reach the public realm.[10]

The desire to keep the report secret was matched by increasing mistrust by the American population and a gnawing sense that the government was withholding information that the public had a right to know. Only a few years earlier, in 1966, the Freedom of Information Act (FOIA), requiring release by request of nonpublic governmental information, was signed into law, due in large part to the unyielding determination of Congressman John Moss and significant lobbying efforts by the American Society of Newspaper Editors.[11] But an FOIA request could only be made if someone knew the information existed. The Pentagon Papers report remained entombed in the inaccessible files controlled by the White House and its proxies until Daniel Ellsberg decided to steal them, copy them, and share their contents with his friend, *New York Times* journalist Neil Sheehan.

Daniel Ellsberg was a brilliant researcher and military strategist. He held a PhD in economics from Harvard, where he met and collaborated with Henry Kissinger, a well-known war hawk. The latter served as national security advisor and secretary of state under President Richard M. Nixon. Ellsberg served in the Marines from 1959 to 1964. Later he worked at RAND Corporation, a civilian think tank that worked closely with the Pentagon, and then at the Department of Defense where he assisted in making strategy and policy decisions regarding the Vietnam War.[12] Initially, Ellsberg supported US efforts in Vietnam. Most noteworthy, when he returned to RAND in 1967, he served as a contributor to the study that eventually became known as the Pentagon Papers report.

Between August 1969 and May 1970, Ellsberg had an opportunity to read the entire Pentagon Papers report. At the time, he was tasked with writing a memorandum for Kissinger outlining Nixon Administration options in the war.[13] The Top Secret designation of the report required that Ellsberg's access be severely restricted. He could read it only while he was on campus at RAND Corporation in Santa Monica, California, and when it was not in his physical possession, he was required to store the papers in a secure safe. He was specifically prohibited from copying them.[14] Indeed, he had signed a security statement to that effect.[15]

Ellsberg's support for the war had already been waning. The study included the data and analysis he needed to buttress his suspicions: The war in Vietnam was unwinnable, a hopeless stalemate.[16] Ellsberg was convinced the details of the report needed to be revealed. In October 1969, he snuck the report out of his office volume by volume, waving to security guards on his way out.[17] He photocopied virtually the entire report using a Xerox machine located in the reception area at a nearby ad agency in West Hollywood, where his friend was employed. It was a slow process; he had to copy each page individually.[18] The first copying excursion, which was obviously conducted after business hours, had him at the agency until after 5:00 a.m.[19]

Ellsberg's efforts to deliver the information in the Pentagon Papers to the American people also did not go quickly. Throughout 1969 and 1970, he attempted to convince lawmakers to publicize it, including Senator George McGovern, who would eventually become the 1972 Democratic nominee for president running on an antiwar ticket. Once the reports were published, McGovern expressed, somewhat disingenuously, anger over the secrets the Johnson Administration had failed to reveal.[20]

Frustrated in his attempts to get legislators to take action, Ellsberg contacted his friend at the *New York Times*, Neil Sheehan. Ellsberg met Sheehan in 1967 when they were both in Vietnam. Ellsberg was on a fact-finding mission for the government, and Sheehan was there reporting on the war. While in Vietnam, Ellsberg and Sheehan developed a friend-ship grounded on a shared cynicism about US efforts in the region. Ells-berg traveled the region and, witnessing untold horrors, was becoming increasingly convinced that the US should withdraw. Sheehan wrote ar-ticles that included reports on North Vietnamese troop strength that contradicted Johnson Administration spin on the issue. Some of the material included in those articles was garnered from leaks of classified information provided to Sheehan by Ellsberg.[21]

In March 1971 in Washington, DC, and then again in Cambridge, Massachusetts, Ellsberg met with Sheehan. The original descriptions of the exchange were that, after receiving assurances from Sheehan that he would do his best to get the information published, Ellsberg provided Sheehan with a copy of the papers.[22] The real story is much more inter-esting. The whole episode reads like a spy novel, complete with clandes-tine meetings and double-dealing. Sheehan agreed to reveal the true details of the Ellsberg-Sheehan exchange in an interview with Janny Scott, a reporter for the *Times*, on the condition that the content of the interview would not go to press until after Sheehan's death. Sheehan died on January 7, 2021, and that same day the paper ran the story Shee-han disclosed to Scott under the headline, "Now It Can Be Told: How Neil Sheehan Got the Pentagon Papers."[23]

It seems, at every turn, that the possession and retention of the Pen-tagon Papers included an element of duplicity. During their initial meet-ings, Ellsberg agreed to provide Sheehan access to the papers but not possession. Sheehan could only read them and take notes. Sheehan agreed but quickly decided he would not keep his word. Sheehan be-lieved Ellsberg was rightly concerned about ending up in jail, but in at-tempting to avoid that fate, Ellsberg had been careless. Sheehan was afraid knowledge of the leaked papers would get to the Justice Depart-ment, which would shut down publication before the *Times* was ready to go to print. At first, Sheehan was stuck in Ellsberg's Cambridge apart-ment with Ellsberg and the report, but when Ellsberg left on vacation, Sheehan took the opportunity presented to him. He duplicated the key

Ellsberg left him, then duplicated Ellsberg's copy of the report. Sheehan took the pilfered copies and flew back to DC. Taking every necessary precaution, he did not check his bags; he purchased an extra seat and the suitcase containing the copies was belted in. Later, a few weeks before publication, upon request, Ellsberg agreed to give Sheehan a copy. Sheehan kept up the farce. He collected the copy from Ellsberg, then he stored some of the papers and destroyed the rest. Later, according to Scott's reporting, Sheehan denied that either Ellsberg or he had stolen the papers. As reported, Sheehan told Ellsberg, "Those papers are the property of the people of the United States. They paid for them with their national treasure and the blood of their sons, and they have a right to it."[24]

The documents Sheehan clandestinely copied were reviewed by a team of *New York Times* reporters and editors at a Hilton Hotel in New York City. No one else at the newspaper knew what they were doing. The documents, weighing sixty pounds,[25] were transferred from the *Times* to the hotel in shopping bags and grocery carts through Times Square by reporters "trying to appear as innocent as possible."[26] That is not to say that the group was unconcerned about the gravity of the undertaking. Betsy Wade, who made history as the first woman copy editor at the *Times*,[27] remembers it this way: "I came into the Pentagon Papers project a week before publication began, when Al Siegal [then foreign affairs editor at the *Times*] asked me if I wanted to join Project X, and did I mind going to jail?"[28] During the review process and before publication, the team often engaged in acrimonious debate about the wisdom of the endeavor and argued about whether their actions were patriotic, self-serving, or treasonous.[29] Once the articles were ready to print, ignoring the warnings from their legal counsel, the editorial board decided that the information in the report was essential to maintaining an informed electorate, a core principle of democratic governance, and chose to publish the material.

Sheehan won the 1972 Pulitzer Prize for his writing on the series for the *Times*.[30] One of the most damning revelations was about the origins of the Gulf of Tonkin Resolution, a congressional resolution passed on August 7, 1964, which provided the Johnson Administration with significantly increased authority to engage in military operations in Vietnam and led to a substantial escalation in the war. The administration had framed the resolution as a necessary response to an aggressive, un-provoked attack by the North Vietnamese on American ships in the Gulf of Tonkin. That frame was, at best, misleading and, at worst, an outright lie. The truth was that for months preceding the North Vietnamese attack, the Americans had been engaged in a shadow war, sponsoring incursions into North Vietnamese territory. The attack by the North Vietnamese was reactive, not aggressive. The administration had engaged in a sleight of hand that cost thousands of Americans their lives.[31]

According to Sheehan, he never revealed Ellsberg's identity. Apparently, a journalist who was not employed by the *Times* blew Ellsberg's cover.[32] After that, Ellsberg granted numerous interviews to newspapers and television stations. He insisted that it was not his intention to bring down the structures of government. Instead, it was his desire and intent to educate the American public and force a reckoning that would end the war.[33]

The events of the two weeks following publication by the *Times* unfolded with head-spinning speed. The first article was printed on June 13, 1971. In the introductory article, the newspaper described the treatise as revealing "a great deal about the ways in which several administrations conducted their business on a fateful course, with much new information about the roles of dozens of senior officials of both major political parties and a whole generation of military commanders."[34] A second article was printed the following day. That night, the *Times* received a telegram from Attorney General John Mitchell (later jailed for his role in the Watergate scandal) insisting the paper immediately cease publication, asserting that circulating the contents of the report was a violation of the Espionage Act and that continued disclosures would "cause irreparable injury to the defense interests of the United States."[35] The Pentagon also released a public statement characterizing some of the report's evidence as highly classified and sensitive.[36] According to a *Times* article printed on June 14, the editors refused to comply with the demand, stating, "The Times must respectfully decline the request of the Attorney General, believing that it is in the interest of the people of this country to be informed of the material contained in this series of articles."[37]

On that same day, US Justice Department lawyers filed a lawsuit on behalf of the government in the US District Court for the Southern District of New York. They sought an **injunction** to stop publication. The government, represented by Solicitor General Erwin Griswold, argued that the Pentagon Papers' continued publication put national security at stake. These were Top Secret, classified documents that, by definition, required that the information written on those pages should not be revealed. The government made this argument even though many of the documents published were decades old, and none were more recent than three years in the past. Max Frankel, the *New York Times* bureau chief, was nothing short of incredulous. He insisted on filing a sworn statement with the court explaining the realities of information exchange in Washington and the government's self-serving actions in labeling information Top Secret. His words are stinging:

> [T]he Government and its officials regularly and routinely misuse and abuse the "classification" of information, either by imposing secrecy where none is justified or by retaining it long after the justification has become invalid, for simple reasons of political or bureaucratic convenience. To hide mistakes of judgment, to protect reputations of individuals, to cover up the loss and waste of funds, almost everything in government is kept secret for a time and, in the foreign policy field, classified as "secret" and "sensitive" beyond any rule of law or reason. Every minor official can testify to this fact.[38]

On June 15, 1971, Judge Murray Gurfein granted the government a **temporary restraining order** requiring the *New York Times* to immediately stop publication of the story and the documents until further hearings could be scheduled. This was not the first time that the US government sought to restrict the publication of information that the government deemed harmful or embarrassing. In most of those cases, the government pursued the publishers after the fact and sought post-publication punishment. In other, relatively rare circumstances, publications are blocked by executive action. For example, most individuals employed by US intelligence agencies must submit any writings for publication, whether they be fiction or nonfiction, for prepublication review. If the government can prove a compelling national security interest in maintaining secrecy regarding the material proposed for publication, the publication can be blocked.[39] This, however, was the first time in United States history that a newspaper had been forbidden by order of a US federal court to print a story.[40] Before being silenced, the newspaper had only published three installments of what it titled "The Vietnam Archives."[41]

The *Times* was muted, but the injunction only applied to that singular newspaper. During the period in which the *Times* was prohibited from publishing, Ellsberg distributed all or portions of the Pentagon Papers to approximately twenty different newspapers, including the *Washington Post*, which then stepped in to fill the void.[42]

The *Post* began publishing and providing commentary starting on June 18, 1971. In response, the Justice Department filed a lawsuit against the *Post* that was virtually identical to the one in New York, but this time in the US District Court for the District of Columbia. After a series of hearings, that court refused to issue an order requiring that newspaper to cease publication of the Pentagon Papers. The result was that the *Post* could publish the story, but the *Times*, which had the story first, could not.

A word on process here: As you know, we have two court systems in the United States. The individual states each have a court system that adjudicates issues raised by state law or within state borders. State courts are physically located across the geography of the individual states. For instance, in Georgia, there are state courts located in Atlanta, and there are state courts located in Augusta, as well as other parts of the state. They are responsible for adjudicating issues in the geography they serve. There is also a federal court system that, for the most part, adjudicates issues related to the Constitution, violations of federal laws, controversies between states, disputes between parties from different states, and lawsuits in which the federal government is a party. Federal courts are physically located across the United States. In the federal court system, there are ninety-four district or trial courts, called US district courts. There is at least one district court in each state as well as the District of Columbia. The ninety-four federal judicial districts are grouped into twelve regional circuits. Given that there are only twelve circuits, each circuit obviously spans a geography that might include more than one state. Appeals from the district courts go to an assigned appellate court in its regional circuit. Appeals from the district trial court in DC, where the *Washington Post* lawsuit was filed, are assigned to the US Court of Appeals for the District of Columbia. Appeals from the district trial court in the Southern District of New York, where the *New York Times* lawsuit was filed, are appealed to the US Court of Appeals for the Second Circuit.

Both cases, the one in New York and the one in DC, were appealed to their respective appellate courts. The effect of the appeals was to maintain the status quo. The *Post* was free to publish, the *Times* was not (unless it wanted to be held in contempt of court). With the conflicting decisions among the federal courts, time was of the essence.

Given that this was an issue of national importance, the Supreme Court agreed to an expedited process. Within days, both newspapers and the Justice Department crafted their arguments and filed their **briefs** (structured legal arguments) with the Supreme Court. To further illustrate the danger, one of the government's briefs was sealed and designated as Top Secret. Included within its pages were references to specific parts of the Pentagon Papers, the disclosure of which the government alleged could affect, among other things, the government's ability to negotiate for peace and a return of prisoners of war. Congress weighed in on the legal arguments as well. Twenty-seven members of Congress submitted an **amicus curiae** (friend of the court) brief arguing that the Pentagon Papers should be published and urging the justices to act as a curb on executive branch overreach and consider the legislature's right to know.[43]

On June 30, 1971, just fifteen days after the *Times* published its first article, the court made its decision. The newspapers won. Publication of the Pentagon Papers would continue to inform an increasingly interested public.

In the opening paragraphs of the 6–3 decision, the court in *New York Times Co. v. United States* quickly designated the injunction imposed in the New York case as a **prior restraint** against political speech. Prior restraint is censorship pure and simple: Speech is eliminated, nothing is published or communicated.[44] There is only silence. Prior restraint has been described as "the single most intrusive and dangerous form of government conduct threatening freedom of expression."[45]

No single justice wrote for the majority, but uncharacteristically, each of the justices wrote a separate opinion. Six justices wrote concurring opinions, each describing the aversion the First Amendment has to prior restraint, and the extraordinary burden the government must meet before the court will support censorship. The government had argued that under the banner of national security, publication of the Pentagon Papers should be censored and public discourse stifled. However, neither within its brief nor at oral argument was the government able to provide evidence of the criteria it used to determine what information should be designated Top Secret. At least for a majority of the justices, that was the fatal flaw in the government's case.

Even those who had testified at the trial level in support of banning publication could not articulate national security fears. In New York, Vice Admiral Francis J. Blouin, deputy chief of Naval Operations for Plans and Policy, had testified not to any specific harm the publication would cause but only that "there is an awful lot of stuff in [the Pentagon study] that I would just prefer to see sleep a while longer."[46] William B. Macomber, deputy undersecretary of state for administration, testified, "I just don't see how we can conduct diplomacy with this kind of business going on."[47] To the majority of justices, his recitation sounded more like embarrassment than danger. As such, a majority of the justices determined that this argument was not strong enough to overcome the hurdles the First Amendment placed upon a prior restraint.

Justice Black commended the newspapers for their courageous reporting and acknowledged that by printing the report, the newspapers did "precisely that which the Founders hoped and trusted they would do."[48] The publication of the Pentagon Papers was "current news of vital importance to the people of this country."[49] He insisted that national security claims at the cost of an informed public provided no security at all.

Justice William O. Douglas asserted that government secrecy was antidemocratic, and he reiterated the constitutional imperative of open and robust debate. Justices Brennan and Stewart described the tentative nature of the government's argument and insisted that only substantial evidence of irreparable harm could support a prior restraint:

> The entire thrust of the Government's claim throughout these cases has been that publication of the material sought to be

enjoined "could," or "might," or "may" prejudice the national interest in various ways. But the First Amendment tolerates absolutely no prior judicial restraints of the press predicated upon surmise or conjecture that untoward consequences may result. . . . [W]hen everything is classified, then nothing is classified, and the system becomes one to be disregarded by the cynical or the careless, and to be manipulated by those intent on self-protection or self-promotion. I should suppose, in short, that the hallmark of a truly effective internal security system would be the maximum possible disclosure, recognizing that secrecy can best be preserved only when credibility is truly maintained.[50]

The opinions of all six concurring justices continue to this day to guide government actions regarding issues of censorship. In denying the government's request to prohibit publication of the Pentagon Papers, the court relied upon the strong presumption in favor of political speech. The court steadfastly defended the importance of political speech as a fundamental element of a functioning democracy. As a cornerstone of democratic governance and champion of the marketplace of ideas, the First Amendment required that in the absence of strong evidence of harm, the public had a right to know about the inner workings of government and governmental decision making.

Each of the dissenting justices also filed written opinions. They did not address the First Amendment issues presented. Instead, they lamented the procedural history of the case. They argued that the race to the Supreme Court was unseemly in its haste. Justice John Marshall Harlan recited the timeline: It was a mere six days from the filing of the petition for a writ of certiorari to the delivery of the decision.[51] Generally, cases take months, even years, or in some instances, decades, to reach the Supreme Court. Justice Warren E. Burger argued further that the *Times* had the documents for three to four months; why all of a sudden did the public have an immediate right to know?[52]

In hindsight, whether it was necessary for the Pentagon Papers to be published with immediacy or not, it appears their publication did affect debate and likely accelerated decisions that led to US withdrawal. It also prompted an investigation into the secret classification system employed by the executive branch, thereby increasing the effectiveness of the Freedom of Information Act.[53]

Upon the release of the Supreme Court decision, the *Times* recommenced publication and continued until the final installment on July 5, 1971. The *Washington Post* completed its publication as well. The Pentagon Papers, in their entirety, were declassified in 2011 and are currently available in PDF format from the National Archives.[54] For a more entertaining experience, the story of the *Washington Post*'s role in the Pentagon Papers is recreated in the movie *The Post*, released in 2017, starring Meryl Streep and Tom Hanks.

BESETTING KRYPTONITE UPON THE SUPERPOWER OF THE FIRST AMENDMENT

Until now, the First Amendment has been the most potent force against the government seeking to halt the publication of government secrets. Today, it seems the internet might be a powerful, even indestructible, ally. Anyone with access to the internet can disseminate information across the world over the course of minutes. The government is virtually powerless to halt the publication of stolen or leaked materials, immobilizing the weapon of prior restraint. Release of classified information by WikiLeaks proves the point.

In 2010, Chelsea Manning, then serving as an army intelligence analyst using the name Bradley Manning, started downloading and saving classified information to which she had access. The information included approximately 250,000 diplomatic cables and incident reports from the wars in Iraq and Afghanistan as well as dossiers on enemy combatants detained at Guantánamo Bay, Cuba.[55] Like Ellsberg, Manning was convinced she was in possession of information that needed to see daylight. In an online conversation with a celebrity hacker who eventually alerted the FBI to her exploits, Manning explained, "i want people to see the truth . . . because without information, you cannot make informed decisions as a public."[56]

Manning reached out to the *Washington Post* and the *New York Times* but was ignored. Then she turned to WikiLeaks. At the time, WikiLeaks was a relatively unknown volunteer organization that served as a portal to the internet for disclosure of leaked or stolen government information; publishing the Manning material put WikiLeaks on the map. Following the WikiLeaks disclosures, much of the material was published by the *Times* and the *Post*. Unlike during the Vietnam era, there was no opportunity for the US government to stop publication, leaving the weapon of censorship out of its arsenal and that particular First Amendment debate largely eliminated.

The truth is that the government and the press have a complicated relationship with regard to government information. As detailed by Max Frankel in his affidavit in *New York Times v. United States*, the government leaks like a sieve, and more often than not, the leaks serve the government's interests. Frankel is not alone in that knowledge. As it happens, his statement is supported by data. In 2013, the *Harvard Law Review* published a study that detailed the symbiotic nature of government officials, their secrets, and the press.[57] It describes the situation as a "permissive culture of classified information disclosures."[58] That having been said, the government wants to be in the driver's seat in determining whether or not something will be disclosed.

A TACTICAL POWER PLAY

In actuality, the internet's power is not limitless, nor is the government powerless. While the government might not be able to stop publication, it may seek to prosecute the leaker. Indictments against leakers are carefully drawn to seek punishment for stealing information. Punishment is sought against illegal behavior, not speech. Both Ellsberg and Manning were prosecuted under the Espionage Act of 1917 for, among other things, stealing government documents.

The government wasted no time in its quest to punish Ellsberg. At the same time the government was fighting publication of the Pentagon Papers, Ellsberg was charged with fifteen counts of theft of government documents and espionage. He faced up to 105 years in prison.[59] Ellsberg surrendered to authorities on June 28, 1971, two days before the Supreme Court rendered its decision on the publication of the Pentagon Papers.[60] As in all things Pentagon Papers, the coda to the Ellsberg trial reads like a spy novel.

The criminal trial against Ellsberg lasted eighty-nine days. On that final day, Judge William Byrne dismissed all charges against Ellsberg and barred the government from retrying him. The judge took this extraordinary action not because Ellsberg was innocent but because the government had engaged in horrific prosecutorial misconduct. It turned out that during the trial, G. Gordon Liddy and E. Howard Hunt hatched a plan. Liddy and Hunt, later indicted and jailed for their role in the Watergate break-in, were members of the White House Special Investigations Unit, known internally as the Plumbers, a reconnaissance unit tasked with plugging White House information leaks. Their plan, approved by John Ehrlichman, a member of President Nixon's inner circle who served as counsel to the president and assistant to the president for domestic affairs, included burglarizing and photographing medical records from Dr. Lewis Fielding, Ellsberg's psychiatrist.[61] The apparent purpose of the plan was to discover information that could be used to blackmail or, at the very least, discredit Ellsberg. On September 3, 1971, the three men executed the plan, which was later revealed to Judge Byrne.[62] In dismissing the case, the judge registered his disgust, writing:

> [T]he conduct of the Government has placed the case in such a
> posture that it precludes the fair, dispassionate resolution of these
> issues by a jury. . . . The totality of the circumstances of this case,
> which I have only briefly sketched, offend "a sense of justice." The
> bizarre events have incurably infected the prosecution of this case.[63]

The Manning prosecution reads more like a horror story than a spy novel. Chelsea Manning was raised as a boy in a small town north of Oklahoma City, a place she characterizes as "highly evangelical."[64] Manning described herself as small and effeminate and the target of intense bullying. She was exceedingly smart and particularly excelled in math and science. She came out as gay to her friends when she was thirteen. At the urging of her father, Manning enlisted in the military in 2007. At the time, the military no longer prohibited gay individuals from joining its ranks, but they didn't want to know about it. They wouldn't ask recruits about their sexual orientation, but the recruits were also expected to keep it under wraps. The policy was aptly named "Don't Ask, Don't Tell."

As a gay man in the army, Manning was again bullied and isolated. Over time, she began to experience gender dysphoria symptoms, which confused her and added to her already stressful living situation. Manning was a computer geek, so her placement as an intelligence analyst was well considered, and she received extensive intelligence training. In 2009, despite concerns about her mental health, Manning was deployed to Iraq. Her skills were in demand, so it seemed her health would have to take a back seat. In Iraq, Manning worked grueling hours. She was lonely and angry. Secluded and friendless, she used some of her time to snoop around war logs and files to which, given her wide-ranging security clearance, she had access.[65]

Manning was arrested on May 27, 2010, and charged with twenty-two violations of the Uniform Code of Military Justice and the Espionage Act, including stealing US government property and aiding the enemy.[66] For eleven months, she was held in solitary confinement, sometimes forced to sleep naked.[67] She was convicted of seventeen of the twenty-two charges against her and sentenced to thirty-five years in prison. It was the longest sentence ever imposed on a leaker.[68] While she was serving her sentence, Manning came out as a trans woman and fought for the right to live as a woman. Denied her requests, she tried to commit suicide twice.[69] Finally, the army agreed to provide her with hormone therapy and allowed her to undergo gender transition surgery. The surgery, however, was not completed prior to her release.[70] In January 2017, President Obama commuted her sentence after hearing convincing arguments that the sentence was excessive. She had served nearly seven years.

The founder of WikiLeaks, Julian Assange, is under US federal indictment and is likely to spend years fighting extradition to the United States. Prosecutors have subpoenaed Manning to testify before a grand jury investigating Assange. She has been given immunity, so she cannot be assessed any penalty for incriminating information she reveals during her testimony. But she has refused on the grounds that she is fundamentally opposed to the secrecy surrounding grand jury investigations, which are conducted behind closed doors and outside of public view.[71] Her refusal landed her in jail again for over a year. She was released on March 12, 2020, and because she has proven that she will not be coerced into testimony, she will not likely be incarcerated for her refusal again.[72]

The demand for Manning's testimony is significant from a First Amendment perspective. Prosecutors hope to find evidence that Assange helped Manning retrieve and download the information from classified files. If so, like Ellsberg and Manning, Assange can be prosecuted for leaking information. If there is no evidence to tie Assange to the retrieving and downloading, then the government may be limited to prosecuting him for publishing. In that situation, Assange's position would shift to be more analogous to the *New York Times* and the *Washington Post* in the Pentagon Papers case. It is true that the *Times* and the *Post* are newspapers, each with an editorial staff that decides which part of the news is fit to print, and WikiLeaks exercises little, if any, editorial control over content. WikiLeaks serves as a publisher of original source material, most particularly "large datasets of censored or otherwise restricted official materials involving war, spying and corruption."[73] Any editorial use of the information retrieved from WikiLeaks is controlled by the user. However, from a First Amendment perspective, both the newspapers and WikiLeaks differ very little, so that, if Assange's relationship to the release of the information is as a publisher rather than a leaker, the First Amendment will very likely shield him from any criminal liability.

Another recent infamous leak case involves Edward Joseph Snowden. Snowden was a former computer technician with the CIA and was later hired as an independent contractor for Booz Allen Hamilton. In 2013, Snowden leaked classified information to the *Guardian*, an internet-based news and media website, revealing global surveillance programs conducted by the United States National Security Agency.[74] He fled to Russia, where he continues to enjoy asylum. He has been charged with two counts of violating the Espionage Act.[75] His US passport has been revoked, but should he return to the country he will be arrested for the theft of the classified material. The *Guardian* and its editors and reporters have not, to our knowledge, been criminally charged for publishing the documents, likely because the First Amendment would provide them a very strong, if not impenetrable, defense.

There comes a time when one must take a position
that is neither safe, nor politic, nor popular, but he
must take it because conscience tells him it is right.
—*Martin Luther King Jr.*[1]

The First Amendment serves its highest purpose as protector of political speech, and it is for that reason that censorship is so profoundly assailed. **Political speech** is not merely communication transmitted during campaigns or among politicians, legislators, lobbyists, and activists. Any person expressing an opinion or engaging in debate on a matter of public concern, whether that be matters of policy, morality, economics, or the like, is engaging in political speech.

Political speech is not always pleasant or courteous or comforting. It is often caustic, troublesome, or based on false ideas. Even so, the constitutional character of political speech will not change; it will continue to enjoy the most robust protection offered by the First Amendment. In 2011, this principle saved the Westboro Baptist Church and its members from bankruptcy.

Until shortly before his death in March 2014, the Westboro Baptist Church was led by its patriarch, Fred W. Phelps Sr. He was a person of deep contradictory character. In 2007, the BBC dubbed his "the most hated family in America."[2] He had been a preacher all of his adult life: he preached sermons full of firebrand and bile about the sin he believed was engulfing the United States, secure in his knowledge that he knew God's will and was his loyal servant.[3] But during the 1960s, 1970s, and much of the 1980s, Phelps also served as a well-respected civil rights lawyer. In Kansas, the state that has the dubious distinction of providing the Supreme Court with the grounds to overturn the "separate but equal" segregation doctrine, he spearheaded a class action lawsuit on the twentieth anniversary of *Brown v. Board of Education*,[4] alleging schools had not lived up to the Supreme Court's dictates and that the schools in Kansas remained unintegrated and unequal.[5] His courtroom demeanor was described as impressive and his oratory as blistering. He had been honored multiple times for his civil rights work. In 1986 he received the Omaha Mayor's Special Recognition Award, and in 1987 he received an award from a local branch of the NAACP for his extraordinary work pursuing civil rights justice for Black people in Kansas.[6] He was a man of great passion and understood the Constitution's power to protect the most vulnerable. His passion, often transforming his otherwise charming manner into anger, ultimately got the better of him. He was stripped of his state license to practice law in 1977 and his federal license in 1989, both times for his unrelenting misuse and manipulation of the legal system.

Phelps drew national attention in 1998 when, at his direction, his church members picketed the funeral of Matthew Shepard, a young college student who was targeted, tortured, and murdered because he was gay. Church members arrived at the funeral along with their signature sign, "God hates fags." Additional signs included the phrases "Fags are nature freaks" and "Matt in hell."[7] It shocked the community. This, however, was just the beginning of the church's multistate, multimediated funeral-protest campaign where they demonstrate against what they describe as America's moral decay.

Despite its title, the church is not affiliated with any particular religious denomination. The Anti-Defamation League and the Southern Poverty Law Center identify the Westboro Baptist Church not as a religious organization but as a hate group. Their preferred targets: the LGBTQ community, the Jewish community, and any individual or group that does not abide by their mantra of "Repent or Perish."

The small congregation is based in Topeka, Kansas. Most of the church members are also members of the large Phelps family, which numbers about seventy. They reside on the church compound in several modest houses. The compound, bounded by chain-link and wood fencing, includes a swimming pool, a running track, tennis and basketball courts, and a children's playground. The Canadian and American flags are flown over the compound upside down.[8] A competing symbol sits across the street, crafted by the organization Planting Peace, which purchased the neighboring property and then painted their building the rainbow colors of the LGBTQ rights movement.[9]

Almost two decades after Matthew Shepard's funeral, the group was still traversing the United States, spreading its message. On March 10, 2006, in the middle of a record-setting heat wave, they arrived in Maryland, signs in hand.[10] Phelps and six of his followers, including two of his daughters, Rebekah Phelps-Davis and Shirley Phelps-Roper, traveled there to protest the funeral service honoring the life of Marine Lance Corporal Matthew Snyder. Snyder died on March 3, 2006, from a noncombat-related accident in Anbar Province, Iraq, while supporting Operation Iraqi Freedom. The Phelps family gathered approximately one thousand feet from the Catholic church, where the funeral service was being held. In full compliance with all state and local regulations, they peacefully and silently marched on the sidewalk, holding signs that read:

God Hates the USA
Thank God for 9/11
America is Doomed
Don't Pray for the USA
Thank God for IEDs
Fag Troops
Semper Fi Fags
God Hates Fags
Maryland Taliban
Fags Doom Nations
Not Blessed Just Cursed
Thank God for Dead Soldiers
Pope in Hell
Priests Rape Boys
You're Going to Hell
God Hates You

All of the signs were produced and printed at an on-site facility at the family compound where they also create videos that are uploaded to their website: godhatesfags.com. Fortunately, Matthew's father, Albert Snyder, did not see the signs until later that day when he watched the news after the burial had concluded. The broadcasted images portrayed his son's funeral as a media circus rather than a somber reflection of a life cut short far too soon. After the group returned to Kansas, they produced a video titled *Epic* that they uploaded to their website. Snyder discovered the video after conducting an internet search of his son's name. Shirley Phelps-Roper narrated the video, in which she charges that Snyder and his former wife "taught Matthew to defy his creator," "raised him for the devil," and "taught him that God was a liar."[11]

Seeing the images of the protest and watching his family's lives and reputation besmirched online caused Albert Snyder to become physically sick and emotionally distraught.[12] He then sued Phelps and the Westboro Baptist Church for intentional infliction of emotional distress, intrusion upon seclusion, and civil conspiracy. A jury awarded Snyder $10.9 million. Phelps and his church appealed the ruling alleging, among other things, that the picketing was protected political speech under the First Amendment, and as such, any award of damages to Snyder, whether he had been disturbed or not by the picketing, was unconstitutional. In an 8–1 decision the Supreme Court agreed with Phelps and the church; the speech was protected political speech.[13] The verdict was set aside, and Snyder did not collect any of the award.

The court acknowledged that the signs, particularly when displayed at the funeral of a fallen soldier, were disturbing, but the signs were nonetheless political speech. The ideas expressed in the signs served as a commentary on public policy. They represented one side of the debate on issues of government responsibility to legislate morality and the role of religion in the public sphere. Therefore, they were protected by the First Amendment. The court was clear:

> [S]peech on matters of public concern . . . is at the heart of the
> First Amendment's protection. The First Amendment reflects a
> profound national commitment to the principle that debate on
> public issues should be uninhibited, robust, and wide-open. That
> is because speech concerning public affairs is more than self-
> expression; it is the essence of self-government. Accordingly, speech
> on public issues occupies the highest rung of the hierarchy of First
> Amendment values and is entitled to special protection. . . . While
> [the signs and their] messages may fall short of refined social or
> political commentary, the issues they highlight—the political and

moral conduct of the United States and its citizens, the fate of our Nation, homosexuality in the military, and scandals involving the Catholic clergy—are matters of public import.[14]

Political speech has been enjoying all the firepower the First Amendment promises since the middle of the last century. Writing for the majority, Chief Justice John Roberts Jr. once again clarified the constitutional prohibition of punishing speech simply because it is offensive: "If there is a bedrock principle underlying the First Amendment, it is that the government may not prohibit the expression of an idea simply because society finds the idea itself offensive or disagreeable."[15] Justice Samuel Alito disagreed with the chief justice's characterization of the language used by the Westboro Baptist Church as merely "offensive or disagreeable." In his lone dissent, he insisted, "[i]n order to have a society in which public issues can be openly and vigorously debated, it is not necessary to allow the brutalization of innocent victims like [Albert Snyder]."[16]

The cases asserting the preeminence of political speech in First Amendment jurisprudence reflect the constitutional struggle between protecting speech and protecting the rights of those who are injured by the speech. Speech by one, as a measure of their liberty, might under some circumstances conflict with another person's right to pursue happiness. Such was the case with the disturbing pronouncements of the Westboro Baptist Church. Their expressions of morality, politics, and religious ideology conflict with the natural right of liberty and the pursuit of happiness of their targets. It is in these situations that the measure of the protection offered by the First Amendment is most apparent.

Muting and muzzling political speech is repugnant to the First Amendment. Critical and robust debate is necessary to ensure the proper functioning of our government and democracy. Time and time again, when the content of speech is defined by the courts as political, they rely on the default position that the speech should be protected.

Notwithstanding claims of national security.[17]

Notwithstanding claims of potential violence.[18]

Notwithstanding claims of emotional distress.[19]

Notwithstanding claims of vulgarity or tastelessness.[20]

The list goes on.

But, as we shall see, the list is not endless.

NOT TODAY, FRED

Those who are offended by the antics of the Westboro Baptist Church and others who proselytize intolerance and hate are not defenseless. They, too, can claim the protection of the First Amendment's superpower. And they do.

In 1998 Romaine Patterson, a Wyoming native, organized a group of people to counterprotest against church members who supported Matthew Shepard's murderers during their criminal trial. The counterprotesters arrived in white capes, dressed as angels. When the church members raised their signs, the angels spread their wings, obscuring the offending words. Now, angels often appear across the nation to conceal the church members and protect those in mourning.[21]

An angel of a different variety addressed the church on September 11, 2001. That day, the angel had no wings and was singular in his quest. On September 11, 2001, a lone young man stood in front of the church compound in Kansas. He held a simple, hand-painted sign that read, "Not today, Fred." The next day he was joined by ninety others.[22]

7 : WARNING! DANGEROUS SPEECH AHEAD

Some people's idea of [free speech] is that they are
free to say what they like, but if anyone says anything
back, that is an outrage. —Winston Churchill[1]

In the early part of the last century, Americans were happy to remain isolated from the nationalistic disputes brewing in Europe. Most Americans had little interest in a war "over there." American indifference was shaken when a German U-boat attacked and sunk the British ocean liner *Lusitania*. Almost 2,000 people died in the attack, including 128 Americans. After an international outcry, Germany agreed to halt attacks on nonmilitary vessels without fair warning. Two years later, Germany resumed unrestricted submarine warfare, fueling American war fever.[2]

The march toward war was swift. On April 2, 1917, President Woodrow Wilson addressed a joint session of Congress and requested a declaration of war against Germany. On April 4, the US Senate voted in favor of the declaration. The House gave its assent two days later, and on April 6, the United States of America entered World War I.[3] US war efforts quickly ramped up.

On April 13, in an effort to increase public support for the war, President Wilson signed an executive order creating the Committee on Public Information. The committee was charged with producing what many today recognize as state-sponsored propaganda.[4] President Wilson also publicly encouraged citizens to report any suspicious or subversive activity to the Justice Department. In other words, any activity that did not support the war was assuredly frowned upon and possibly illegal.

Six weeks later, on May 17, Congress passed the Selective Service Act of 1917, giving the president power to draft soldiers into combat. (It was this act, as amended in 1965, that put David Paul O'Brien in jail.) Then, on June 15, in response to administration lobbying efforts, Congress passed the Espionage Act of 1917. (Yes, the same Espionage Act under which, decades later, Daniel Ellsberg, Chelsea Manning, and Edward

Snowden would be charged.) Among other things, the Espionage Act made it a crime to interfere with recruitment or military operations and was broadly defined to include "refusal of duty or disloyalty."[5]

Fearful of efforts by pacifists, anarchists, and socialists to impede the war effort, less than a year later Congress passed the Sedition Act of 1918, which amended the Espionage Act and expanded its reach. While the Espionage Act targeted organized efforts that promoted resistance to the war or disrupted the objectives of the armed forces, the Sedition Act criminalized speech that the government feared would undermine the war effort. A conviction under the Sedition Act could result in a twenty-year jail sentence.[6] It appeared that the government intended to eliminate opposition to the war, and only fealty to the cause would be tolerated.[7] Those who dared to protest the war or government policies that supported the war effort were in danger of being arrested and prosecuted.

CLEAR AND PRESENT DANGER

Three months after Congress instituted the draft, the Philadelphia branch of the Socialist Party met and directed its officers to craft a document outlining steps to take in furtherance of the group's opposition to the government's war strategy. In August 1917, Charles T. Schenck was completing his term as general secretary of the political organization. Following the party's direction, he, along with Elizabeth Baer, a physician and executive committee member of the party, drafted and printed a single-page, two-sided leaflet.[8] One side was titled "Long Live the Constitution of the United States," and the other side was titled "Assert Your Rights."[9] The contents described the war draft as "despotism in its worst form, and a monstrous wrong against humanity." It urged readers not to submit to the draft and thereby "submit to intimidation."[10] Approximately 15,000 copies were mailed to draftees and others. Schenck and Baer were arrested, tried, and convicted under the Espionage Act.

Their conviction rested only on evidence of their intent to obstruct the draft.[11] No evidence was submitted at the trial that the leaflets persuaded anyone to avoid the draft or otherwise resist war efforts. Schenck, described as a "small, nervous man,"[12] was sentenced to six months in prison; Baer was sentenced to ninety days.[13] They appealed their convictions, arguing that their speech was political and that the First Amendment protected them from government prosecution. However, political speech had not yet obtained its primacy in the First Amendment constellation of protections. The government was suspicious of minority views and consequently speech that appeared to undermine government policy was suspect, and the courts were disinclined to provide such views constitutional safeguards. So, at the time, asserting First Amendment protection for speech critical of the government as protected political speech was a novel argument.[14] Realistically, the Supreme Court was unlikely to embrace broader speech protections under the then-current circumstances. The war fever created great stress in the citizenry, to which the court was not immune. This was not a time to upset the status quo. To the contrary, the court was quite comfortable allowing the views of the majority to bend the will of the individual.

In a unanimous decision, the Supreme Court of the United States upheld the conviction; Schenck and others could not use the First Amendment as a bulwark against criminal liability. Writing for the court, Justice Oliver Wendell Holmes Jr. explained that attempts to obstruct the government from performing its responsibilities created a **clear and present danger** to the citizenry's safety and security and therefore were not protected. Such attempts could be prohibited and even criminalized. Justice Holmes did not dismiss First Amendment protections but insisted that under these circumstances, they were not enough to save the defendants from criminal punishment. In perhaps his most famous quote, the justice reminded us: "The most stringent protection of free speech would not protect a man in falsely shouting fire in a theatre and causing a panic."[15] Schenck and Baer remained convicted criminals and were required to serve their full terms in jail.[16]

In subsequent cases in the lower courts and the Supreme Court, the clear and present danger test was used to identify speech that purportedly had a natural or probable effect of inciting illegal activity; this speech was then stripped of First Amendment protection. The test seemed to imply that the audience has no free will, that words directed toward an audience have an immediate effect. The courts embraced the accepted social scientific paradigm of the time that speech alone could produce harm to the public. In other words, speech can cause or create an effect on an audience and induce behavior.

Academicians described the theory at the time as the **hypodermic needle theory**, which analogized communication to vaccinations—all recipients have the same response to the inoculation, or in this case, the communication. It was also called the **magic bullet theory**, imagining the audience as monolithic, uncritical, and easily manipulated. It followed that an easily manipulated audience, one that can be vaccinated by a hypodermic needle or influenced by a magic bullet of words, is dangerous to the public welfare. As such, the government, in its paternalistic capacity, was duty bound to protect the nation's health and well-being.[17] If speech appeared capable of inducing an audience to subvert a government policy, then the speakers should be punished.

The *Schenck* clear and present danger test was liberally utilized for the next fifty years to criminalize speech that the government found might influence the target audience to behave in a manner that could lead to criminal activity, including violence or obstructing the government in its regular functions. Hundreds were arrested, prosecuted, and convicted under the Espionage and Sedition Acts. Among the most notable was a group of five Russian-born immigrants: Jacob Abrams, Hyman Rosansky, Hyman Lachowsky, Samuel Lipman, and Mollie Steimer. The group politically identified as anarchists and produced an underground newspaper, *Der Shturem* (The Storm), and later, *Frayhayt* (Freedom). The papers' editorial posture exhorted against the evils of capitalism and the American war effort. Conversely, the papers urged support for socialism and the Bolshevik Revolution in Russia.

Mollie Steimer was the star of the group. A diminutive provocateur, she emigrated to the United States from Russia in 1913 at the age of sixteen and was employed in New York City as a seamstress in the garment district.[18] She lived in an apartment in Harlem with several friends, including Jacob Abrams. Born Jacob Abramovsky, he changed his name upon his arrival at Ellis Island at twenty-two.[19] Abrams worked as a bookbinder and ultimately became president of the local union chapter of the International Brotherhood of Bookbinders.[20]

The immigrant anarchists were alarmed when American troops arrived in Russia during the spring and summer of 1918. Abrams and company firmly believed the troops would interfere in the Bolshevik cause, so they went back to the presses, located in the basement of a building in East Harlem, New York. They proceeded to print leaflets in opposition to the military action.[21] They printed 5,000 copies each of two leaflets, one in Yiddish and one in English.[22] The leaflets included language that accused President Wilson of being a hypocrite and a coward and further called for a general strike against government work that produced "bullets, bayonets, cannon and other munitions of war the use of which would cause the murder of Germans and Russians."[23] Steimer and Rosansky distributed many of the leaflets around the city. Later, Steimer dumped the remainder out of an upper-floor bathroom of the factory in which she worked.[24] The papers were collected by a group of men on the street and delivered to the local police. The police arrived at the building and arrested the only person present at the time: Hyman Rosansky. A young, now frightened idealist, he quickly revealed the identity of his comrades. The police moved on to the apartment where the group lived and arrested Abrams and another man, Jacob Schwartz. Abrams and Schwartz were beaten on the way to the station. Schwartz later died, most likely from the injuries he sustained from the beating. Over the next few days, the rest of the group was rounded up. They were charged and tried under the Espionage Act, as amended by the Sedition Act.

The presiding trial judge was Henry DeLamar Clayton Jr., a visiting judge from Alabama. He exhibited a breathtaking bias at the trial. In one exchange with the defendants, he asked them why they simply didn't return to Russia. And in another exchange with their lawyer, Howard Weinberger, Judge Clayton said, "I have tried to out-talk an Irishman, and I never can do it, and the Lord knows I cannot out-talk a Jew."[25] In his summation, Weinberger argued that the Abrams defendants were not subversives; they were merely idealists.[26] It was the government, he argued, that was subverting the First Amendment.

The jury deliberated only one hour and six minutes before finding the group guilty.[27] After berating the defendants, Judge Clayton imposed the maximum sentences allowable by law: twenty years for the men, and for the lone woman, Mollie Steimer, fifteen years.[28] Hyman Rosansky was sentenced to three years, as recognition for the assistance he had provided in the others' arrest and conviction.[29]

The Supreme Court confirmed their convictions; however, due to their attorney's enormous lobbying efforts, their sentences were commuted, and they were released from prison after serving three years and deported to Russia.[30] Steimer and Abrams continued to support the Bolshevik cause in their homeland but eventually became disenchanted, and both lived out their lives with their companions in Mexico City. They remained friends all their lives. Steimer was at Abrams' bedside the day he died from lung cancer on June 10, 1953.[31] The life stories of Lachowsky and Lipman are much more tragic: Lipman died at the hands of the Bolsheviks, and Lachowsky at the hands of the Nazis.[32]

Although the Supreme Court upheld the convictions in *Abrams v. United States*, unlike the *Schenck* decision, the *Abrams* decision was not unanimous.[33] Two justices disagreed with the majority decision and dissented: Holmes and Brandeis. Justice Holmes, who crafted the clear and present danger test in the Schenck case, wrote the dissenting opinion in the *Abrams* case. While Justice Louis Brandeis did not write his own opinion, he acknowledged his agreement with Holmes by concurring in Holmes' dissent. Justice Holmes argued the Abrams leaflet was silly, drafted by an unknown man and unlikely to produce any action on the part of the target audience. Justice Holmes insisted the First Amendment was never intended to restrict such inconsequential speech. Rather, he argued, speech should receive full First Amendment protection "unless [the words] so imminently threaten immediate interference with the lawful and pressing purposes of the law that an immediate check is required to save the country."[34]

Justice Holmes' dissenting opinion in *Abrams* represented a reinterpretation of the First Amendment. In it Holmes asserted that the First Amendment provided more robust and extensive protection than had been granted in the past. Even the other justices were disturbed, if not confused.[35] It is hard to reconcile why Justice Holmes believed Charles Schenck was a criminal and the *Abrams* five were not. Holmes himself explained his momentous change of posture from *Schenck* to *Abrams*, plainly stating, with regard to his *Schenck* decision, "I was simply ignorant."[36] Of course, Holmes' evolution on speech protections was not simple or plain but the result of profound intellectual exploration and debate.

In fact, subsequent to the *Schenck* case, Holmes spent a great deal of time rethinking his position. To that end, he spoke, argued, and considered the positions of several colleagues and friends, including Judge Learned Hand, Justice Louis Brandeis, Harold Laski, Zechariah Chafee, and Walter Lippmann, all recognized today as giants in the world of First Amendment legal doctrine.[37] He was under significant pressure from these men who met with him in person, wrote letters, and even joined him on a train ride, imploring him to reevaluate his limited view of First Amendment protections as articulated in *Schenck*. The turning point for Holmes was an article written by Chaffee in the *Harvard Law Review*, which provided Holmes with the intellectual and legal support for his paradigmatic shift.[38]

The impact of Holmes' turnabout cannot be overstated. He, like all of the justices, admitted an abiding belief in the law and precedent. It was rare for any justice to make such a titanic change. The law required consistency; anything less would lead to confusion regarding legally accepted parameters of behavior. Notably, it was exactly the free exchange of ideas to which Holmes referred in his dissent that moved his soul and changed his mind.

It was in this dissent that Justice Holmes articulated the now well-accepted justification for free speech protections as necessary to maintain a free and open marketplace of ideas. The opinion remains one of the preeminent statements of the fundamental value of free speech in a democratic society. Quoted again here, it is well regarded by legal scholars and jurists for its brilliance and its poetry: "[T]he ultimate good desired is better reached by free trade in ideas—that the best test of truth is the power of the thought to get itself accepted in the competition of the market, and that truth is the only ground upon which their wishes safely can be carried out."[39]

TOWARD A GRADUAL PHILOSOPHICAL RECALIBRATION

The expansion of speech protections was slow in coming. The Sedition Act was repealed less than two years after it was signed into law, but as we know, the Espionage Act remains on the books and is actively enforced even today. Additionally, the Espionage Act served as the model for state criminal syndicalism acts. **Criminal syndicalism laws** criminalized certain types of advocacy directed at political, industrial, or social change. More particularly, these laws were used by states to incarcerate dissidents who supported labor unions and socialist or communist ideologies and political platforms. Between 1917 and 1919, twenty-three states passed criminal syndicalism laws. California enacted its criminal syndicalism law on April 30, 1919;[40] it was not repealed until 1991.[41] One of the most prominent persons prosecuted under the California Syndicalism Law was Charlotte Whitney.[42]

Charlotte Whitney was a descendant of the Mayflower Pilgrims, the niece of a former Supreme Court justice, and an avowed communist.[43] Whitney was a lifelong advocate for social justice. As a trained social worker, she led the Associated Charities of Alameda County, California. She was instrumental in creating a juvenile court in the county and served as its first juvenile probation officer. She was a member of the NAACP and was dedicated to the women's suffrage movement.[44]

During the summer of 1919, Whitney attended the Communist Labor Party (CLP) convention as a delegate. There, despite her opposition, the CLP adopted a platform that specifically called for "organizing the workers as a class in a revolutionary class struggle to conquer the capitalist state for the overthrow of capitalist rule, the conquest of political power and the establishment of a working class government."[45] On November 28, 1919, she delivered a speech before the Women's Civic Center of Oakland, a group she had helped to found. Her topic was "The Negro Question," wherein she discussed her intention to protest recent lynchings and race riots. At the conclusion of the speech, she was arrested. She was charged under the California Criminal Syndicalism law for participating in the CLP convention that past summer as a delegate, and by that action, supporting an organization that advocated for the overthrow of the government.[46] Three months after she was arrested, she was tried. The trial lasted four long weeks, but the jury convicted her after deliberating only six hours, ostensibly for associating with and lending support to others who advocated for a violent revolution. At the age of fifty-two, for her first criminal offense, she was sentenced to fourteen years in San Quentin prison.[47] Three hundred people who worked with Whitney in the social services community attended her sentencing. They stood in tribute to her as she entered the courtroom and remained standing until the sentence was delivered.[48] Many leaders in the community were horrified and immediately began a petition seeking a pardon from the governor. Whitney herself was not part of that movement, asserting she should not be treated any differently than those with less social stature who were arrested, awaiting trial, or convicted under the same statute. Whitney need not have bothered; Governor Friend W. Richardson denied the pardon.[49]

Whitney chose to continue the fight through the courts and appealed the decision on several grounds, including that the California Criminal Syndicalism Law unconstitutionally infringed on liberties of assembly and speech. She argued that none of her actions could be considered an incitement to violence, and as a result, she was protected from criminal liability by the First Amendment. Fortunately for her, Whitney was able to post bail and await the long appellate process outside of the prison walls, because it took a full seven years before her case landed on the Supreme Court's steps.[50] All hope of reprieve was lost on May 27, 1927, when the court issued its unanimous decision upholding Whitney's conviction. The court found that the statute was a reasonable regulation designed to discourage activities the state deemed dangerous to public peace and security.[51]

Both Justice Holmes and Justice Brandeis believed the California law unconstitutionally punished speech; however, they concurred in the majority opinion because of procedural abnormalities.[52] This time, Justice Brandeis took the lead and wrote the concurring opinion that, for all intents and purposes, reads like a dissent. While Justice Holmes was described as aloof in demeanor, Justice Brandeis was engaging. At least in *Whitney*, his opinion matched his personality, and Brandeis offered a full-throated defense of speech protections even for ideas we hate.[53] He warned of the dangers of repression and insisted that debate and discussion were the only appropriate antidote to "noxious doctrine."[54] Brandeis argued that the foundational principle for self-government is liberty, and the freedom to speak without fear of punishment is an essential part of liberty.

Justice Brandeis warned that advocacy alone is not enough to move an audience to passion and violence. The speaker must intend for the words to incite action, and the words must have the power to arouse the audience to action. Brandeis explained that imminent danger from words exists only if there is insufficient time and space for cooler heads to prevail. He insisted that speech should be silenced only in emergency situations when a mob mentality overtakes reasoned reactions. He explained that when speech overtakes reasoned reactions, it obstructs debate and reflection and threatens public safety. In the absence of those conditions, even speech that advocates for the destruction of the government and its processes should be subject to the glare of discussion and debate. It is nearly impossible to properly paraphrase Brandeis's own words:

> [D]anger flowing from speech can be deemed . . . present [only if] the incidence of the evil apprehended is so imminent that it may befall before there is opportunity for full discussion. If there be time to expose through discussion the falsehood and fallacies, to avert the evil by the processes of education, the remedy to be applied is more speech, not enforced silence. Only an emergency can justify repression. Such must be the rule if authority is to be reconciled with freedom.[55]

Brandeis's concurring opinion represented part of a culture-wide shift that embraced a more nuanced understanding of the effects of speech on an audience and the ability to process and understand messages based on intellect, culture, and education.[56] Without explicitly referring to it, Brandeis relied upon the currently well-accepted limited effects theory of audience response. The **limited effects theory** recognizes that audiences are composed of individuals who listen to a message for different reasons, with different levels of attentiveness that elicits different kinds of responses. He relied upon the rational response of audience members, even when the speech is incendiary. Brandeis's opinion has been hailed as one of the most powerful justifications for First Amendment protection of political dissent, and it eventually became the guiding principle for greater speech protection.[57]

Fortunately, Whitney's freedom was restricted for only a few days after the trial, and she never spent time behind bars again. She was granted a pardon by another California governor: C. C. Young. Whitney died in 1955, a hero to the communist movement in the United States. Her greatest legacy lies in the opinion written in her defense.

The criminal syndicalism laws under which Charlotte Whitney was prosecuted and convicted remained in full effect and increased in number as the upheavals of the 1960s, calls for civil rights reform, and withdrawal from the bloody and unpopular Vietnam war took center stage. Indeed, it was the use, or perhaps the abuse, of criminal syndicalism laws by state governments to curtail the dissenting voices of that era that induced the court to revisit the clear and present danger line of cases and the philosophy that underpinned so many criminal convictions.

And we fight. We fight like hell. And if you don't fight
like hell, you're not going to have a country anymore.
—*Former President Donald J. Trump, January 6, 2021*[1]

Charles Brandenburg worked as a TV repairman for his day job. At night, he wore a red hood and carried a gun in his role as the leader of a local Ku Klux Klan (KKK) chapter in Hamilton County, Ohio.[2] While he was obviously a racist and a White nationalist, he was the lucky recipient of the burgeoning First Amendment philosophy that was moving toward greater speech protection.

In the summer of 1964, Brandenburg organized a rally on a farm in his hometown. He telephoned a local television reporter and invited the reporter to film the rally. The reporter accepted the invitation and filmed portions of the gathering, which was attended by ten to twenty members of Brandenburg's KKK compatriots, all carrying firearms. As they gathered around a burning cross, Brandenburg castigated his listeners:

How far is the n——ger going to—yeah.
This is what we are going to do to the n——gers.
A dirty n——ger.
Send the Jews back to Israel.
Let's give them back to the dark garden.
Save America.
Let's go back to constitutional betterment.
Bury the n——gers.
We intend to do our part.
Give us our state rights.
Freedom for the Whites.[3]

Later during the rally, Brandenburg made a short, somewhat grammatically challenged speech, which was later broadcast on the local Cincinnati station and across the national network:

N——ger will have to fight for every inch he gets from now on. This is an organizers' meeting. We have had quite a few members here today which are—we have hundreds, hundreds of members throughout the State of Ohio. I can quote from a newspaper clipping from the Columbus, Ohio, *Dispatch*, five weeks ago Sunday morning. The Klan has more members in the State of Ohio than does any other organization. We're not a revengent organization, but if our President, our Congress, our Supreme Court, continues to suppress the white, Caucasian race, it's possible that there might have to be some revengeance taken.

We are marching on Congress July the Fourth, four hundred thousand strong. From there, we are dividing into two groups, one group to march on St. Augustine, Florida, the other group to march into Mississippi. Thank you.[4]

Brandenburg was arrested on August 6, 1964, at his place of business.[5] He was charged and convicted of violating Ohio's Criminal Syndicalism Law, which prohibited advocating violence as a means of accomplishing industrial or political reform. He was sentenced to one to ten years in the Ohio Penitentiary and a $1,000 fine. He remained free on a $5,000 bond while he pursued his appeals and took that opportunity to move to Seattle, Washington.[6]

During oral argument before the Supreme Court on February 27, 1969, his attorney, Allen Brown, apparently no fan of his client, argued that Brandenburg and crew were no more than "stupid and senseless figures" and that the things they said were only "absurd hyperbole."[7] The justices agreed with both descriptions and, in a unanimous decision, overturned the conviction. As part of the decision, the court specifically overruled their decision in *Whitney v. California* so that it was no longer valid. Having been overruled, the justifications set forth in the *Whitney* decision no longer provided guidance and had no legal effect. In its place, the Supreme Court adopted the justifications proposed by Justice Brandeis in his concurring opinion in *Whitney* and drew a constitutional distinction between advocacy and incitement: Advocacy is protected speech, incitement is not. Advocacy is an integral element to political speech, incitement is not.

The court noted that context counts. Speech designed to inform or affect belief is not the same as speech that stimulates and incites the target audience to action. In the words of the court, "the mere abstract teaching . . . of the moral propriety or even moral necessity for a resort to force and violence, is not the same as preparing a group for violent action and steeling it to such action."[8] Speech that incites must evidence some immediacy that harm will occur. In his concurring opinion in *Brandenburg*, Justice Douglas quoting Justice Holmes put it best:

> Every idea is an incitement. It offers itself for belief, and, if believed, it is acted on unless some other belief outweighs it or some failure of energy stifles the movement at its birth. The only difference between the expression of an opinion and an incitement in the narrower sense is the speaker's enthusiasm for the result.[9]

According to the *Brandenburg* rationale, three elements must be met to criminalize speech for inciting unlawful action by the audience. First, there must be a determination that the speaker intended to incite violence or crime in the moment, not conditioned on a secondary event or passage of time. Second, the expressions and vocabulary used by the speaker must reveal that their purpose was to produce violence or crime. In other words, there must be an immediate call to action, either explicit or implied. Third, there must be an objective likelihood that the speech would cause the audience to engage in violence or crime, directly and currently, taking no opportunity for rational reflection—so that there must be an explosive or combustible aspect to the situation. The *Brandenburg* test ensures that punishment will be levied only against speech that shows immediacy, gravity, and a high probability of agitating or provoking an audience to break the law.

The court does not require that violence must be in progress before the speech can be prohibited or punished. The burden often falls on law enforcement's shoulders to strike the appropriate constitutional balance: protect the speaker and their speech as they forcefully advocate their position or, if they appear to be prompting the audience to impending violence, shut it down before someone gets hurt. Law enforcement professionals and the courts are advised to focus on the proximity of the danger to public welfare caused by the speech, providing much more space for freedom to speak, assert, and advocate.

The speech-protective *Brandenburg* test continues to be the guiding standard in combustible situations where speech appears to encourage lawless action. However, the court has never wholly abandoned the clear and present danger test, and that particular phrase often appears in political debate. Some legal theorists argue that the clear and present danger test still has application in situations where national security is at stake, and questions of imminence or immediacy can be somewhat attenuated in favor of staunching the damage to national interests. Even in the face of this confusion, the Supreme Court and most lower courts have continued to apply the sanctuary provided to speech by the *Brandenburg* test.

It is indeed ironic that the court articulated the First Amendment doctrine that provided cover to the sometimes vitriolic and even violent language of the civil rights movement on behalf of a racist. However, the protections announced in *Brandenburg* were essential in bringing the civil rights debate into the political marketplace of ideas and ultimately forced the campaign for equality forward. The *Brandenburg* test provided the court the opportunity to revise the boundaries between the language of debate, deliberation, and advocacy, which is safeguarded by the First Amendment, and the language of incitement, which is not.

STRETCHING THE BOUNDARIES OF PROTECTED SPEECH

In 1966, in Claiborne County, Mississippi, a group of Black citizens formed a Human Relations Committee. That committee drafted a petition titled "Demands for Racial Justice," which set forth nineteen specific demands. Included among them were:

- Desegregating all public schools and public facilities
- Hiring Black policemen
- Making public improvements in Black residential areas
- Selecting Black people for jury duty
- Integrating bus stations so that Blacks could use all facilities

- Ending verbal abuse by law enforcement officers
- Addressing Black citizens as *Mr.*, *Mrs.*, *or Miss*, consistent with the respect shown to White citizens, instead of using offensive terms such as *boy*, *girl*, *shine*, and *uncle*[10]

The petition was presented to public officials of Port Gibson and Claiborne County, but it was ignored. On April 1, 1966, members of the Claiborne County NAACP held a meeting attended by several hundred people. The purpose of the meeting was to address the mounting frustration of the Black community arising from the lack of response to their demands. By unanimous vote, they agreed to boycott all White-owned businesses in Port Gibson and Claiborne County. After suffering the effects of the economic protest for three years, the White business owners retaliated in court, seeking to recover their losses from the boycott leaders and prohibit the Black community from continuing to promote the embargo. Importantly, the business owners argued that Black patrons had been forced to support the boycott by threats of violence.

The owners provided evidence at trial that revealed tactics used by the organizers. Some of the tactics included the use of store watchers to report any Black persons who patronized the White-owned stores. Black patrons were often surrounded by boycotters who insisted they not enter the targeted stores.[11] Black persons who were caught breaking the boycott had their names published in a paper titled the *Black Times*, and their names were read aloud at meetings of the Claiborne County NAACP. At two such meetings, Charles Evers, the NAACP field secretary in Mississippi, and brother of the assassinated civil rights leader, Medgar Evers, addressed the group and warned that those who violated the community-endorsed action would be disciplined and "have their necks broken."[12] Another time, during a speech at the local courthouse, Evers warned: "If we catch a Negro at any store, we will get his name, address, and phone number and take care of him later."[13]

The case bounced between state and federal courts, accumulating more than a 16,000-page record after an eight-month trial. On appeal, the Mississippi Supreme Court ruled that the boycott was an illegal conspiracy, but that the $1.25 million in damages awarded at trial was excessive. It took twelve years for the case, NAACP v. *Claiborne Hardware*

Co.,[14] to reach the Supreme Court. In a prophetic twist of fate, by the time the case reached the Supreme Court, the boycotters' demands had largely been met. Control of county government had passed into Black hands, and many store owners and managers were Black.[15] So, too, Evers went on to become a national civil rights leader in his own right. In 1969 he was elected the first Black mayor of Fayette, Mississippi, in more than a century. He is credited with coining the phrase, "Hands that picked cotton can now pick the mayor." That phrase has been reused and paraphrased by many over the last fifty-plus years. The divisions in the Black community stimulated by the boycott have largely been erased. Some even describe it as a unique moment of solidarity, having provided the local population with identity and purpose.[16]

By unanimous decision, the Supreme Court found the boycott itself was protected symbolic communication. Even speech that seemed to threaten was described by the court as highly charged political rhetoric lying at the core of the First Amendment that could not be subject to civil penalty.[17] The court recognized that emotion is a necessary element of persuasive speech and applied the *Brandenburg* test. Writing for the court, Justice John Paul Stevens explained, "Speech does not lose its protected character . . . simply because it may embarrass others or coerce them into action."[18] The court explained that an advocate must be free to stimulate their audience with spontaneous and emotional appeals for unity and action in a common cause. When such appeals do not incite lawless action, they must be regarded as protected speech.[19]

IS IT ADVOCACY OR IS IT INCITEMENT?

The debate over when emotional appeals metamorphosize from advocacy to incitement took center stage many times during the presidency of Donald J. Trump but reached its apex after the 2020 election. Over the course of several weeks, culminating on November 3, 2020, a total of 155,506,321 people cast their vote for the president of the United States. Joseph R. Biden won, garnering 51.3 percent of the total to Trump's 46.8 percent of the total. Despite assurances from his own administration officials that this had been the most secure election in US history, Mr. Trump disagreed.[20] Citing conspiracy theories and unproven, even disproven, events, Trump insisted the election was ripe with fraud, and the truth was that he had won "in a landslide."[21] Thus began an unprecedented campaign by Mr. Trump, some officials of his administration, and many of his devoted followers to "stop the steal" and reverse the election results.[22] Trump continued his campaign for seventy-seven days.[23] Those who deny the former president's claims have labeled his false assertions The Big Lie.[24]

The Stop the Steal movement had been foretold by the former president himself. As early as July 2020, President Trump refused to say whether he would accept the election results, and in August, he proclaimed that the only way he could lose was if the election was "rigged."[25] Following the election, the Trump campaign and the president's allies filed over sixty-two lawsuits making various and sundry claims, all aimed at overturning the election results. None of the lawsuits succeeded in providing evidence of widespread, systemic fraud.[26] As Trump's frustration mounted, so did the frustration of his supporters. Tempers were flaring. Trump explicitly and tacitly approved the violent rhetoric of his supporters, much of it communicated over social media, threatening violence in order to ensure the return of Donald Trump to the White House on January 20, 2021, Inauguration Day.[27]

Between November 3 and December 14, 2020, each individual state certified its election results. On December 14, the winning slate of electors of each state met in their respective state capitals and cast their votes, solidifying Biden's electoral victory. Then, on January 6, 2021, as part of its historical and constitutional responsibilities, Congress met in joint session to count the electoral votes. The vice president was in attendance as he was required to fulfill his ceremonial role and declare the winner.

Mr. Trump and his supporters were incensed. On December 19, Trump announced via Twitter that there would be a "big protest" in Washington, DC, on January 6, 2021. What was dubbed the "Save America Rally" was hosted by a pro-Trump nonprofit group: Women for America First. According to the public gathering permit filed by the organization, the rally was labeled a First Amendment rally "to demand transparency and protect election integrity."[28] Trump promised that the protest would "be wild."[29] Later, additional rallies were planned, and the event was renamed The March to Save America.[30] The event was widely advertised over social media platforms. In addition, during the weeks preceding the January 6 rally, far-right militia groups used social media platforms to coordinate plans to storm the Capitol Building.[31] At around noon on January 6, Trump arrived at the Ellipse near the White House and began a one-hour speech denouncing the election and trumpeting the postulates that buttressed The Big Lie. His listeners, who numbered in the thousands, many in military attire and holding items that could be used for combat, cheered his speech and shared portions of it via social media. His language was peppered with words that portended violence:

> [Y]ou'll never take back our country with weakness. You have to show strength and you have to be strong. We have come to demand that Congress do the right thing. . . . But it almost seems that they're all going out of their way to hurt all of us and to hurt our country. To hurt our country. . . . They also want to indoctrinate your children in school by teaching them things that aren't so. They want to indoctrinate your children. It's all part of the comprehensive assault on our democracy, and the American people are finally standing up and saying no. . . . These people are crooked. They're 100 percent, in my opinion, one of the most corrupt . . . this is the most fraudulent thing anybody has, this is a criminal enterprise. This is a criminal enterprise. . . . And we fight. We fight like hell. And if you don't fight like hell, you're not going to have a country anymore.[32]

At the close of the speech, by invitation of the president to "walk down Pennsylvania Avenue,"[33] the rally attendees turned and marched toward the Capitol Building, where they joined an already violent crowd. The Joint Session of Congress was underway. For 224 years, the United States proudly ushered a peaceful transition of power. On January 6, 2021, that shining tradition came to a deadly end. The burgeoning crowd breached the Capitol grounds, shouting threats at lawmakers hidden in terror. Personal and government property was damaged and stolen, several other people died, and hundreds were injured.

By eight o'clock that night, Congress had been secured, and the violence subdued. Vice President Mike Pence, who during the insurrection had been whisked off to a secure location while the crowds screamed "Hang Mike Pence" and erected a gallows, returned to the building and called the Senate back to order.[34] The electoral votes were counted, and Joe Biden was declared the winner. Then, on January 13, 2021, Donald J. Trump, the forty-fifth president of the United States, was impeached for the second time in his tenure. The charge of high crimes and misdemeanors specifically accused Mr. Trump of inciting the insurrection on January 6.

The House drafted a single article for this second impeachment trial of President Trump, and in its brief devoted an entire section to debunking any freedom of speech claims the president might make in his defense. The House impeachment managers who authored the brief argued, "the First Amendment protects private citizens from the government; it does not protect government officials from accountability for their own abuses in office. Therefore, as scholars from across the political spectrum have recognized, the First Amendment does not apply at all to an impeachment proceeding."[35] In other words, as per the intent of our Founders, the US Constitution in general and the First Amendment in particular protect citizens from government overreach, and do not provide cover for government officials to violate their oath of office. But, the impeachment managers argued, even if examination of First Amendment principles was warranted, Mr. Trump's speech fell squarely within the parameters of the *Brandenburg* incitement test, and he should be held accountable.

The president's lawyers argued that Mr. Trump's language at the Ellipse on January 6 did not encourage violence and did not incite a riot. They specifically referenced a part of Trump's speech in which he said, "I know that everyone here will soon be marching over to the Capitol building to peacefully and patriotically make your voices heard."[36] Moreover, they argued that since the insurrection had been preplanned, Mr. Trump, by definition, could not have incited the crowd to violence.[37] As became painfully clear, in many of the criminal charges filed against the insurrectionists, they came armed and ready to destroy democracy. Social media posts are evidence of their intent to engage in violence. And if there were any doubt, the warm-up rally on the night of January 5 planned by the Eighty Percent Coalition was evidence enough. The rally that night was attended by many wearing helmets and Kevlar vests and carrying bats, clubs, and knives.

The House managers had a counterargument to that too. It was true that the planning for an operational event by Trump supporters began in the days and hours after major media outlets called the election for Biden; however, Trump's own pre-rally rhetoric fueled rioters who attacked the Capitol.[38] The House impeachment managers argued that context counts. With calls to "take our country back," the president's attacks and his rhetoric for seventy-seven days built the fire, twig by twig, match by match. And he fed the fire as it burned. At 2:24 p.m. on January 6, as Mike Pence was being ushered out of the Capitol with his family by the Secret Service, President Trump tweeted, "Mike Pence didn't have the courage to do what should have been done to protect our Country and our Constitution, giving States a chance to certify a corrected set of facts, not the fraudulent or inaccurate ones which they were asked to previously certify. USA demands the truth!"[39]

The impeachment trial lasted less than a week. Upon its conclusion, a majority of the Senate voted that President Trump had, indeed, incited a riot. However, conviction in the Senate requires a supermajority of two-thirds. The vote fell short by ten. While Trump remains the only president impeached twice by the House of Representatives, he was acquitted by the Senate. Mitch McConnell, the minority leader of the Senate, who voted to acquit, spoke for many of his colleagues when he explained that his vote rested on technical grounds. He did not believe a former president can be impeached. Nonetheless, he believed the House managers had proved their case. On February 13, 2021, Minority Leader McConnell spoke from the well of the Senate:

> There is no question that President Trump is practically and morally responsible for provoking the events of that day. The people who stormed this building believed they were acting on the wishes and instructions of their President. And their having that belief was a foreseeable consequence of the growing crescendo of false statements, conspiracy theories, and reckless hyperbole which the defeated President kept shouting into the largest megaphone on planet Earth.[40]

The events that led to the January 6 insurrection were like tinder for a fire. The constant repeating of fraud, theft, and fear made the situation even more combustible. All of the elements necessary for a conflagration were present. Should President Trump have known the situation was so volatile? If so, given the context, were his words sufficient to incite the crowd to violence? Or to continue the metaphor, if the fires were already burning, was Mr. Trump responsible then for fanning the flames? The debate regarding whether or not Trump's words met the high bar set by the *Brandenburg* court will rage for a long time.

INCITEMENT AND THE INTERNET

The internet and social media have complicated the communication environment. Justice Brandeis argued in *Whitney* that a speaker should be charged with inciting the audience only in those situations in which there was no time for reflection. Later, context became a central element of the *Brandenburg* equation.

However, context is disembodied in internet speech. There are some who hide in the deep recesses of the internet, seeking to build terror networks or entice lone wolves to attack innocents. The dark web provides cover to those that seek to do harm. It agitates and promotes terror and criminal behavior. 8chan is the current favorite posting place for wannabe mass murderers. They post kill counts and livestreams of murderous rages. Internet service providers have shut down 8chan and many other dark web sites, but these forums are like multiheaded hydra; once shut down, they seem to find other online spaces that will host them.

Hate, fear, violence, and death are not linked to geography. Moreover, messages are sent and received asynchronously, so that the concept of imminent harm is hard to apply. Today, those who use the internet to target the willing have time on their side; they lure their prey. The speakers do not seek, nor do they implore immediate action; they preach stealth and opportunity. And they preach to a global audience across multiple channels. Can the *Brandenburg* test survive the dilemmas posed by this new medium, or will we need a more sensitive test that continues to protect speech despite the terrors posed by bad actors?

There are no clear answers.

9 : STICKS AND STONES AND
WORDS THAT HARM

Hate begets hate; violence begets violence; toughness
begets a greater toughness. We must meet the forces of
hate with the power of love. —Martin Luther King Jr.

The historical link between cross burning and the KKK can be traced to the 1915 movie *Birth of a Nation*, adapted from the pages of Thomas Dixon's book *The Clansman: A Historical Romance of the KKK*. Both the book and the movie denigrated and maligned Black Americans and presented the hate group as a heroic force of White supremacy. Cross burnings were described and portrayed as celebratory events glorifying the executions of former slaves. The movie sparked White supremacist violence across the nation, and since then, cross burning in the United States has been recognized as a symbol of malevolence and a harbinger of harm.

A burning cross can paralyze its victim with fear. The Heissers, a Black family in Westminster, California, testified to the terror experienced by those targeted by that particular symbol. At 4:30 a.m. on August 8, 1988, the eighteen-year-old daughter of Alvin "Ted" and Lillie Heisser was awakened by a noise. She rose from sleep and peered out of her bedroom window to see a three-foot-by-three-foot cross burning on the front lawn. She ran to her older brother's room and woke him, and he, in turn, ran to their parents' room and alerted them. Upon seeing the fire, Mrs. Heisser fell to her knees and wept. In a community meeting four days later, Mr. Heisser, who had formerly served as the president of the Santa Ana, California, chapter of the NAACP, was also moved to tears.[1]

Gary Skillman, a twenty-four-year-old local boat repairman was responsible for the act, which was described by Assistant US Attorney Thomas Umberg as an attempt by Skillman to earn his White supremacist credentials. Skillman was apprehended, brought to trial, convicted of a felony, and sentenced to thirty-seven months in prison.[2] At the trial, Mrs. Heisser described the fear, frustration, and intimidation she experienced in that moment and in the days and months that followed: "Murder, hanging, rape, lynching. Just anything bad that you can name. It's the worst thing that could happen to a person."[3]

TRUE THREATS

Cross burning, named cross lighting by the KKK so as not to be confused with destroying a religious icon, is not mediated by speech or the written word but rather through action or image. It is symbolic speech. It is instantly understood as a hostile symbol and frequently as a powerful threat to the lives and livelihoods of many, particularly to people of color.

Many states have sought to criminalize the burning of a cross as a true threat. The constitutional question is whether communication that induces fear can be punished or whether the First Amendment will provide cover for one speaker to frighten another. The court has consistently held, sometimes to the shock and even rage of American citizens and those who reside among us, that speech can be restricted and punished only in the narrowest of circumstances. Threatening language is often discharged during emotional confrontations; as such, mere threatening language is constitutionally protected. **True threats**, however, are not.

Speech, symbolic or otherwise, is a true threat only if the clear intent of the speaker is to put the target in fear of their life or safety. Threatening language is often intimidating; it may anger the target or unnerve them. It can nonetheless claim the protection of the First Amendment. In contrast, a true threat induces a sense of dread in the victim such that they fear violence or death. True threats are criminal, and the First Amendment will not shield the perpetrators from punishment.

The unconstitutional nature of a true threat focuses on the language used and the terror it induces, even if the action threatened is never commenced and even if there was never any real intent by the speaker to actuate the threat. The fear produced by communicated true threats is similar to the fear produced by terrorism or by a physically threatened assault. The target of a person waving a fist, a gun, or a knife will fear for their bodily safety. A true threat breeds the same kind of panic. Former Justice Sandra Day O'Connor, speaking for the court, defined true threats this way:

True threats encompass those statements where the speaker means to communicate a serious expression of an intent to commit an act of unlawful violence to a particular individual or group of individuals.... The speaker need not actually intend to carry out the threat. Rather, a prohibition on true threats protect[s] individuals from the fear of violence and from the disruption that fear engenders, in addition to protecting people from the possibility that the threatened violence will occur. Intimidation in the constitutionally proscribable sense of the word is a type of true threat, where a speaker directs a threat to a person or group of persons with the intent of placing the victim in fear of bodily harm or death.[4]

Proof of a true threat is exacting and difficult. The proof must include evidence of intent to victimize the target and further evidence that the victim was reasonable in the fear that the threat generated. Absent clear intent to terrorize, separate from the threatened act itself, the speech is something less than a true threat and will be protected.

In 1996, the State of Virginia tried its hand at crafting legislation that specifically made it a criminal felony to burn a cross with the intent to intimidate another person or group. The statute specified the criminal liability attached if the cross was burned "on the property of another, a highway or other public place." In May 1998, Richard Elliot and his one-time friend Jonathan O'Mara burned a cross in Virginia Beach, Virginia, in James Jubillee's yard. Both Elliot and O'Mara were White; Jubillee was Black.

It seems Elliot was a gun enthusiast, and he enjoyed shooting as a hobby, so he created a firing range in his backyard. Jubillee found the constant sound of firearms being discharged unnerving and complained to Elliot's mother. Elliot was none too pleased, and he decided to seek revenge by placing a cross on Jubillee's lawn and igniting it. Jubillee did not witness the event as it was happening, but he noticed the remnants of the charred cross the next morning. Jubillee was overwrought. He understood the message as a warning: the first round in events that were planned for the future.[5] Elliot and O'Mara, both nineteen at the time, were convicted under the Virginia cross-burning statute for their actions, sentenced to ninety days in jail, and fined $2,500.

In an unrelated event later in August of that same year, Barry Black, also White, organized a KKK rally of about twenty-five to thirty people on a privately owned open field bordered by a state highway in Cana, Virginia. The property was public facing, so this event fell within the dictates of the statute. Several participants spoke at the rally. Their speeches were filled with enmity, including one by a rally participant asserting his desire to shoot Blacks. At the conclusion of the rally, a twenty-five to thirty-foot cross was burned as the crowd circled around and cheered. Black was convicted and also fined $2,500.

All three defendants appealed their convictions, each arguing that they burned the cross as a means of expressing their views about particular people and issues. They argued their expression was speech, albeit symbolic speech, and it was protected from criminalization by the First Amendment. The cases essentially raised the same legal issue regarding the constitutionality of the statute, so they were consolidated in their appeal to the Virginia Supreme Court. Four years after the events, the justices of the United States Supreme Court agreed to hear *Virginia v. Black*, the consolidated cases.[6]

The decision by the Supreme Court is complicated. The cases against all three defendants were sent back to the lower courts and had to be retried, not because the defendants were innocent but because it was difficult to determine whether the jury properly considered the intent of the defendants. If there was evidence that proved that the defendants did not intend to terrorize but rather only intended to communicate their political beliefs in support of White supremacy or to simply communicate their anger at particular individuals, then they were not engaging in true threats.

Cross burning can be a statement of political ideology, such as White supremacy. It can be a statement of anger at the government or individuals. It can be a statement of solidarity to group identity. Or it can be a threat of violence and death. It can be a tangled warren of intentions to mine. And therein lay the problem. The justices in *Virginia v. Black* were somewhat split on how to navigate the labyrinth.

The justices took note that "[b]urning a cross in the United States is inextricably intertwined with the history of the Ku Klux Klan," and "the history of violence associated with the Klan shows that the possibility of injury or death is not just hypothetical."[7] They also made clear that "[t]o this day, regardless of whether the message is a political one or whether the message is also meant to intimidate, the burning of a cross is a symbol of hate."[8] To be sure, the court noted that even "[a] white, conservative, middle-class Protestant, waking up at night to find a burning cross outside his home, will reasonably understand that someone is threatening him. His reaction is likely to be very different than if he were to find, say, a burning circle or square. In the latter case, he may call the fire department. In the former, he will probably call the police."[9] Still, the court observed that some cross burnings might not give rise to a constitutionally unprotected true threat. There must be evidence that the communicator intended to induce mortal fear. As disturbing as it might be, cross burnings that are not intended as a true threat but are instead intended to communicate a message of White supremacy or anger are protected speech.[10] As a relief to some of us, in the second round, the trial courts found each of the defendants indeed had a specific intent to express a true threat, and the convictions were reinstated.

FIGHTING WORDS

Similar to language that incites, and similar to true threats, fighting words are not shielded by the First Amendment from prosecution. These exclusions from First Amendment protection are unique content-based exceptions. As noted in earlier chapters, generally the government may not target speech as out of bounds based on the subject matter of the communication or even offensive use of language. The government may restrict or prohibit speech only if it can prove that restricting the speech is related to an essential responsibility of the state. The means used by the state to restrict the speech must be limited and narrowly tailored to support only that essential interest. The power of the government to punish words that incite and words that are a true threat would seem to fit within those boundaries. The same might be said of fighting words, but in fact, the court used a different rationale when it came to fighting words and designated them to be part of a group of words that had little or no value. The First Amendment was simply too important to be wasted on them. The doctrine was first announced by the Supreme Court in *Chaplinsky v. New Hampshire*.[11]

Walter Chaplinsky was a Jehovah's Witness. As a matter of religious conscience, Jehovah's Witnesses refuse to serve in the military, recite the Pledge of Allegiance, and engage in other civic duties. Particularly in the 1940s, as the United States battled the Axis Powers in World War II, and patriotism was equated with the war effort, Jehovah's Witnesses were subject to vitriol, ridicule, and even mob violence. Their persecution was not limited to vigilante attacks, but also included legislated discrimination.[12]

Chaplinsky was uniquely dedicated to his faith. He had earned the title of "special pioneer," which required him to apply extra effort in seeking converts to his faith. As a young man in his mid-twenties, Chaplinsky frequently preached in the northeastern regions of the United States. On April 6, 1940, the eve of his twenty-sixth birthday, Chaplinsky returned to one of his favorite spots in Rochester, New Hampshire, a mill town close to the Maine border, and proceeded to deliver one of his fiery street-side sermons. He preached against the Catholic faith and the military, calling priests racketeers and denouncing President Roosevelt's efforts in Europe. He was joined by four young men who distributed pamphlets that also attacked the Catholic Church and various veterans' organizations.[13]

While Chaplinsky might have enjoyed his moment, many of the citizens of Rochester did not. A crowd of about fifty men angrily surrounded Chaplinsky and the boys, taunting and even threatening them. Others complained to James Bowering, the city marshal, and reported that they were offended by Chaplinsky's speech. Bowering, a former football player, approached Chaplinsky and, towering over him, urged Chaplinsky to tone down the rhetoric.[14] Chaplinsky ignored Bowering and continued, further enraging the growing crowd. One military veteran, William Bowman, became so angry that he assaulted Chaplinsky. At one point, Bowman lunged at him with a flag-draped pole, trying to impale him. Bowering witnessed the attack but refused Chaplinsky's request that Bowering arrest Bowman. That assault encouraged others, and Chaplinsky was attacked and punched by a number of men. Chaplinsky was shaken but not badly hurt and was able to regain his footing. As he did so, he was grabbed by a police officer, Gerald Lapierre, and was pushed and shoved toward the police station. Lapierre later testified that Chaplinsky was escorted away from the melee for his own protection, but other witnesses testified that Chaplinsky was manhandled by the officer and the four or five other officers that had joined him. Again, Chaplinsky demanded that his attackers be arrested too. Bowering refused and told Chaplinsky to "Shut up, you dumb bastard and come along."[15] Frustrated, Chaplinsky shouted at Bowering: "You are a damn fascist and a racketeer."[16] That is when the real troubles started for the young man.

Chaplinsky was criminally charged and convicted for violating a New Hampshire law that made it illegal to use offensive, derisive, or annoying language aimed at another person on a public street.[17] The law was rarely used. In fact, during that year, only two people had been arrested under that statute, and both were Jehovah's Witnesses. Alfred Albert, Chaplinsky's attorney, tried to make an issue at trial of the police conduct, arguing that Chaplinsky had lashed out at the city marshal only after he had been physically and verbally attacked.[18] His argument fell on deaf ears. The jury deliberated all of fifteen minutes before finding Chaplinsky guilty.[19] Chaplinsky was sentenced to six months at a prison farm in Strafford County, New Hampshire.

Chaplinsky appealed his conviction all the way up to the Supreme Court, but to no avail. The Supreme Court denied Chaplinsky's assertion of First Amendment protection. The court found that Chaplinsky's angry outburst directed at Bowering was personally abusive and was "not in any proper sense communication of information or opinion safeguarded by the Constitution."[20] This all occurred during the time that the court supported the speech-restrictive clear and present danger test. The 1919 Holmes dissent in *Abrams* and the Brandeis concurrence in *Whitney* were in the history books, but the courts had yet to endorse the full potential of the words "Congress shall make no law . . . abridging the freedom of speech." The court reasoned that the statute properly criminalized speech that was likely to cause the targeted audience to become agitated and cause a disturbance. The court identified these types of words as **fighting words**.

Fighting words did not enjoy First Amendment protection because, the court said, fighting words do not enhance the marketplace of ideas or otherwise promote debate and deliberation. The court went on to define fighting words as those "which, by their very utterance, inflict injury or tend to incite an immediate breach of the peace."[21] They "are no essential part of any exposition of ideas, and are of such slight social value as a step to truth that any benefit that may be derived from them is clearly outweighed by the social interest in order and morality."[22]

Fighting words are assaultive speech. Fighting words provoke a reaction from the target, often toward the speaker. The words are inflammatory; they are calculated to bait the target into action and, for that reason, according to the Supreme Court, deserve no constitutional protection. The court declared that by arresting and prosecuting Chaplinsky, the state properly exercised its obligation to preserve the public peace.

When Chaplinsky arrived at the prison to serve out his sentence, he was warned not to preach. Ever the faithful servant, Chaplinsky ignored the warning and was punished with six weeks of solitary confinement. Despite his trials and punishment, he remained devoted to his faith throughout his long life.[23]

It is highly likely that today, the court would not find the language used by Chaplinsky as rising to the level of fighting words. However, the rationale behind the fighting words doctrine remains strong. Numerous provocateurs have been jailed or fined by juries and judges for speech designed to induce a response. Notably, courts pointedly apply the fighting words only in contexts where there is a clear intent to cause a breach of the peace. They have required that unprotected fighting words must be face to face and designed to elicit a response.[24] Importantly, the courts have held that when directed at a police officer, even profane, boorish, or swear words are protected speech. The courts reason that because of the nature of their job, police should not be baited by such language, and so, the requirement that the words are intended to elicit a violent response cannot be met.[25] In contrast, alcohol-fueled aggressive, sexually explicit talk by a bar patron was unprotected speech. The aggressive language was fighting words which, by their very nature, intended to provoke a response.[26]

Fighting words and true threats are more than merely offensive. They do more than disturb sensitive souls or cause hurt feelings. They are assaultive and provocative in a physical sense. Anger, frustration, and even hatred can find expression, but if the words used are, by their very nature, brutalizing or induce mortal fear, the speaker will be silenced or punished.

FIGHTING WORDS AND THE HECKLER'S VETO

Odious speech that is not directed at a target audience or intended to elicit an angry response is not incitement and it is not fighting words. The distinction is difficult to apply, but it is an important one. Once again, context counts—just ask the Bible Believers of Michigan.[27]

Dearborn, Michigan, is home to one of the largest Arab American populations in the United States. Beginning in 1996, the city hosted an Arab International Festival to celebrate Arab heritage and culture. The festival took place over the course of three days and by 2012 attracted more than 300,000 people from all over the world. It was the largest festival of its kind in the United States.[28]

In 2012, a group of evangelical Christians attended the festival for the express purpose of converting nonbelievers and calling upon them to repent. Rather than seek converts by preaching love and peace, they assailed the festivalgoers with messages of intolerance and animus. They wore T-shirts and carried signs proclaiming:

Islam Is a Religion of Blood and Murder
Jesus Is the Way, the Truth and the Life. All Others Are Thieves and Robbers
Turn or Burn[29]

They paraded with a severed pig's head, with the full knowledge that pork is prohibited for those that celebrate the Islamic faith.[30] One of the speakers addressing a crowd of teenagers warned that they should not follow "a false prophet," who was nothing but an "unclean drawing" and "a pedophile."[31] Not surprisingly, the teens reacted angrily and began throwing debris at the speaker.

The police escorted the Bible Believers out of the festival on the grounds that they were instigating a breach of the peace. While it is clear the language used by the Bible Believers is offensive, it was not targeted at the audience in an effort to elicit a violent response. Perhaps unrealistically, it was intended to elicit a religious conversion. In contrast to the Supreme Court's support of the police action against Walter Chaplinsky, the Michigan federal court admonished the police. The Michigan court noted that the violence was reactive to the speech, but not caused by it. The members of the crowd had caused the violence by throwing debris, and they should have been escorted out, not the Bible Believers. The court held that the Bible Believers were engaging in religious speech, and the police had an obligation to protect their speech from the heckler's veto of the crowd. The court explained, while the messaging of the Bible Believers was loathsome, they did

> "not advocate for, encourage, condone, or even embrace imminent violence or lawlessness . . . The Bible Believers did not ask their audience to rise up in arms and fight for their beliefs, let alone request that they hurl bottles and other garbage upon the Bible Believers' heads . . . The hostile reaction of a crowd does not transform protected speech into incitement.[32]

A heckler's veto occurs when speech is cut off, not because the speaker is engaging in unprotected expression but because the audience, offended by the content of the speech, reacts forcefully. When an audience responds by engaging in combative behavior—not because the audience is provoked by the speaker but instead because the audience disapproves of what it hears—it is the audience who must desist, not the speaker. Any other action would be tantamount to censorship of unpopular views, which we know is an abhorrence to the First Amendment.

The Bible Believers did not incite violence, and they did not use fighting words. Unlike the inebriated bar goer who deliberately enrages their target, the Bible Believers did not project their language toward any individual for the purpose of provoking an unlawful response. They were preaching a sincere, if ugly, belief in their faith. The Michigan court explained that "the state cannot sanction speech . . . solely on the basis that it stirred people to anger, invited public dispute, or brought about a condition of unrest."[33]

Action against a speaker requires more than a desire by law enforcement to protect the peace and tranquility of the community. The caveat is, of course, if the crowd reaction cannot be controlled. Then, in an effort to keep the public safe, the police might be justified in removing the speaker without trespassing on the First Amendment.

HATE SPEECH

The moral boundaries within which we can confine hate speech are relatively easy to find. Constitutional boundaries are much more elusive and fraught. Still, those who argue the First Amendment should not offer protection to hate speech insist that the marketplace of ideas is not enhanced by hate. Hate does not enlarge debate; it contracts it. Hate speech diminishes the marketplace because it silences victims' voices and causes emotional and psychological harm.

In fact, several European countries have legislation that criminalizes hate speech, including Germany, which criminalizes Holocaust denial; Denmark, which penalizes persons who threaten or degrade others based on race, national or ethnic origin, faith, or sexual orientation; and France, which prosecutes incitement to discrimination, hatred, or violence on the basis of one's origin or membership in an ethnic, national, racial, or religious group, or based on sexual orientation. However, European courts in each of the countries that criminalize hate speech have struggled with creating objective and measurable criteria for determining the nature of speech that can be punished.

The legislatures and the courts in the United States are facing similar problems. Are there specific words or phrases that are to be eliminated from the lexicon—and if so, which words? Should those words be punishable in all circumstances? Will we then have to ban particular books, poems, movies, performances, etc.? It is easy to claim hate speech ought to be penalized; putting a plan into action that supports First Amendment principles and does not overly restrict expression is much more difficult.

While fighting words and true threats are defined, in part, by the response they induce from the target, hate speech does not lend itself to that kind of definition. However, the fighting words and true threats doctrines might provide some avenues to balance the right to feel safe and the right to speak freely. The fighting words doctrine requires that the right to speak freely ends at the point where a person is assaulted by words whose "very utterance, inflict injury or tend to incite an immediate breach of the peace."[34] And the true threats doctrine prohibits speech that places the victim in reasonable fear of life and safety. This makes it so that, if hate speech falls within these narrow limits, the government might be able to halt the speech and punish the speaker. If speech falls outside of those confines, it seems we all must continue to rely on the power of words of tolerance as a constitutional antidote.

Interestingly, evidence of hate as a motive to commit a crime can be considered by a jury when they are deliberating the verdict and can ultimately lead to an enhanced sentence. Such was the fate of nineteen-year-old Todd Mitchell who, with about ten of his friends, accosted and brutally beat fourteen-year-old Gregory Reddick. The assault followed a heated discussion between Mitchell and his friends after they had watched the film *Mississippi Burning*. The scene that triggered the boys' intense anger depicted an attack by a Klansman upon a Black boy knelt in prayer. Mitchell and his friends are Black. As they talked and fumed, Mitchell spotted Reddick walking on the other side of the street. Reddick is white. Mitchell turned to his friends and said: "You all want to fuck somebody up? There goes a White boy; go get him."[35] He counted to three, and the group assaulted Reddick. The beating left Reddick hospitalized and in a coma for four days. At trial, the prosecutor described the attack as so severe that Reddick had been "nearly stomped to death."[36] Some of the younger teens were sentenced to juvenile supervision; Jermaine Mitchell, Todd's brother, was sentenced to a ten-year prison term, and another adult was sentenced to eight years.[37] Todd Mitchell was sentenced to two years for his role in the assault, and then another two years was added to his punishment pursuant to the Wisconsin Penalty Enhancement Statute, which allows for enhanced sentencing if a perpetrator chooses their victim based on the victim's race, religion, or color.[38]

Appealing his conviction, Mitchell argued that the enhanced sentencing statute provided an unconstitutional incursion into his First Amendment right because it effectively imposed punishment for his thoughts and beliefs. In *Wisconsin v. Mitchell*, the Supreme Court rejected that argument. The court held that "the First Amendment . . . does not prohibit the evidentiary use of speech to establish the elements of a crime or to prove motive or intent."[39] The Supreme Court ridiculed the notion that a bigot's First Amendment right to declare their hate for another would somehow be chilled, knowing that such utterances could be used as evidence of motive in a criminal trial or as support for enhanced sentencing. Bigots will not be censored because they are concerned that the hate they spew may increase a prison term for a crime they commit. Mitchell served his time, and tried to put the incident behind him. Reddick fortunately recovered from his injuries—he too simply sought to move on with his life.[40]

INCITEMENT, FIGHTING WORDS, TRUE THREATS, AND THE INTERNET

Abusive speech on the internet and social media are particularly concerning, especially because of the anonymity of that forum, which emboldens the speaker and can paralyze the target with fear. The internet as a medium for speech, however, has not changed the nature of First Amendment protection; not yet.

Speech that incites an audience to violence is not protected. But the *Brandenburg* incitement test requires a temporal connection. The disorder and destruction must imminently follow the inciting speech. Given the asynchronous nature of speech posted on the internet, without an expansion of the concept of imminence or proof of criminality such as conspiracy, speech that advocates violence is protected.

Fighting words, by definition, require face-to-face contact. Digital communication is facilitated by cell phones and computers; there is no opportunity for in-person contact. At least in the lower courts, the lack of in-person, face-to-face contact, even when words are provocative, saves the messenger from criminal prosecution.[41] Some European countries require social media platforms to monitor posts and delete hateful language on pain of penalty, but as discussed in later chapters, internet-based companies are not government owned; in the United States, they are treated only as staging areas for speech and are further protected by statute from liability for the harmful speech of their users. In the United States, under current law, imposing liability on social media platforms for user-generated posts is unlikely.

True threats require a specified target. True threats do not necessitate a temporal connection or a face-to-face interaction, so that it might be easier to prosecute the offender of a true threat broadcast over the internet, but only if the offender is identifiable. Such was the case against Anthony Douglas Elonis. Mr. Elonis clearly had anger issues. By May 2010, after seven years of marriage, his wife had had enough, and she left him, taking with her their two children. Over the next several months, Elonis crafted numerous graphic and violent posts on Facebook.[42] Many of his posts were directed at his soon-to-be ex-wife, including this post, published after she was successful in obtaining a restraining order against him:

> Fold up your [protection-from-abuse order] and put it in your pocket
> Is it thick enough to stop a bullet?
> Try to enforce an Order
> that was improperly granted in the first place.
> Me thinks the Judge needs an education
> on true threat jurisprudence
> And prison time'll add zeros to my settlement . . .
> And if worse comes to worse
> I've got enough explosives
> to take care of the State Police and the Sheriff's Department.[43]

He drafted another post describing a school shooting. A grand jury indicted him for making threats to, among others, his estranged wife and a kindergarten class. He was convicted and sentenced to serve three years, eight months in prison and three years of supervised release.[44] He appealed his conviction. The Supreme Court in *Elonis v. United States* remanded the case back to the lower court because it was unclear whether the jury properly considered whether Elonis specifically intended to engage in a true threat.[45] But nothing changed when the case was reargued.[46] It was determined that Elonis intended to terrorize his victims; he had engaged in a true threat and was required to serve his time. In this case, the medium, ultimately, had no effect on the message. Plainly, forty-four months behind bars was not sufficient time for Elonis to reconsider his behavioral choices. He was back behind bars in 2015 for violating the terms of his supervised release, having been arrested and charged with assault associated with domestic violence and harassment.[47]

If the user is anonymous, it might require the assistance of the social media platform or the internet service provider to expose the speaker. Requiring assistance from platforms and providers to identify anonymous participants in conversations might run afoul of Fourth Amendment protections against unreasonable searches and seizures (that are beyond the scope of this book), but if there are no barriers to identification, the true threats doctrine might offer the best constitutionally sanctioned method of punishing purveyors of terror, hate, and fear over the internet.

10 : WHAT THE #@*%!

School Speech, Campus Codes, and Cancel Culture

History teaches that grave threats to liberty often come in times of urgency, when constitutional rights seem too extravagant to endure. —Justice Thurgood Marshall[1]

SCHOOL SPEECH

Fourteen-year-old Brandi Levy characterized her somewhat crude snapchat as venting. Even so, Supreme Court Justice Stephen Breyer did not treat her rants as trivial and unworthy of the grandeur of First Amendment protection. While her words were profane, Levy was expressing her point of view about school policy and practice, certainly something that was central to her political world. As was true of Paul Robert Cohen when he paraded in public in a jean jacket with the words "Fuck the Draft" emblazoned on the back, Levy's words and gestures were communicative of her frustration.[2] If her word choice was "superfluous," Justice Breyer insisted "sometimes it is necessary to protect the superfluous in order to preserve the necessary."[3] Breyer's recognition of First Amendment protection for student speech relied squarely on that same protection called into service by another set of young students fifty years earlier.

In *Tinker v. Des Moines School Dist.*, decided by the Supreme Court in 1969 and widely celebrated for affirming students' rights to free speech in public schools, the Court upheld the right of sixteen-year-old Christopher Eckhardt, fifteen-year-old John F. Tinker, and his thirteen-year-old sister Mary Beth Tinker to wear a black armband as a means of political protest because it did not disrupt any school activity.[4] The *Tinker* case declared that students do not lose their First Amendment rights at the schoolhouse gate; however, those rights are balanced against the schools' duty to educate our youth and provide models for civil and civic obligations. Public schools cannot restrict speech, particularly political speech, simply because the speaker advocates unpopular views. Still, they may limit speech if it "materially and substantially interferes with the requirements of appropriate discipline in the operation of the school."[5] Notably, student speech cannot be regulated merely because teachers and administrators seek to avoid discomfort or unpleasantness or upon an undifferentiated fear of disturbance.[6] In other words, schools do not have the power to ensnare student speech that they do not like simply by branding the speech as disruptive to the school environment.

Guided by the principal that the school environs are an essential place where students are exposed to a "robust exchange of ideas which discovers truth out of a multitude of tongues,"[7] the Supreme Court as well as federal and state lower courts have spent the last half century sculpting nuanced details into the broad framework of *Tinker*. They have been assisted by students and their parents who have tested the patience and the power of the schools to promote their educational mission in the hundreds of cases brought before the courts, some providing rather entertaining reading to be sure.

On April 26, 1983, despite warnings from his teachers, Mathew Fraser took to the stage at a school-sponsored educational program in self-government that was attended by 600 of his peers and offered the following as reasons for those assembled to vote for his friend:

> I know a man who is firm—he's firm in his pants, he's firm in his shirt, his character is firm—but most of all, his belief in you, the students of Bethel, is firm.
>
> Jeff Kuhlman is a man who takes his point and pounds it in. If necessary, he'll take an issue and nail it to the wall. He doesn't attack things in spurts—he drives hard, pushing and pushing until finally —he succeeds. . . .
>
> Jeff is a man who will go to the very end—even the climax, for each and every one of you. . . . So vote for Jeff for A.S.B. vice-president —he'll never come between you and the best our high school can be.[8]

During the delivery, students hooted and yelled and simulated the sexual activities alluded to in Fraser's speech. The speech clearly caused a substantial disruption at a planned educational event. Fraser was thereafter suspended for three days and prohibited from being considered as a speaker at the school's commencement exercises. Relying on *Tinker*, the Supreme Court affirmed the suspension on the grounds that the speech undermined the school's basic educational mission. However, the court acknowledged that had the speech been delivered off school grounds, it might very well have been protected—the lewd nature of Fraser's speech was problematic only because it occurred on campus. (It seems that Fraser might have gotten the last word. Many years later he proudly served as coach and program director for the Stanford University Debate Society.)

Then in 2002, Joseph Frederick tested the geographic boundaries of the campus only to find himself enfolded within them while participating in a school sponsored activity. In *Morse v. Frederick*[9] the Supreme Court upheld Frederick's suspension for unfurling a large banner during a school outing to observe the Olympic Torch Relay that read, "BONG HITS 4 JESUS." Once again relying on *Tinker*, the Court cited the special characteristics of the school environment to "safeguard those entrusted to their care from speech that can reasonably be regarded as encouraging illegal drug use"[10] Critical to the Court's decision in *Morse* was that Frederick unfurled the banner while attending a school-sanctioned activity and in the presence of students, staff, and administrators. That he held the banner aloft across the street from the school campus did not call the First Amendment into action.

The *Tinker* decision has served as the benchmark for school speech cases for over fifty years, but its current prominence in the free speech constellation of cases is likely to be diminished by Levy's case, which required the court to assess the scope of school power to restrict speech created off-campus but disseminated online and therefore accessible to students and staff.

In 2017, Brandi Levy was completing her freshman year at Mahanoy Area High School (MAHS) in Pennsylvania. She had a successful year as a junior varsity (JV) cheerleader and was proud of that accomplishment. At the end of the cheerleading season, Levy tried out for the varsity squad. She didn't make it and would have to spend a second year on the JV squad. Worse still, a rising freshman jumped over her and was awarded a spot on the varsity team. As many teens do, she sought to unleash her frustration in a barrage of f-bombs. Her medium of choice: the social media app, Snapchat. It might have been the perfect communication channel. Snaps are digitally created communication that are sent to a customized list of Snapchat friends. It remains visible for only twenty-four hours after it has been posted. By the time the snap disappeared, her anger would have dissipated, and she could move on. The snap, however, was captured and it survived much longer than its intended twenty-four-hour lifespan.[11]

Levy fashioned the snap while hanging out with a friend on a Saturday afternoon at the Cocoa Hut, a local convenience store. She took a photo of herself and her friend, both with their middle fingers raised. She captioned the photo with "Fuck school fuck softball fuck cheer fuck everything," and then added, "Love how me and [another student] get told we need a year of jv before we make varsity but that's [sic] doesn't matter to anyone else? [upside down smiley face emoji]."[12] The snap was visible to Levy's 250 Snapchat friends, one of whom was a cheerleader and the daughter of one of the cheerleading coaches. That friend took a screenshot of the snap, which in 2021 landed on the Supreme Court docket.

The snap was composed from Levy's personal cell phone, off the school grounds. It did not include any school logos or the names of any school officials. It did not include any threatening language or language that could be categorized as harassment. School officials admitted that while some students were visibly upset by the snap, there was no substantial disruption to the school learning environment.[13] Further, both cheerleading coaches acknowledged that this type of friction was typical of teenage teammates and that it often occurred on social media. Nevertheless, the cheerleading coaches decided that Levy had violated two cheerleading rules that she had agreed to abide by. The rules required that the teammates show respect for one another, the coaches, the school, and opposing teams. The cheerleaders were expressly prohibited from using foul language, inappropriate gestures, or posting negative information about the squad or the coaches on the internet.[14] To "avoid chaos and maintain a team-like environment," the coaches suspended Levy from the squad for the entirety of her sophomore year.[15]

Alleging that MAHS violated Levy's First Amendment rights by disciplining her for off-campus speech, Levy and her parents sued the school and demanded she be reinstated onto the squad and her disciplinary record be expunged. The district court granted the requested relief and held that Levy's speech was immunized by the First Amendment because there was no evidence that it caused or was likely to cause a substantial disruption to the educational environment of the school. MAHS appealed the lower court decision to the Court of Appeals for the Third Circuit. That court also ruled in Levy's favor, but it went much further in its rationale. The appellate court held that the power of a school to punish student speech for material disruption of the school environment did not extend to off-campus speech unless it occurred "in a context owned, controlled, or sponsored by the school."[16] The Third Circuit Court of Appeals held that Levy's snap did not meet the conditions necessary for the school to assert disciplinary action and therefore it had no power to punish Levy. The school had unconstitutionally infringed Levy's First Amendment right to criticize and protest.

Once again MAHS appealed the decision—this time to the US Supreme Court, which granted the appeal. In their briefs to the court, MAHS vociferously argued that the Third Circuit, despite its assertions to the contrary, reinterpreted *Tinker* and imposed a territorial test upon school speech. They argued such a test ignores the lack of boundaries inherent in digital communication. The location in which a student presses "send" should not govern restrictions on the power of schools to punish speech that was intended to, or with reasonable foreseeability could be anticipated to, substantially disrupt the school environment. They argued that this is most important in an era when bullying, teen anxiety, depression, and even suicide represent pernicious problems in schools.[17]

The Levy case was argued before the Supreme Court on April 28, 2021. At oral argument, the justices expressed some skepticism about whether Levy should have been punished at all. Justice Brett Kavanaugh, who coaches his daughters' basketball team, was most critical of the school's response, stating, "my reaction when I read this, she's competitive, she cares, she blew off steam like millions of other kids have when they're disappointed about being cut from the high school team or not being in the starting lineup or not making all league."[18] Most of the justices seemed to indicate a reluctance to set forth a broad-based rule and seemed to search for avenues that provided a narrower ruling than that created by the Third Circuit but still empowered the school and protected the student. Supreme Court watchers read the tea leaves correctly.

The justices delivered their opinion in *Mahanoy Area School District v. B.L.*[19] on June 23, 2021. As did both the district court and the Third Circuit Court of Appeals, the Supreme Court found that the punishment meted out to Levy violated her constitutional right to freedom of speech. Justice Breyer wrote the decision for the court and was joined by all of the justices except Clarence Thomas, who dissented. Central to Justice Breyer's decision was his assessment that "America's public schools are the nurseries of democracy."[20] Underlying that assessment is a welcome recognition of the reality of students' lives. Just as their First Amendment rights do not end upon entry onto school grounds, students' thoughts, feelings, and opinions about all things related to school don't stop as soon as they step outside of the school boundaries. Justice Breyer acknowledged this truism, and warned that if regulations of off-campus speech were to be coupled with regulations of on-campus speech, they would "include all the speech a student utters during the full 24-hour day."[21] Providing only limited First Amendment protection to all communication crafted by a student of and concerning school regardless of context would be chilling. It would hardly serve to educate students about the groundings of our democracy.

Justice Breyer rejected the hardline territorial distinction between on-campus versus off-campus speech promoted by the Third Circuit Court. He also declined to provide a broad, general First Amendment rule or a list of criteria identifying the circumstances under which a school could reach beyond its physical boundaries and restrict or punish student speech.[22] He did, however, provide some guidelines—three to be exact.

The guidelines include considerations of geography, context, and the marketplace of ideas. As to geography, Justice Breyer offered that student speech is generally outside of the reach of school disciplinarians when it occurs at a time and place that is within "the zone of parental, rather than school-related, responsibility."[23] In this particular case, while the school might seek to discourage profanity and punish its use, such language, particularly when it is composed off of school grounds and is not specifically directed at any individual, ought to be addressed by parents and guardians of the young, not schoolteachers and administrators. As relates to context, schools should exercise caution regarding efforts to regulate or control student communication that is crafted outside of school-related events. Schools should be particularly reluctant to stifle any political or religious speech. Finally, the school should ensure the free exchange of ideas and may not prohibit or punish speech merely because the speech is unpleasant, and especially when it reflects unpopular views. A strong marketplace of ideas serves to strengthen democracy and provides students valuable lessons about its processes. As was true with the *Tinker* decision, Justice Breyer suggested future cases will necessarily fill in the details and serve to develop more specific criteria.

Brandi Levy is no longer in high school; upon graduation, she enrolled in Bloomsburg University as an accounting major.[24] She is pleased with the Supreme Court's decision and insisted that, "[y]oung people need to have the ability to express themselves without worrying about being punished when they get to school."[25] No doubt, millions of students and their parents too are relieved that teenage growing pains expressed in coarse or inelegant language are less likely to result in suspension from school and school activities.

CAMPUS CODES

Like K–12 public schools, public colleges and universities seek to create an environment that promotes learning. Similarly, they seek to create an environment in which students feel safe from demeaning racist and sexist diatribes. However, unlike K–12 schools, colleges and universities are populated with adults. The free speech standards applied on college campuses are more similar to those applied in the streets and parks than to middle or high school halls.[26] Many public institutions of higher learning have drafted campus speech codes in an effort to walk the free speech tightrope.

Campus speech codes, as evidenced by their very title, target speech. When speech is the target of regulation by the government, as we have already seen, it is considered content based and subject to a strict scrutiny analysis. A strict scrutiny analysis requires a determination that the regulation protects a compelling interest of the government, or in this case, a public college.

Certainly, a college or university has a compelling interest in protecting its students, faculty, and staff's freedom, safety, and integrity. However, as always, the devil is in the details. Crafting a speech code to protect against offense and discomfort requires broad, sweeping prohibitions. However, the First Amendment and the second prong of the strict scrutiny analysis require speech restrictions to be limited and narrow. Unfortunately, seeking to promote an inclusive atmosphere, the codes are too broad and capture otherwise protected speech in their nets. Few of the codes that have been challenged at public colleges and brought under judicial examination in the lower courts have survived. A case in point is *Doe v. University of Michigan.*[27]

During the latter part of the 1980s, the University of Michigan endured a spate of racist and sexist speech on campus, including a flyer distributed across campus that declared open season on Blacks and referred to Blacks in offensive and derogatory terms. In another incident, a KKK uniform was hung outside of a dorm window. The university could never identify the culprits and was later threatened with a class action lawsuit for failing to maintain a nonracist, nonviolent atmosphere. In the midst of the controversies propelled by the crisis, the university president resigned.[28] Evidently shaken and determined to create a positive campus environment, administration efforts moved into high gear to create a policy that circumscribed appropriate behavior on campus. After more than twelve drafts, reviewed by faculty and university lawyers, and a public comment period, the university finally adopted a campus-wide speech code, "The University of Michigan Policy on Discrimination and Discriminatory Harassment." In part, the policy punished verbal behavior that had the effect of stigmatizing or victimizing others based on "race, ethnicity, religion, sex, sexual orientation, creed, national origin, ancestry, age, marital status, [or] handicap."[29]

A graduate student at the university studying biopsychology was in the planning stages of introducing a controversial theory relating to sex and race, asserting that men as a group are more capable with spatially related tasks and therefore better suited for employment as engineers. He was concerned that by promoting his research, he could be sanctioned under the policy. He brought suit against the university in the United States District Court for the Eastern District of Michigan, seeking to have the policy declared unconstitutional based on over-breadth and vagueness. The court agreed that the policy could not with-stand a constitutional challenge. The policy was not narrowly drawn.

In its opening paragraphs, the court stated:

> It is an unfortunate fact of our constitutional system that the ideals of freedom and equality are often in conflict. The difficult and sometimes painful task of our political and legal institutions is to mediate the appropriate balance between these two competing values. . . . However laudable or appropriate an effort this may have been, . . . the Policy swept within its scope a significant amount of verbal conduct or verbal behavior which is unquestionably protected speech under the First Amendment.[30]

Like private K–12 schools, private colleges and universities have greater constitutional leeway than do public ones.[31] A lawsuit for unlaw-ful abridgment of the right to speak freely on a private campus might have more success, alleging breach of contract, false advertising, or discrimination.[32] Another option for college students and employees at both public and private institutions who have been targeted is to al-lege harassment rather than hate speech. On the federal and state lev-els, harassment is generally punished as a pattern of behavior rather than mere speech. If there is evidence of harassment that creates an in-timidating, offensive, or hostile environment, legal remedies are often available.

CANCEL CULTURE

Cancel culture is the other side of the campus speech debate. Cancel culture is measured by the quiet of a speech never heard, where speakers are refused invitations or uninvited. Rather than champion speech and require those who peddle in untruths or encourage rancor and hostility to defend their views and be held accountable for their harm, cancel culture extracts vengeance by rendering speakers mute. Banning speakers from campus affects not only their right to express their views, it also impacts the right of the audience to hear those views.

Such speakers plainly abuse the beneficence of the First Amendment by using it to support their right to speak, but the First Amendment was constructed to withstand such poor treatment. Canceling speech subjects the marketplace of ideas to regulatory control rather than leaving the trade in ideas open to market forces.

In those instances where unpopular speakers are given the stage, the First Amendment gives them cover to deliver their vitriol; however, it also provides an opportunity for opponents to shout extremists down so that their diatribes go unheard. Professor Clay Calvert has described these events as "theatre of the absurd."[33] Professor Calvert was specifically referencing Richard Spencer's appearance at the University of Florida on October 19, 2017. According to the Southern Poverty Law Center, which monitors hate groups, Spencer is a "radical white separatist whose goal is the establishment of a white ethno-state in North America."[34] Anticipating protests against Spencer, the governor declared a state of emergency, and the university deployed taxpayer-funded security to the tune of $500,000.[35] Snipers patrolled rooftops and hundreds of state troopers manned barricades.[36] In the end, no violence was directed at Spencer, and he was provided his soapbox. He did not incite violence, so there was no opportunity for the police to remove him. Nonetheless, his message went unheard. The event devolved into a shouting match, and Spencer's performance never really got off the ground.[37]

Like the angels that block the Westboro Baptist Church's signs, the primary speakers in these shouting matches are silenced; however, the government or controlling authority (the school) has taken no role in the silencing. It is an organic event. The First Amendment, doing what it does best, has provided the stage for speech. The First Amendment is not tasked with controlling the volume, just the space. If the loudest voices are the only ones heard, so be it.

Many lament the college climate that allows some to shout down those whose viewpoints they abhor. It is, they argue, a heckler's veto, and those who participate should be removed from the venue. Others celebrate the power the First Amendment provides opponents to shout over and shout out the ugliness. It is all, it seems, either the First Amendment at its best or its worst.

Cancel culture also seeks to silence speakers by removing them from their jobs or punishing them for views that are disagreeable to those in power or those with the loudest megaphones. Despite the belief by some citizens of public colleges and universities that those who hold intolerant views should be silenced and prohibited from speaking on campus, the First Amendment offers them no solace. Public college employees, like government employees, can invoke First Amendment protections as long as the employee is speaking as a private citizen and not as a representative of the government in furtherance of their employment responsibilities: "A teacher's exercise of his right to speak on issues of public importance may not furnish the basis for his dismissal from public employment."[38] Employees at private colleges cannot necessarily claim the same protections and might be limited to their contractual remedies.

*[O]ur decisions have also made clear that picketing
and parading may nonetheless constitute methods of
expression, entitled to First Amendment protection.*
—*Shuttlesworth v. City of Birmingham*[1]

On April 12, 1960, *New York Times* reporter Harrison E. Salisbury wrote a scathing article describing the racist climate that gripped Birmingham, Alabama.[2] Salisbury observed that the only public facilities shared by Whites and Blacks were the city's streets, the water supply, and the sewer systems. Rather than comply with court orders to desegregate the city's recreation facilities, the city government closed them. They closed sixty-eight parks, thirty-eight playgrounds, six swimming pools, and four golf courses. It remained a crime for people of both races to play cards or checkers with one another. Even libraries were not immune: Administrators banned a book that featured black rabbits and white rabbits.[3]

Salisbury crafted an image of Birmingham as "fragmented by the emotional dynamite of racism, reinforced by the whip, the razor, the gun, the bomb, the torch, the club, the knife, the mob, the police and many branches of the state's apparatus."[4] The Black community in Birmingham was gripped by fear, strife, and terror. So, too, was any member of the White community who dared recognize the humanity of a Black person or supported the call for civil rights. A nineteen-year-old girl had been grabbed by a group of men, self-identified as "floggers," and beaten until she signed a confession admitting she had been dating Black men. The home of a boy who participated in a prayer for freedom was invaded by a band of men "armed with iron pipes, clubs and leather blackjacks into which razor blades were sunk." As the mother protected her son from the blows, her leg was broken, her scalp smashed open, and her hands crushed.[5]

The terror had not abated by 1963; Birmingham was still widely believed to represent the most segregated and virulently racist city in the

United States. So it became the logical target of the burgeoning nonviolent civil rights movement. The Birmingham Campaign was conceived and created by Reverend Fred L. Shuttlesworth, Reverend Dr. Martin Luther King Jr., and the leaders of the Southern Christian Leadership Council (SCLC).

The mission of the campaign was outlined in the Birmingham Manifesto, which was released on April 3, 1963, by the Alabama Christian Movement for Civil Rights.[6] The manifesto served as an indictment against the White citizens of Birmingham and their leaders for illegally enforcing segregation policies. The terms of the manifesto demanded, among other things, immediate implementation of fair hiring practices and equal employment opportunities. It was also a call to action to Birmingham residents and citizens across the nation, Black and White, to unite in protest. Out of that manifesto grew Project Confrontation (Project C), a series of planned demonstrations and boycotts to protest civil rights failures, push forward integration efforts, and execute promised reforms.

At the time, a Birmingham ordinance required that anyone seeking to participate in a parade or procession must first apply for a permit to do so. It required that the application be completed in writing and addressed to a designated commission. Further, it required that the application identify the path of the procession, the number of people anticipated, and the event's purpose. According to the terms of the ordinance, a permit would be granted unless, in the sole discretion of the commission, "the public welfare, peace, safety, health, decency, good order, morals or convenience require that it be refused."[7]

On April 3, Lola Hendricks and Reverend Ambus Hill entered city hall with a written request for a permit to march in protest along Birmingham's streets. The request conformed to all of the requirements mentioned above. Upon entering city hall, Ms. Hendricks and Reverend Hill were greeted by Commissioner of Public Safety Eugene "Bull" Connor. Connor was a former sportscaster who earned the nickname because of the timbre of his voice.[8] He mocked the two advocates, telling them, "No, you will not get a permit in Birmingham, Alabama, to picket. I will picket you over to the City Jail if you don't get the hell out of here."[9]

Bull Connor had a reputation. He was a virulent racist intent on maintaining White supremacist culture. He was known to ride around the city in an armored tank to terrorize Black citizens. In May 1961, Connor gave Klansmen the go-ahead to attack the Freedom Riders, when they arrived in Birmingham. The Freedom Riders were a group of activists, among them the late Congressman John Lewis, who participated in an interracial bus ride across the South to test compliance with two Supreme Court rulings declaring that segregation at lunch counters, bathrooms, and interstate travel facilities is unconstitutional.[10] The Klansmen met the bus at the Birmingham station "wielding baseball bats, pipes and bicycle chains" and, with Connor's full knowledge and consent, beat the activists for fifteen minutes before the police arrived.[11] On May 3, 1963, it was Bull Connor who authorized the use of firehoses and dogs against the civil rights protesters. In hindsight, it is probable that the televised pictures of those horrors moved the needle forward in the fight for equality and catalyzed the passage of the Civil Rights Act of 1964 and the Voting Rights Act of 1965. In 1963, even President John F. Kennedy noted that Connor's actions would likely propel the civil rights movement forward: "The civil rights movement should thank God for Bull Connor. He's helped it as much as Abraham Lincoln."[12]

At the same time that Connor was threatening Ms. Hendricks and Reverend Hill with jail, sixty five young Black citizens were engaged in a lunch counter protest. The large group had divided into smaller groups and each group separately entered a local department store, went to the lunch counter, and sat down. They were met by Birmingham police officers and about two dozen of the protesters were promptly jailed for breaching the peace. The only evidence that supported the arrests was that the accused sought to be served and to purchase lunch at a counter in a local department store reserved for White patrons.

In the wake of those arrests, Project C recommitted to larger, more public protests led by key figures in the movement. Tensions escalated. Hoping to interrupt Project C's growing momentum, the local government, led by Connor, turned to the courts. They sought and were granted an injunction. The injunction mandated that by order of the court, the group was prohibited from marching without a permit—the same permit Bull Connor had already forecast would not be granted.

The nonviolent civil rights movement was premised on the moral responsibility to dismantle unjust laws. In his famous "Letter from Birmingham Jail," Dr. King defined unjust laws this way: "An unjust law is a code that a numerical or power majority group compels a minority group to obey but does not make binding on itself."[13] Dr. King and his followers sought to dismantle unjust laws not by evading them, but rather by submitting to them. In the letter he explained: "In no sense do I advocate evading or defying the law, as would the rabid segregationist. That would lead to anarchy. One who breaks an unjust law must do so openly, lovingly, and with a willingness to accept the penalty. I submit that an individual who breaks a law that conscience tells him is unjust, and who willingly accepts the penalty of imprisonment in order to arouse the conscience of the community over its injustice, is in reality expressing the highest respect for law."[14] In other words, punishment for breaking laws, jail time, must be endured so that the courts could have the opportunity to review and invalidate unjust laws. The movement relied on the judicial precepts of fairness and justice and the belief that eventually the courts would employ the wheels of justice to arrive finally at the truth.

The court order secured by Conner et al. smacked of injustice. This put the movement in the impossible situation of reliance upon a judiciary that the movement believed had abused its judicial power and turned a blind eye to its responsibilities. For the first time in the movement's history, Dr. King chose to disobey a court order. After consulting with the international jazz singing star Harry Belafonte and securing funding for what was sure to be mass arrests, Project C protesters continued their plan to march on April 12, Good Friday.[15] That day, knowing he would be arrested along with everyone else, Dr. Martin Luther King Jr. stepped to the front and led the demonstration.

At about 2:30 p.m., King, Shuttlesworth, and an additional fifty volunteers walked out of church and onto the streets. The protesters were controlled and disciplined. They did not obstruct traffic or other pedestrians. Hundreds of onlookers lined the streets. The protesters walked for about four blocks before Connor and the police met them. Upon receiving Connor's order to stop, the group knelt in prayer. Dr. King and the other protesters, were summarily seized and hauled off to jail. Notably, it was during this incarceration that Dr. King penned the "Letter from Birmingham Jail" referenced above. He wrote his thoughts on the margins of a newspaper. They were collected by another leader of the movement, Wyatt Tee Walker, the executive director of SCLC, typed up, and returned to King for editing.[16]

Shuttlesworth, described in his *New York Times* obituary, printed on October 5, 2011, as a man who had "no equal in terms of courage and putting his life in the line of fire to battle segregation,"[17] was the first to post bond and be released from jail. Later, he was tried and convicted for violating the permit ordinance. Shuttlesworth stood in stark contrast to his ally Dr. King. He was "blunt where King was soothing, driven where King was leisurely, and most important, confrontational where King was conciliatory."[18] Attacked with bicycle chains and brass knuckles by Klansmen in 1957, he responded to a doctor's surprised observation that he had not suffered a concussion with, "Doctor, the Lord knew I lived in a hard town, so he gave me a hard head."[19]

Shuttlesworth was sentenced to ninety days imprisonment at hard labor, payment of a seventy-five-dollar fine, and court costs totaling twenty-four dollars. He appealed and remained free on bond.[20] Throughout the Alabama court system, as many as 1,500 protesters were awaiting trial related to a number of protests and marches across the state. Their cases were stayed pending Shuttlesworth's appeal.[21] It took two years for the Alabama Court of Appeals to overturn the conviction. That court described the march as a group of people taking a walk and, more importantly, found the ordinance unconstitutionally vague and overbroad.[22] It was another two years before the Alabama Supreme Court reversed the Alabama Court of Appeals' decision and reinstated the conviction. It was not until five years after the original conviction that the case was heard at the US Supreme Court, which finally and permanently overturned the convictions—an absurd amount of time to wait for permission to march in protest of current events.[23]

PROTECTING THE PUBLIC FORUM

The march for which Shuttlesworth and his colleagues were convicted took place on Birmingham's public streets. Using public streets and parks to protest is part of the history and heritage of the

United States.[24] In constitutional parlance, these places are labeled **public forums**. Public forums are generally open to speech and debate such that content-based restrictions directed at their use will be subject to a strict scrutiny analysis. They are, in essence, held in trust for public use. However, that use is not absolute and can be subject to meaningful content-neutral limitations regarding time of day, location, and even means of expression. Often these limitations are described as time, place, and manner restrictions. That the Birmingham ordinance required a permit to march was not, by itself, an unreasonable restriction. There is little dispute that municipalities have a duty to maintain and control access to sidewalks and streets for the public's convenience and safety.[25] Requiring a permit provides notice to the municipality of the possible need for additional police presence. It allows the municipality to control the time and manner of the march so it can balance the needs of the community against the rights of the speakers. However, constitutional application of a statute or ordinance also requires that such an ordinance be fairly and objectively enforced. As written, the Birmingham ordinance unconstitutionally provided unbridled discretion to a commission regarding whether or not to grant a permit. Indeed, a permit could be refused for no other reason than the march was inconvenient. Discretion of that nature smacked of unchecked power. The United States was born out of a war that scorned such power and sought fairness and justice in governance. Applying such discretion as a means to shut down protest amounted to a prior restraint on speech.

As we already know, prior restraint is censorship, plain and simple, and the First Amendment abhors a prior restraint. Those seeking civil rights for all were doing so in the pursuit of freedom and dignity. Their means of communicating through direct action and marching was speech through action. Like the expressive jean jacket Paul Robert Cohen would wear to court a few years later and, even further in the future, the flag Gregory Johnson would burn in protest, it was symbolic speech. The First Amendment was their shield. While the protesters' march could be constitutionally managed regarding the time of day, route, and method, absent compelling reasons, they could not be censored or restrained from speaking. The ordinance was unconstitutional.

TIME, PLACE, AND MANNER RESTRICTIONS

The complicated case of the "buffer zone" serves as an interesting illustration of the importance geography plays in First Amendment conflicts.

When patients and opponents meet at the doors of a facility that provides abortion, the interactions are often heated and can sometimes become physical. Women who seek abortions are taking action following a profoundly personal choice about their bodies and their lives. Abortion providers seek to protect their patients as they enter their premises to pursue treatment or undertake a medical procedure that will terminate a pregnancy. Abortion foes seek to change minds, policies, and procedures so as to protect the life of the unborn. Steadfastly believing that abortions are wrong, many seek to dissuade women from seeking them or, if they are unsuccessful in doing so, to actively block the entrances so that women cannot use their services. In a Colorado court hearing, testimony confirmed the contentious nature of the abortion protests:

> A nurse practitioner testified that some anti-abortion protesters "yell, thrust signs in faces, and generally try to upset the patient as much as possible, which makes it much more difficult for us to provide care in a scary situation anyway."
>
> A volunteer who escorts patients into and out of clinics testified that the protesters are flashing their bloody fetus signs. "[T]hey are yelling, you are killing your baby. . . . they are talking about fetuses and babies being dismembered, arms and legs torn off. . . . [A] mother and her daughter . . . were immediately surrounded and yelled at and screamed at."[26]

In 1993, the Colorado legislature enacted a statute in response to anti-abortion protests that regularly occurred at abortion clinics or medical facilities that performed abortions. The stated purpose behind the legislation was to balance a person's right to protest against a patient's right to seek treatment. Specifically, the statute created a buffer zone between protesters and patients attempting to enter the clinic. Once a patient was within one hundred feet of the clinic entrance, the patient was protected by an eight-foot bubble. Within that eight-foot bubble, only after a patient accepted the request of a protester, could a protester approach a patient.

Groups representing the anti-abortion movement argued that the eight-feet-within-one-hundred-feet buffer zone on a public street was an unconstitutional content-based restriction on free speech. In the case *Hill v. Colorado*,[27] six of the nine justices disagreed with the anti-abortion advocates and held that the statute created a reasonable time, place, and manner restriction. The court reiterated the accepted doctrine that a public forum will earn the strongest protection from the First Amendment unless there are compelling reasons to withdraw the protection. However, reasonable limitations on the place, the time, and sometimes even the method used to speak will be upheld as long as the state or municipality asserts a valid and significant interest in creating the regulations. The regulations must be narrowly tailored, meaning that they do not burden substantially more speech than is necessary, and there must remain ample alternatives for the speaker to communicate their message.

The majority found that the State of Colorado had a significant interest in providing unrestricted access to medical facilities. Moreover, the court held that the regulations were aimed not at the content of the speech but at the geography: the area where the speech could take place. The justices insisted the geographical limitations went only as far as necessary to meet the state interest of protecting its population's health and safety. No speech was censored. The protester's speech could continue unabated as long as the patient agreed to be approached. If the request was refused, the protester could choose to march outside of the clinic on the public sidewalk as long as the march was one hundred feet from the clinic entrance.

The three dissenting justices were fierce in their arguments that the statute unconstitutionally restricted speech. The dissenting justices accused the majority of failing to recognize the value and importance of medium to message. Counseling and hand billing cannot occur within an eight-foot barrier. Just as Paul Robert Cohen's choice of an expletive emblazoned on his jean jacket was crucial to his message opposing the draft, so, too, is the need to approach a pregnant woman and speak to her in close proximity to persuade her not to follow through with her intent to abort. Restricting the medium of the anti-abortion advocates' message effectively censored the speech. Justice Anthony Kennedy best articulated the point:

The means of expression at stake here are of controlling importance. . . . Nowhere is the speech more important than at the time and place where the act is about to occur. . . . Colorado and the Court have it just backwards. For these protesters the 100-foot zone in which young women enter a building is not just the last place where the message can be communicated. It likely is the only place. It is the location where the Court should expend its utmost effort to vindicate free speech, not to burden or suppress it.[28]

The majority spent a good portion of its decision defending the public's right to be free from unwanted speech—the right to be left alone. It described the audience approaching a health facility for treatment as captive, one who could not avoid unwanted messaging simply by averting their eyes or ignoring what they heard. The dissent swiftly dispensed with that reasoning and countered that there is no First Amendment right to be free from hearing speech one finds disturbing. Unless the speech is incitement, fighting words, a true threat, or obscene, the First Amendment does not countenance limiting speech in the public forum. The dissent argued that this was not merely a restriction on the location of speech but a restriction focused on antiabortion speech. It was content based, and worse, it was **viewpoint discriminatory**. From a First Amendment perspective, viewpoint discrimination is the worst kind of content-based restriction, because it targets only one side of the debate. The disfavored side is muted, but the favored side is allowed full expression.

Justice Scalia was among the most strident of the dissenters. He insisted that the court did no favor to democracy and warned that rather than protect unwilling listeners from disturbing speech, both the State of Colorado and the court ensured that the speech of the protesters would only get louder in an effort to breach the divide created by the buffer zone:

Those whose concern is for the physical safety and security of clinic patients, workers, and doctors should take no comfort from today's decision. Individuals or groups intent on bullying or frightening women out of an abortion, or doctors out of performing that procedure, will not be deterred by Colorado's statute; bullhorns and screaming from eight feet away will serve their purposes well.

But those who would accomplish their moral and religious objectives by peaceful and civil means, by trying to persuade individual women of the rightness of their cause, will be deterred; and that is not a good thing in a democracy.[29]

Of course, this wasn't the end of the story. We met Eleanor McCullen earlier. Her attack on the Massachusetts buffer zone statute was mounted fourteen years after the decision in *Hill v. Colorado*. Unlike the Colorado statute, which created a "floating buffer zone," the Massachusetts statute created a static buffer zone. As you might recall, Mrs. McCullen, a grandmother and devout Catholic, wanted to counsel women against terminating their pregnancies; however, she was required to stay thirty-five feet away from a person entering a facility that provides abortions. Mrs. McCullen argued that the statutory restriction effectively prohibited her from engaging in any conversations with the pregnant women entering the facilities. The government argued that the law was drafted not to affect speech but to prohibit protesters from blocking clinics' entrances, accosting patients, taking their picture, and throwing literature at them.[30] The Supreme Court agreed with Mrs. McCullen. The court held that the Massachusetts buffer zone was an unconstitutional time, place, and manner restriction.

Are the variances between the Colorado and Massachusetts statutes a distinction without a difference? Maybe. The *McCullen* decision was unanimous. The court found that the statute was overbroad, and despite the justifications offered by the government, the statute placed an undue burden on speech. For our purposes, the point is that public streets, as constitutionally protected public forums, remain open for debate, conversation, and protest. Under some circumstances, the forum can be temporarily closed, moved to another location, or rescheduled to another time of day, but only if those restrictions offer adequate protection for robust speech.

THE PRICE OF PROTECTING THE PUBLIC FORUM

A government regulation that allows any kind of arbitrary judgment regarding the time, place, or manner of speech creates the potential means for suppressing a particular point of view. Even fees assessed to offset municipal costs are suspect.

On January 24, 1987, Cumming, Georgia, the county seat for Forsyth County, was the location of the largest civil rights protest since the 1960s. Forsyth County had a troubled past. In 1921, all of the Black Americans who lived there were driven out of town after one man was lynched and another was beaten over the alleged rape and murder of a White woman. From 1921 until sometime in the 1990s, not a single Black person called Forsyth County home.[31] On that January day in 1987, over 20,000 civil rights advocates descended on the county. They came in response to a racist brawl that had occurred the week before, when a small group marched there in celebration of the Martin Luther King holiday. The civil rights advocates were met by about a thousand White supremacists; some dressed in camouflage fatigues, and others dressed in the standard KKK uniform of a white hood and gown. All of the participants were protected by approximately 3,000 state and local police and National Guardsmen. Over fifty people were arrested, many for illegal possession of weapons, including bows and arrows.[32] Permits for the demonstrations had been properly filed, but the cost, mostly borne by the local municipality, exceeded $500,000.[33]

To avoid another economic tsunami, the Forsyth County Board of Commissioners enacted an ordinance that sought to defray the municipal costs for maintaining safety and order during parades and marches. The fees were adjusted for each event based upon the expected level of conflict between marchers and counterprotesters.[34] In January 1989, the Nationalist Movement, an organization that maintained an independent affiliation with the KKK, planned another rally in Forsyth to protest national recognition of the Martin Luther King Jr. holiday. They sought a permit for the march, and pursuant to the ordinance, the county administrator assessed a fee of one hundred dollars. The group refused to pay the fee, canceled the rally, and sued the county, alleging that the county ordinance did not prescribe adequate standards for the levying of a permit fee by the county administrator. They argued that discretionary assessment of a permit fee imposed an unconstitutional condition upon the exercise of a First Amendment right. The lower federal courts reached opposite conclusions regarding the constitutionality of the fees.[35] The Supreme Court made the final determination.

In *Forsyth County, Georgia v. Nationalist Movement*, the Supreme

Court held that the statute created a legislated sanction for a heckler's veto. Costs for demonstrators were assessed by a county administrator's estimations of the community's response to the demonstration. Those estimations are not narrow, objective, definitive standards; essentially, the freedom to speak is left to a county administrator's whim and good will. In the words of the court, the ordinance was unconstitutional because it allowed the county to charge a premium "in the case of a controversial political message delivered before a hostile audience."[36] The First Amendment will not countenance bestowing the government with that kind of power.

PUBLIC PROPERTY, NOT PUBLIC FORUM

The First Amendment may not be used as an entry point onto all property owned by the government. Simply because a property is owned or maintained by a municipality and supported by the government through tax dollars does not automatically make it a public forum.

As we've already mentioned in our discussion of the Bork nomination, Richard Nixon was running for his second term of office in 1972. The Democrats nominated George McGovern. Nixon won reelection with 60 percent of the vote, only to resign in disgrace over the Watergate scandal two years later. Nixon and McGovern were not the only two candidates running for president, however. Benjamin Spock was running as the candidate for the People's Party; his vice presidential nominee was Julius Hobson. Linda Jenness was running for president on the Socialist Workers Party platform, and her vice presidential pick was Andrew Pulley. All four of those candidates wanted to hold a meeting to discuss election issues with the servicemen and servicewomen who were posted at Fort Dix in New Jersey. They properly sought permission from the commander of the military base, who promptly rejected the request. The Supreme Court held that the rejection was constitutional.[37] The court explained that property owned by the government, which is used for a specified purpose, in this case a military base, can be limited to that use as long as the limitation is objectively applied and not applied to restrict the content of particular messages.

PUBLIC FORUM FOR A LIMITED PURPOSE

On the other hand, once the government opens a tax-funded property to the public for a limited use, the government must keep the property available for all speech that meets the limited use criteria. For example, if a municipally owned performance space is open to theatrical and musical productions in general, it cannot be closed to a particular production that offends the sensibilities of some of the population.[38] That noteworthy piece of constitutional law came as a complete surprise to the Tennessee board of trustees of the Tivoli Theater in Chattanooga.

In October 1971, Southeastern Promotions applied for permission to mount a performance of the musical *Hair* at the Tivoli, a municipally leased theater in Chattanooga, Tennessee. It was operated by a nonprofit board appointed by the mayor and confirmed by the city's board of commissioners. The board's mission was to promote the auditorium as a "community center of Chattanooga, where civic, educational, religious, patriotic and charitable organizations and associations may have a common meeting place to discuss and further the upbuilding and general welfare of the city and surrounding territory."[39] The board apparently did not find the musical *Hair* to meet those criteria.

Hair was described at the time by theater critic Clive Barnes as a tribal rock musical. It celebrated the energy, music, and movement of 1960s hippie culture, which included antiwar messages and typical antiestablishment themes of the time. It was, at its core, a political message of youth empowerment and protest. One scene in the musical had all of the characters on stage disrobe and stand nude in front of the audience. There was quite a bit of profanity in the dialogue and scenes of simulated sex. It was considered radical at the time.

The municipal board rejected the request to perform *Hair* on the grounds that the performance was not in the best interests of the Chattanooga community. At trial, defending the board's decision, Commissioner Conrad stated that the board sought to promote only those theatrical productions that were "clean and healthful and culturally uplifting."[40] *Hair*, he believed, did not meet that standard.

The Supreme Court ruled that the action by the board was unconstitutional. Refusing to allow speech before any sound is uttered is censorship. The theater was a publicly available forum for artistic performances. As such, it was open to all performative speech. A prior restraint will not be tolerated in a public forum, even a public forum contained by walls and a roof.[41] The court insisted that the performance could not be censored and should have been allowed to proceed. Once the performance began, if the performance was obscene or incited the audience to imminent lawless action, it might lose the protection of the First Amendment, but that determination could only be made after the fact.[42]

A public forum democratizes speech opportunities to all regardless of socioeconomic, ethnic, racial, religious, and sexual considerations. Restrictions on speech in a public forum cannot be imposed because the community leaders do not like, are uncomfortable with, or even are afraid of the content of the speech. If a government property is otherwise open for expressive activities, the government must maintain its open character and provide the fullest and broadest speech protection.

IS SOCIAL MEDIA A PUBLIC FORUM?

Yes and no. It's complicated. Social media is a vast platform for expression, a virtual public park or street. That definition reads as strikingly similar to the definition of a public forum. However, a fundamental element in the public forum doctrine is that the spaces are publicly owned and supported by tax dollars. Social media is not a public forum because social media platforms do not belong to the government. Social media platforms, such as Facebook, YouTube, and Twitter, are owned by shareholders, which include private citizens and corporations. Rules of access to the platforms are created and enforced by their governing bodies (the board of directors, for instance). The platforms themselves can place limitations on the speech they will support. It is for this reason that, at present, they can cleanse their sites of hate speech and fake news without running into First Amendment barriers. In fact, those platforms, had they wished to, could have blocked Lester Gerard Packingham.

Packingham was a registered sex offender in North Carolina. As a twenty-one-year-old college student, he had sex with a thirteen-year-old girl. He pleaded guilty to the charge, received a suspended sentence, and was subject to twenty-four months of supervised probation, which he completed without any trouble or complications.[43] Eight years later, he was back in court for a traffic violation, which was later dismissed. He celebrated the successful outcome of that case by posting on Facebook: "Man God is Good! How about I got so much favor they dismissed the ticket before court even started? No fine, no court cost, no nothing spent . . . Praise be to GOD, WOW! Thanks JESUS!" However, his celebration was short-lived. The Durham police department recorded Packingham's post, and he was arrested and convicted for violating a North Carolina law that prohibited a registered sex offender from accessing any "social networking Web site where the sex offender knows that the site permits minor children to become members or to create or maintain personal Web pages."[44] There was no evidence that Packingham had attempted to contact a minor.

The North Carolina statute was enacted in 2008.[45] From 2008 to 2010, it had been used to prosecute a thousand other men who were registered sex offenders and had accessed social media sites.[46] Packingham appealed his conviction, asserting that restricting his social media access in this manner was an unconstitutional burden on his First Amendment rights. It took six long years as the case worked its way through the appellate process before the Supreme Court made its final decision. The justices agreed with Packingham. The court found the statute overbroad. While Packingham could be prohibited from unauthorized contact with minors on the internet, he could not be prohibited from generally accessing social media. As part of its decision, the court analogized the internet to a "modern public square."[47]

Using the same analogy, in *Knight First Amendment Institute v. Trump*,[48] the Court of Appeals for the Second Circuit held that the interactive spaces on President Trump's twitter account, @realDonaldTrump, were public forums. Like Facebook, Twitter is not government owned, but according to the Second Circuit Federal Court of Appeals, a public official can transform their own space on social media into a public forum. President Donald Trump did just that with his Twitter account. The president and members of his administration described all of the president's Twitter feeds, including @POTUS and @whitehouse, as official accounts. In particular, the president used the @realDonaldTrump account "to announce, describe, and defend his policies; to promote his

Administration's legislative agenda; to announce official decisions; to engage with foreign political leaders; to publicize state visits; [and] to challenge media organizations whose coverage of his Administration he believes to be unfair."[49]

It seems Mr. Trump was angered by individual Twitter followers who criticized him, and he blocked those followers from his Twitter account. As a result, those users were unable to view the president's tweets directly and unable to reply to them, limiting their ability to engage in discussion with the president and the rest of his Twitter followers. The court held Mr. Trump's actions were unconstitutional. By his own hand, he had created a public forum by opening up his tweets to comments and shares by retweet. As such, it was subject to the same constitutional restraints as any other public forum. The president could not restrict speech based on content. The court was careful to limit its decision to this particular set of facts, and the court explicitly did "not consider or decide whether an elected official violates the Constitution by excluding persons from a wholly private social media account." Nor did the court decide "whether private social media companies are bound by the First Amendment when policing their platforms."[50] Of course, now, private citizen Trump can ban as many people from his account as he chooses.

BACK TO CAMPUS SPEECH

Speech on a public university campus is generally subject to the same constitutional guidelines as speech in a public forum.[51] As we learned in the discussion of campus speech codes, if a public college or university imposes a regulation on speech that is directed at content or viewpoint, it will be subject to a strict scrutiny analysis, which is difficult to overcome.[52] Any restrictions on speech must be content neutral and satisfy all elements of that constitutional test.[53]

Nonetheless, public colleges and universities are not obligated to make available all parts of the university at all times for speech. Although the Supreme Court has yet to rule on this issue, generally, the lower courts have found that classrooms are not public forums and may be subject to reasonable content-based restrictions. For example, in 1988, plaintiff Christina Axson-Flynn was studying at the University of Utah's Actor Training Program. During her audition for entry into the program, and then again during class exercises, Axson-Flynn explained that she would not use swear words or any words that took God's name in vain. When required to recite scripts that were contrary to her standards and beliefs, she refused to utter the offending language. Under pressure to either modify her values or leave the program, she chose to leave the program and sue the school for violating her First Amendment rights by seeking to compel her to speak.[54] As we will discover in later chapters, the First Amendment protects both the right to speak and the right to refuse to speak.[55] The US Court of Appeals for the Tenth Circuit found that a classroom is not a public forum of any kind and, as such, teachers and administrators are free to impose reasonable guidelines regarding speech within the classroom walls.[56] The only restriction is that the curriculum requirement is reasonably related to pedagogical concerns. As long as the rules and regulations are not a pretext for discrimination, courts will defer to the educator's decision.[57]

12 : THE MESSAGE AND THE MEDIUM

We shape our tools, and thereafter, our tools shape us.
—*John Culkin*[1]

The impact of the medium upon the message is incalculable. Visual, aural, and written messages all communicate by activating distinct sensors and particular parts of our brains. Different media have different emotional and intellectual impacts upon the target audiences. Those who authored the First Amendment in the latter part of the eighteenth century were undoubtedly visionaries, but they weren't clairvoyant. They surely could not envision a world of cable television and internet streaming. Crafting First Amendment jurisprudence to meet the ever-expanding communication landscape has been, in a word, challenging.

NEWSPAPERS

In 1972 the *Miami Herald*, a daily newspaper, had a bone to pick with Pat Tornillo, who was a candidate for the Florida House of Representatives. Since 1962, Tornillo, described as a "classic power broker" and "political strongman," had served in the leadership of the South Florida teacher's union, the United Teachers of Dade (UTD).[2] The editorial board wrote a scathing piece about Mr. Tornillo besmirching his politics and his character:

> For years now, he has been kicking the public shin to call attention to his shakedown statesmanship. He and whichever acerbic prexy is in alleged office have always felt their private ventures so chock-full of public weal that we should leap at the chance to nab the tab, be it half the glorious Leader's salary or the dues check-off or anything else except perhaps mileage on the staff hydrofoil. Give him public office, says Pat, and he will no doubt live by the Golden Rule. Our translation reads that as more gold and more rule.[3]

Mr. Tornillo demanded that according to Florida's right to reply law, the newspaper was obligated to provide him equal space and equal prominence in the paper to answer the accusations. The paper refused.

Tornillo argued that newspapers, as "surrogates for the public," had a fiduciary obligation to ensure that the marketplace of ideas remained robust. The government, he contended, had a responsibility to enforce that obligation.[4] In opposition, the newspaper replied that enforcing the statute would create a chilling effect. Rather than face the financial burden of adding pages to the newspaper or paying government-imposed fines, the newspaper might decide not to print content that would create a liability. The marketplace of ideas would contract, not expand. More importantly, the newspaper asserted that the First Amendment does not provide the public or the government the right to dictate to the press the form and content of its news columns or the opinions expressed in its editorials.

In *Miami Herald Publishing Co. v. Tornillo*,[5] a unanimous Supreme Court agreed with the newspaper. The *Miami Herald* had full editorial control over its pages, and the Florida law that sought to compel the newspaper to print content was unconstitutional. The court explained that, as a medium of communication, print is treated similarly to speech, and so, speech published in a newspaper is given the fullest First Amendment protection.

The court decision was grounded upon the fact that newspapers are private enterprises. They are not an arm of the government, and government cannot transform newspapers into a public forum. A newspaper reflects the editorial choices of its editors or owners. They are not required to serve as a platform for opposing views. Significantly, as a business enterprise, there are economic concerns regarding space allocation and advertising, and requiring a newspaper to provide space to all those who wish to publish might create undue financial burdens. Of course, there were still options available to an individual who took issue with a publication. They could sue the newspaper for defamation. However, as we shall see later, that option is not quite as simple as it seems.

In his concurring opinion, Justice Byron White acknowledged that failing to require a right to reply might, in some instances, skew the debate, but he maintained that "the balance struck by the First Amendment with respect to the press is that society must take the risk that occasionally debate on vital matters will not be comprehensive, and that all viewpoints may not be expressed."[6]

In hindsight, one might wonder what defense Tornillo might have offered had he been given the right to reply. Thirty years later, he plead guilty to federal charges of tax evasion and mail fraud for having used UTD money "to fund his lavish lifestyle."[7] He was sentenced to twenty-seven months in prison and required to pay restitution in the amount of $650,000, a $25,000 fine, and $160,000 in unpaid federal income taxes.[8] He was released after having served twenty-two months. Only then did Tornillo have his opportunity to reply in the pages of the newspaper. Upon his release from prison, Tornillo published this apology in the *Miami Herald*:

> I write to apologize with the deepest sense of humility to the teachers and children of Miami-Dade County . . . to the United Teachers of Dade . . . to the union members who believed in me and stood with me through demonstrations and rallies and civil disobedience as we fought for collective bargaining and teacher rights.[9]

Tornillo died two years later, in 2007, from a variety of health issues.[10]

BROADCAST AND CABLE

Unlike newspapers, which theoretically can be operated by anyone with the ability to print, the radio and television broadcasts of the last century could be operated only under limited circumstances, so the application of First Amendment principles was a bit more complicated. Broadcast transmissions rely upon radio waves and electromagnetic signals. There are only a finite number of radio waves and electromagnetic signals from which broadcast radio and television stations can operate. As a result, they are considered a scarce resource. Using the foundational principles of the **scarcity rationale**, the government created the Federal Communications Commission (FCC) and empowered it to issue and enforce licenses and guidelines for the use of the waves and signals. The purpose of the guidelines was to preserve the marketplace of ideas and encourage a diversity of viewpoints as well as enhance educational programming and protect children from indecent content.

Until 1987, under FCC rules, licensed broadcast producers were obligated to follow the **Fairness Doctrine**, which required that they dedicate airtime to all sides of a controversial issue to allow for a balanced discussion of opposing views. The Supreme Court gave its stamp of constitutional approval to that doctrine in *Red Lion v. FCC*.[11]

The Red Lion Broadcasting Company owned a radio license, giving it spectrum rights over the airwaves in Pennsylvania. On November 27, 1964, the author Fred J. Cook was the subject of an editorialized attack aired by Red Lion. In that broadcast, Cook was accused by the Reverend Billy Jay Hargis of making false charges against city officials and working for Communist-affiliated organizations, a still-frightening accusation ten years after the McCarthy-era Red Scare. Cook demanded free airtime to reply to the accusations. In stark contrast to the (later) decision in *Tornillo*,[12] the Supreme Court held that Cook should be given equal time to reply to the attack pursuant to the Fairness Doctrine. While the court refused to acknowledge a fiduciary responsibility of newspapers, they imposed that responsibility on broadcast license holders. The court described broadcast license holders as trustees; that designation required them to share the riches of free speech that the megaphone of radio or TV spectrum rights provides.

Under the dictates of the Fairness Doctrine, radio and TV broadcasters' own First Amendment protections were secondary to the First Amendment rights of listeners and viewers. Broadcasters were not free to proselytize in favor of their worldview to the exclusion of other worldviews. To allow such broad editorial control over content would "snuff out" the free speech of all those with whom the broadcaster disagreed and thereby limit free exchange in the marketplace of ideas.[13] Without requiring fair balance, the Supreme Court warned, the broadcasters would fail in their duty of providing full disclosure of conflicting views on issues of public importance.

Then, in 1985 the FCC released a report that determined that an unintended consequence of the Fairness Doctrine was that broadcasters were limiting their programming so as to avoid running afoul of the doctrine and were refusing to broadcast anything that might produce controversy.

The doctrine was reducing, not expanding, the marketplace of ideas. In 1987, the FCC abandoned most of the Fairness Doctrine requirements as too restrictive and having a chilling effect on free speech. The doctrine's repeal is largely believed to have opened the floodgates for the proliferation of ideologically based programing such as conservative talk radio.

Indeed, the conservative talk show megastar, the late Rush Limbaugh, was able to rise to fame and fortune from the abyss created by the Fairness Doctrine repeal. At the time of his death in 2021, Limbaugh's audience numbered in the multiple millions.[14] In 2011, he was the subject of the bestseller, *The Most Dangerous Man in America: Rush Limbaugh's Assault on Reason*, which describes Limbaugh as vicious, venomous, and polarizing.[15] He was an equal opportunity offender, having disparaged people of all races, genders and sexual orientation, as illustrated by some of his comments catalogued in an article by CBS News:

> "I think it's time to get rid of this whole National Basketball Association. Call it the TBA, the Thug Basketball Association, and stop calling them teams. Call 'em gangs."
>
> "Have you ever noticed how all composite pictures of wanted criminals resemble Jesse Jackson?"
>
> "The NAACP should have riot rehearsal. They should get a liquor store and practice robberies."
>
> "Feminism was established so as to allow unattractive women access to the mainstream of society."
>
> "Women should not be allowed on juries where the accused is a stud."
>
> "When a gay person turns his back on you, it is anything but an insult; it's an invitation."[16]

Comments like these drew applause from his followers and jeers from his detractors, but there was no opportunity for the targets of his attack to respond on Limbaugh's platform. Of course, other platforms were available, particularly in this burgeoning age of digital media, but they often miss Limbaugh's audience, who relied exclusively on him to learn about politics and policy.

By 2011, all but two remnants of the Fairness Doctrine had hit the dustbin, but nostalgia for an era when balance in broadcasting was required remains, and in 2019, Hawaii Congresswoman Tulsi Gabbard introduced a bill to reinstate the Fairness Doctrine in its entirety. The bill is floating in permanent congressional limbo. The two remaining vestiges of the Fairness Doctrine are the Reasonable Access Rule and the Equal Time Rule,[17] both related to political speech. Those rules remain in effect even today.

The Reasonable Access Rule simply requires broadcasters to permit candidates for federal office reasonable access to purchase time on their airwaves.[18] The more interesting and controversial rule is the Equal Time Rule. The Equal Time Rule is a more limited version of the Fairness Doctrine. The Equal Time Rule only applies to candidates running for public office, whereas the Fairness Doctrine applied to all matters of public import. The Equal Time Rule seeks to prevent a single candidate from hijacking broadcast time. The rule was applied in the 2016 presidential election when Donald Trump hosted Saturday Night Live (SNL). He was on air for over twelve minutes. As a result, NBC affiliate stations were required to offer equivalent time to all other candidates running for president that requested equal time. The network was not obligated to provide competitors with a spot on SNL, but it had to be a broadcast time of equivalent value and exposure.

Another remnant of the scarcity rationale still in place today is the Safe Harbor Rule. This vestige of broadcast regulation focuses on decency standards, which were crafted to protect children from some of the more harmful effects of television and legacy analog radio. One of the more entertaining stories of the government seeking to restrict the broadcast transmission of material inappropriate for children concerns the late comedian George Carlin's monologue "Filthy Words."

In the early afternoon on October 30, 1973, John H. Douglas, who happened to be a planning board member of Morality in Media, was driving in the car with his fifteen-year-old son. As many do, they turned on the radio. They were listening to WBAI-FM in New York, which was owned by the Pacifica Foundation. To Mr. Douglas's horror, the station was playing Carlin's satiric routine in which he discussed the seven filthy words you could not say on television. Those words, which he often repeated to peals of taped live audience laughter were: shit, piss, fuck, cunt, cocksucker, motherfucker, and tits. In fact, the entire monologue is appended to the Supreme Court decision about the broadcast and makes for some unusual reading.[19]

Mr. Douglas wrote a letter of complaint to the FCC, asserting that the broadcast was inappropriate for the middle of the day when children might hear it. The FCC was authorized to fine broadcasters for any radio communication deemed obscene, indecent, or profane. None of the parties argued that the language was obscene. Obscenity, discussed in greater detail in a later chapter, has a very particular definition in First Amendment parlance. Obscene speech, which is not protected by the First Amendment, must appeal to "prurient interest" and lack "serious literary, artistic, political, or scientific value."[20] Carlin's monologue did not appeal to prurient interest and the parties agreed that it had at least some artistic and political value, but the FCC did find the language patently offensive and indecent.[21] The FCC defines indecent broadcasts as those that depict or describe "sexual or excretory activities and organs in terms patently offensive as measured by contemporary community standards for the broadcast medium."[22] The FCC declined to formally sanction Pacifica Foundation for the broadcast; instead, it posted a warning in Pacifica's file that might affect future licensing options. Pacifica objected to the FCC action and took the issue to court.

Pacifica correctly described Carlin as "a significant social satirist who like Twain and Sahl before him, examines the language of ordinary people. . . . Carlin is not mouthing obscenities, he is merely using words to satirize as harmless and essentially silly our attitudes towards those words."[23] The FCC responded that it did not intend to censor the language and prohibit its broadcast but rather ensure that this type of broadcast, or any otherwise indecent or profane broadcast, was limited to hours when children were not likely to be in the audience.

The Supreme Court upheld the FCC action. The court specifically noted that "each medium of expression presents special First Amendment problems."[24] The court went further and explained that due to the broadcast medium's unique contours, it has limited First Amendment protections. The medium pervades the sound space and is easily accessible by children. The justices, many of them parents and grandparents in their own right, noted that upon hearing such a broadcast, a young child's vocabulary could be frightfully broadened "in an instant."[25]

After years of wrangling and numerous court cases that followed the *Pacifica* decision, a standard was finally developed and enforced. The FCC created a **Safe Harbor Rule**, which demarcates the time during which indecent speech may be legally (safely) broadcast. According to the Safe Harbor Rule, programming and advertising that is inappropriate for children and families can only be broadcast between 10:00 p.m. and 6:00 a.m. However, this didn't end the concern by the FCC, Congress, and others regarding profanity and indecency over the airwaves.

During the January 2003 Golden Globe Awards, U2 lead singer Bono let the expletive "fuck" fly two times during his acceptance speech. The following year, Janet Jackson and Justin Timberlake caused quite a scandal at the close of their 2004 Super Bowl halftime performance when Timberlake pulled on a part of Jackson's costume, revealing her right breast covered only with a nipple shield. It is thanks in large part to these two incidents, known affectionately as the "fleeting expletive problem" and "Nipplegate," respectively, that live sports and entertainment broadcasts are now subject to delays of several seconds. The delays provide time for control rooms to bleep out any offending material.

The Safe Harbor Rule has been defended as nothing more than a time, place, and manner restriction, but in fact it has had a demonstrable effect on the content of broadcast media. Failure to abide by that regulation can result in fines or the removal of the broadcast license. Many broadcasters report self-censorship by eliminating or editing programming, even removing or sanctioning on-air hosts for failing to abide by decency dictates. Radio stations that aired shock jock hosts such as Howard Stern incurred so many fines for violating the rule that the stations merely included the penalties as a cost of doing business. Ultimately, the shock jocks migrated to satellite and digital programming that was not restricted by the Safe Harbor Rule because satellite and digital programing is not part of the broadcast spectrum regulated by the FCC.

Today, more households rely on cable and digital than broadcast media. Moreover, according to the Digital Transition and Public Safety Act of 2005, all full-power analog television broadcasting was required to convert to the digital medium. All this virtually eliminates the problem of spectrum scarcity. Nonetheless, legacy broadcasters are still carefully monitored to abide by the reasonable access, equal time, and safe harbor restrictions.

Finally, while no one under forty years old knows or cares to know the difference between cable and broadcast media, suffice it to say that cable television has never been designated a scarce resource, unlike broadcast TV and radio. Therefore, regulations regarding cable TV are focused more on the details of delivery and access for local and other commercial channels.[26] Justifications for regulations over cable systems rely on municipalities' power to grant or deny permission to build cable infrastructure over public rights of way and easements. The courts have been more willing to protect cable operators' editorial authority and less willing to view any efforts to control the medium.[27]

Food for thought: In this digital era, the number of newspapers has declined in the face of an explosion of other media available to publish just about anything. It leads one to wonder if, today, both the broadcast spectrum and newspapers are limited resources.

THE INTERNET

Broadcast media use scarce radio and electromagnetic waves to reach their audiences. Cable systems use infrastructure restricted only by property boundaries and the inability to access public rights of way and easements. Entry points onto the internet are effectively limitless. To access the internet, all one needs is a keyboard and a connection. Moreover, as discussed earlier, the court has defined the internet as a vast democratic forum, similar in dimensions to a public forum, and we know that regulations to restrict access to or use of a public forum must meet a high constitutional standard. So far, most efforts by Congress to craft rules of access to and use of the internet have failed to meet the standard.

In 1996, Congress passed the Communications Decency Act (CDA). Section 223 and Section 230 of the CDA immediately became the subject of comment and litigation. Section 223 required Internet Service Providers (ISPS) to regulate access by children under eighteen to pornographic material. While obscene material does not enjoy constitutional protection, pornography is not always considered obscene. Maintaining the metaphor of a public forum, the government argued that the protections offered by section 223 of the CDA were no more than cyberzoning (an analogy to geographical zoning in a community)—creating time, place, and manner restrictions. However, the court in *Reno v. American Civil Liberties Union*[28] rejected the analogy, asserting the restrictions were based on content.

Congress may have been well intentioned, but good intent is not enough to overcome constitutional proscriptions. As a content-based restriction, Section 223 of the CDA had to survive a strict scrutiny analysis. As we know, there are two parts to a strict scrutiny analysis. First, the regulations must be directed at a compelling state interest, and second, the regulations must be crafted so they affect speech by the least intrusive means possible.

Undeniably, protecting children from harm is a compelling state interest, and the disputed parts of Section 223 targeted those interests. However, Section 223 failed the second part of the strict scrutiny analysis. It was overly broad. The effect of the limitations on internet-accessed pornographic material was to reduce constitutionally protected content on the internet to only that which was suitable for children. Such a limitation was a violation of First Amendment principles that promote disseminating information and ideas. The court noted there were (and are) proactive methods available to parents and schools to restrict access by children to inappropriate material. Parents and schools can control the content of material their children see, hear, and experience through filtering technologies, thereby protecting children and respecting the breadth of the First Amendment.[29]

Unlike Section 223 of the CDA, which imposed responsibilities and penalties upon ISPs, Section 230 provided ISPs, and by extension social media platforms, robust protection from liability. One of the early challenges for the legislatures and the courts was determining where accountability must lie for user-generated content on the internet. For instance, if someone uploads a post to an online platform, who is responsible for any ill effects? The speaker or the platform or both? Is YouTube liable for hosting a social media platform that promotes hate, lies, and violence? Is Twitter accountable for a factually inaccurate or an incendiary tweet? If Facebook creates rules to guide user content, but does not take down a post that violates its own rules, is Facebook responsible for any violence, injury, or monetary damages that occur as a direct result of that post? Are any of the platforms liable for taking down posts they deem objectionable, but would otherwise enjoy constitutional protection? The dilemma is apparent. If ISPs or social media platforms undertake monitoring responsibilities, they could become liable for any monitoring failures, which could lead to overcensoring material. If they refuse monitoring responsibilities, the platform may become an open free-for-all for any kind of speech, true or false, hateful or praiseworthy, reconciliatory or incendiary. Either choice erodes the value of the marketplace of ideas. Congress came to the rescue in the guise of Section 230 of the CDA.

Section 230(c)(1) singled out the author of a post as the only party responsible for any damages and injuries resulting from a post. In effect, Section 230(c)(1) protects ISPs, and anyone who publishes material by a third party (Facebook, for instance), from liability as a result of those publications. The application of that part of Section 230 can seem harsh and unfair to the injured party, but taking the long view, it is highly supportive of the wide variety of speech on the internet.

Twitter took refuge under Section 230(c)(1) in response to a lawsuit by the wives of Lloyd "Carl" Fields Jr. and James Damon Creach. Fields and Creach were United States government contractors working in Amman, Jordan. In November 2015, the men were shot and killed by Abu Zaid, who had been influenced by ISIS (Islamic State of Iraq and Syria) posts on Twitter.[30]

The contractors' wives sued Twitter for, among other things, allowing ISIS to sign up for and use Twitter accounts. The women correctly alleged that ISIS uses Twitter as a platform to spread propaganda, recruit members, and encourage terrorism and murder.[31] The First Amendment would not protect the men who murdered Fields and Creach, but Section 230(c)(1) served to protect Twitter from any liability for their deaths. The Federal District Court for the Northern District of California, expressing due respect for the families' anguish, dismissed the lawsuit on the grounds that Section 230(c)(1) protected Twitter from statements published by a third party, a heavy burden only the First Amendment is strong enough to withstand.[32]

Section 230(c)(2), commonly referred to as the "Good Samaritan" provision, which protects ISPS from liability for removing content that the ISP determines is objectionable even if the material would otherwise be constitutionally protected, has come under fire for giving ISPS and social media platforms the power to regulate speech with impunity. As a result of the 2020 postelection vitriol, Twitter permanently banned Donald Trump from using its platform; Amazon booted the social media platform Parler from its services; Facebook removed any content that contained the phrase "stop the steal"; and YouTube removed Alex Jones and *Infowars* from its platform for posts glorifying violence. Some on the political right are crying foul and insisting it is only conservative voices that are being muzzled. And the left is enraged by the length of time it took the social media platforms to take action; they argue the failure of the platforms to properly monitor posts championing conspiracy theories and untruths resulted in a misinformed public and fueled acts of violence by individuals and groups.

ISPS and social media platforms are in a Catch-22: They either have too much power to monitor speech—they create their own regulations regarding hate speech, incitement, and fake news and block posts or users at will—or they are not properly exercising editorial control over content and providing unfettered access to communication channels regardless of injuries or damages that follow harmful speech. No one, it seems, is happy with Section 230 of the CDA. There is a steady drumbeat of legislators insisting Section 230 be completely eliminated or significantly revised. We will just have to wait and see how this all shakes out.

[E]ven though falsehoods have little value in and
of themselves, they are nevertheless inevitable in
free debate. — Hustler v. Falwell[1]

James Carothers Garrison was a colorful figure. He served as district attorney (DA) of Orleans Parish, Louisiana, from 1962 to 1973. He is best known for his prosecution of Clay Shaw, whom he charged with conspiring to assassinate President John F. Kennedy. The jury acquitted Shaw in less than one hour, but Garrison never wavered from his belief that Shaw and others working for the CIA were part of a plot to murder the president. Garrison's book, *On the Trail of the Assassins: My Investigation and Prosecution of the Murder of President Kennedy*, was one of the main texts used by Oliver Stone to script his blockbuster film, *JFK*.

Even in a city known for its eccentricities, Garrison was one of a kind. At six feet, six inches and over 200 pounds, he was an imposing presence. *Washington Post* reporter James E. Clayton described Garrison as "good looking" and "eloquent," "the personification of all the ideas television DAS have created."[2] Garrison understood the value of publicity, good or bad, and used it to make his case inside and outside of the courtroom. He was a storyteller, with a sonorous voice and a poetic ability when it came to language. Alecia P. Long, a professor of history at Louisiana State University, describes Garrison as one of the nation's first reality TV politicians.[3] James Savage, a local Louisiana historian, marveled at Garrison's ability to manipulate his public image in a time before the concept of "spin" had entered the political landscape.[4]

Garrison enjoyed the mantle of law-and-order prosecutor, especially in a town run rampant with establishments that appealed to decadence and debauchery. New Orleans had "an atmosphere steeped in sex broken only by an occasional air of jazz."[5] No stranger to the honky-tonks that made New Orleans famous, he took on Bourbon Street with great zeal, orchestrating vice raids in the French Quarter and successfully arresting and prosecuting prostitutes, pimps, and extortionists who conducted business within city limits. Garrison employed informants to assist him in collecting evidence in support of arrests and subsequent prosecutions. He was particularly angered when one of his informants was assaulted and beaten while on patrol. That event motivated Garrison to redouble his efforts. Within six months, almost half of the strip joints in the nighttime business district were shuttered. He insisted he was not a crusader against vice and, in fact, continued to enjoy the strip joints on his time off. Still, he was determined to eliminate the criminal element from the city.

Some applauded Garrison's attempts to clean up New Orleans; others were suspicious of his passion; and still others, especially those who profited from the city's appeal to humanity's primitive instincts, simply wanted the raids to stop. Eventually, the bar and club owners organized a protest to express their displeasure with Garrison's strong-arming and shut their doors, providing an economic punch to the argument that the city relied upon them for much-needed tourism income.

All declarations to the contrary, Garrison's actions had all the elements of a crusade. The attention he garnered from the press irked the New Orleans Police Department. Generally, the responsibility for investigating crimes and arresting perpetrators belongs to the police department. Moreover, the raids orchestrated by Garrison devoured significant human resources and money. Funds existed to cover the DA's operations, but they required the criminal district court judges' approval. As costs continued to grow, and Garrison's office continued to encroach on the police department's responsibilities, the police department sought help from the criminal district court judges. The department successfully lobbied the judges to reform the funding apparatus. The new funding requirements were far more onerous and offered far less monetary support for Garrison's raids. Garrison clearly understood that political power in New Orleans also required power over the purse. This was a turf war. The police department had won a significant battle, and it infuriated Garrison.

Over several weeks, Garrison used his press contacts to attack the judges and the police commissioner. He defended his public attacks as the only way he could deprive the judges of their status as sacred cows.

He called the judges racketeers and accused them of seeking to obstruct the DA's investigations.[6] The judges crafted their response in the press, but they had been outplayed. The only recourse left to them was to take away Garrison's megaphone. They traveled to Baton Rouge and asked one of the state prosecutors to indict Garrison on charges of criminal defamation and jeopardizing the integrity of the Louisiana judicial system.

DEFAMATION

An action for defamation claims injury to one's reputation. Defamation must be more than hyperbole, parody, or name-calling. It must go to the heart of a person's reputation in the community. Libel and slander are two methods of defamation. Libel is the written form of defamation, and slander is the oral form. Libel is often a more permanent form of harm because it is communicated in a more permanent medium. **Defamation, libel or slander**, must be false and must include three additional elements: (1) a statement by the defendant, the person alleged to have done the speaking or writing, (2) a statement of and concerning the plaintiff, the person complaining of the injury to reputation, and (3) publication, meaning communication, to at least one person. Garrison had publicly accused the judges of greed and criminality. The judges argued that those accusations were malevolent and impugned their reputations. Garrison retorted by claiming he was exercising his well-protected First Amendment right to criticize public officials, the judiciary in New Orleans.

The judges mounted an angry case aimed at Garrison, but he turned the tables on his accusers. At the trial, the judges took to the witness stand and swore under oath that none of their decisions were unduly influenced. However, Garrison's attorneys introduced contradictory evidence establishing that some of the judges played favorites when granting bail requests. Additional evidence showed that some judges had prominent and public friendships with known gamblers and had even been feted by the gamblers upon winning election to the judgeship. And of course, like Garrison, many of the complaining judges enjoyed the company of the women who earned their income as escorts and companions of inebriated patrons in the bars that lined the New Orleans streets.[7] All of these details were breathlessly reported in the local papers. It seemed that the trial was not about Garrison's guilt or innocence but rather about the allegiance of the judges to truth and justice. Garrison decided he wanted to keep the focus on the judges and refused to take the stand in his own defense. He did not wish to become public fodder. His image was too important. He would rather lose the trial and face jail time.[8] The newspaper reports of the trial only bolstered Garrison's image as a crime fighter and reform-minded politician intent on breaking down the good-ol'-boy political machinery that had run New Orleans for decades. Because he refused to take the witness stand, Garrison could not be questioned at trial about his motives. The rules of evidence prohibited others from testifying about Garrison's state of mind. The skeletons in his closet would stay put. Once again, Garrison played the situation so that he looked like the savior of the day against a compromised judiciary.[9]

However, the Baton Rouge court was not as easily manipulated as the public. Judge William Ponder had been appointed by the Louisiana Supreme Court to hear the case. He ruled against Garrison and found him guilty as charged. In a forty-page opinion, the judge asserted that Garrison's media-buttressed accusations against the judges were intended to injure their reputations and question their ethics and moral principles. Garrison was not the angel of truth but instead was motivated by "ill-feeling, spite and enmity."[10] Judge Ponder explained that it did not stand to reason that Garrison honestly believed all eight of the judges were racketeers. On the contrary, Garrison's accusations were malicious and ill-natured. The court held that Garrison could not use the First Amendment to protect himself from prosecution and fined him $1,000 or, alternatively, four months in jail. Rather than accept the decision of the judge and thereby implicitly acknowledge guilt, Garrison appealed the judgment. He lost his appeal to the highest court in Louisiana and sought appeal to the United States Supreme Court.

Eight months before Garrison sought his appeal to the US Supreme Court, the court decided what has come to be a seminal case in defamation law: *New York Times v. Sullivan*.[11] The decision in that case would govern the decision in the criminal prosecution against Garrison.[12] In the *Sullivan* case, the Supreme Court developed a new standard for defamation cases. The public profile of the plaintiff (the person complaining of having been defamed) became a key determining factor in whether and how the defendant (the person who allegedly defamed the plaintiff) could claim First Amendment protection from language that disparaged the reputation of the plaintiff. This new standard was Garrison's get-out-of-jail-free card.

ACTUAL MALICE

The *Sullivan* case was yet another case that grew out of the turmoil of the civil rights protests in the 1960s. On March 29, 1960, the *New York Times* ran a full-page advertisement titled "Heed Their Rising Voices." The ad was written by the Committee to Defend Martin Luther King Jr. and the Struggle for Freedom in the South, and strategically chosen for publication in that newspaper. The *Times* enjoyed journalistic prestige and boasted a vast readership in the northeastern part of the United States, from which the civil rights groups sought sympathy and funds. The ostensible purpose of the ad was an appeal for funds to support the civil rights movement in the South, in general, and the legal defense of Martin Luther King Jr., in particular. At the time, King was defending a perjury indictment in Montgomery, Alabama. As part of the fundraising appeal, the ad detailed a list of offenses that civil rights advocates had endured at the hands of government officials in Montgomery. The ad claimed that Black students who had engaged in nonviolent protests against civil rights abuses in the South were subjected to an unprecedented wave of terror by police. The third and sixth paragraphs of the ad were the focus of this monumental case. The third paragraph read:

> In Montgomery, Alabama, after students sang My Country, 'Tis of Thee on the State Capitol steps, their leaders were expelled from school, and truckloads of police armed with shotguns and tear-gas ringed the Alabama State College Campus. When the entire student body protested to state authorities by refusing to re-register, their dining hall was padlocked in an attempt to starve them into submission.[13]

And the sixth paragraph of the ad read:

Again and again, the Southern violators have answered Dr. King's peaceful protests with intimidation and violence. They have bombed his home, almost killing his wife and child. They have assaulted his person. They have arrested him seven times—for speeding, loitering and similar offenses. And now they have charged him with perjury —a felony under which they could imprison him for ten years.[14]

In March 1960, L. B. Sullivan was the commissioner of public affairs in Montgomery. His duties included supervising the Public Affairs Department, the Fire Department, the Department of Cemetery, and the Department of Scales. Sullivan alleged that, by implication, he had been defamed in the ad. He complained that the word "police" in the third paragraph referred to him and that the "arrests" alleged in the sixth paragraph similarly referenced him in his role as commissioner. Sullivan argued that those statements in the ads injured his reputation by accusing him of acting illegally and immorally in response to the civil rights protesters. In addition, as part of his complaint, he identified several inaccuracies in the ad:

1 The students sang the "National Anthem" and not "My Country, 'Tis of Thee."
2 The students were not expelled for leading the protests; they were expelled for demanding service at the lunch counter in the Montgomery County Courthouse.
3 The general student body protested the students' expulsion by boycotting classes, not by refusing to register for classes.
4 The campus dining room was never padlocked. The only students who might have been refused entry were those who had not properly registered for meal tickets.
5 Although the police had deployed to the campus on three occasions, they did not, at any time, surround the campus.
6 Dr. King was arrested four times, not seven, and although Dr. King had alleged an assault during his arrest, the arresting officer denied it.

At trial, Sullivan presented evidence that the *New York Times* failed to follow its own editorial policies pertaining to the ad. He claimed the

Times knew or should have known, from its own reporting of events in Alabama, that the ad was factually inaccurate, and for that reason, the newspaper was liable for injuries he suffered as a result of the ad's alleged defamatory content. The Alabama courts agreed with Commissioner Sullivan and assessed damages against the *Times* in the amount of $500,000, an extraordinary sum in 1960. Sullivan was only one of several plaintiffs that had sued the newspaper—by the time the jury reached its verdict in the *Sullivan* case, the *Times* was facing possible liability of over $3,000,000 stemming from the ad (worth almost $30,000,000 in today's dollars). The paper appealed the case up to the US Supreme Court, and in a unanimous decision, the Supreme Court overturned the Alabama verdict.

The Supreme Court agreed that the statements were inaccurate and therefore false. The justices also agreed that if the accusations were understood to implicate Commissioner Sullivan, they were injurious to the commissioner's reputation and therefore defamatory. Then, the justices pivoted. The central question was not whether the statements were false and defamatory, but rather whether the ad's inaccuracies and the alleged defamatory nature of some of the statements in the ad stripped the speech of its First Amendment protections.

The court determined that the *New York Times* ad was fundamentally political speech, an expression of grievance and protest, published by the newspaper as an "editorial advertisement."[15] Political speech remains protected whether or not it is true or false. The court explained that erroneous statements or misstatements of fact are a natural part of public debate. To provide breathing room for the process, speech must remain protected. The public must have the opportunity to assess and criticize official conduct without fear of retribution by the official who asserts that the criticism impugned their reputation. Requiring that criticism of public officials adhere to a standard of absolute truth on pain of a judgment of libel, which could amount to devastating monetary awards, would lead to the critic's self-censorship, effectively silencing them. Such a rule would limit the variety of public debate. The court reasserted the elemental principle that "debate on public issues should be uninhibited, robust, and wide-open, and that it may well include vehement, caustic, and sometimes unpleasantly sharp attacks on government and public officials."[16]

The court was insistent that public officials, generally understood to mean those who serve in a governmental capacity, whether elected or appointed, should not use the First Amendment as a shield to protect them from scrutiny. Public officials place themselves in the public eye and into positions of power. Their actions and speech can create community effects far more extensive than a nonpublic official. With the power to influence comes additional scrutiny. The court explained that "public men are, as it were, public property,"[17] and libel "must be measured by standards that satisfy the First Amendment."[18] The court enunciated the principle that a public official can only recover damages for injuries resulting from defamation if the statements were made with **actual malice**. Proof of actual malice requires evidence that the false statement was made with knowledge that it was false or with reckless disregard of whether it was false or not.

The actual malice standard requires that defamatory statements about people in the public eye are protected absent clear evidence of recklessness about their truth. Messengers are protected from liability absent a consciousness that the statements they made are likely false. Negligence is not enough. **Negligence** is defined by Cornell Law School Legal Information Institute as "A failure to behave with the level of care that someone of ordinary prudence would have exercised under the same circumstances. The behavior usually consists of actions, but can also consist of omissions when there is some duty to act."[19] A statement made with actual malice must be constructed with an element of inattention that defies logic. Whereas negligence evinces carelessness, actual malice evidences an utter lack of concern, dismissiveness, or irresponsibility, thereby nullifying First Amendment protection. While the phrase "actual malice" includes the word "malice"—generally understood as an intent or desire to cause injury or pain to another—it is not an element of the constitutional test. The constitutional concept of actual malice does not include intent to cause harm; rather, it includes imprudence, irrationality, or delinquency. In later cases, the court explained that for a plaintiff to prove actual malice, "there must be sufficient evidence to permit the conclusion that the defendant in fact entertained serious doubts as to the truth of his publication."[20]

The actual malice standard has governed libel cases advanced by public officials since the *Sullivan* decision. The standard was extended to apply to public figures as well.[21] The court has defined a **public figure** as a person who has achieved general fame or notoriety or a celebrity who engages the public's attention in the community in which that individual lives, works, or plays.[22] The power of celebrity is undeniable. Public figures often can shape politics and purchases; one simply has to look toward the number of celebrity endorsements sought by corporations and politicians as evidence of their influence. Criticism of those who place themselves in the public eye must be protected. Like a public official, a public figure who sues alleging libel or slander by a critic will be unsuccessful unless there is proof of actual malice.

The point is not that false statements are constitutionally valuable. The point is that requiring perfection from those who choose to engage in public conversation is an impossible standard. Free, uninhibited speech requires considerable latitude; without that latitude debate about public officials, or even public figures, who often wield as much or more power to persuade than public officials, will be silenced for fear of liability, merely for speaking one's mind. The actual malice standard provides the necessary space for robust debate and discussion.

The *Sullivan* case was groundbreaking. It shaped the nature of public criticism for decades, providing depth and breadth to public debate. It shaped today's media landscape, allowing for hasty, sometimes poorly sourced reporting without fear of liability. At the same time, it promoted good investigative reporting, with the knowledge that minor inaccuracies would not result in damage awards that can bankrupt a media defendant. It has increased the volume of the marketplace of ideas, if not always the quality.

The actual malice standard is what the Supreme Court applied in the libel case against James Carothers Garrison. To recover damages, the New Orleans judges were required to prove that Garrison acted with actual malice. They were required to prove that Garrison's statements about the corruption in the judiciary were false and that he acted with reckless disregard as to their falsity. The Supreme Court justices were not blind to the fact that Garrison's accusations were constructed out of spite and calculated to damage reputations. In fact, they required two sets of oral arguments, one in April and one in October of 1964, and circulated more than thirty draft opinions before revealing their decision. Reluctantly, the justices concluded that it did not matter if Garrison spoke out of hatred or even with an intent to injure.[23] It is often the case that a speaker acts with ill will or selfish motives. Ill will and selfish motives are not enough to punish even defamatory speech uttered in criticism of a public official. Even if Garrison had intended to inflict harm on the judges, he did not make the statements with reckless disregard as to their falsity if indeed they were false. In other words, Garrison could be held liable only if he published his statements with actual malice; the fact that Garrison's accusations were embarrassing to the judges or injured their reputations was of no consequence. And so, the Supreme Court reversed the decision of the Louisiana courts. Garrison was not criminally liable for defaming the New Orleans judiciary.

DEFAMATION LAWSUITS AS A CUDGEL AGAINST WEAPONIZED FALSEHOODS

Modern political animosity has created another opportunity to review the constitutional boundaries of defamation law. American history is ripe with stories of loathsome political rhetoric. Few, however, will dispute that the rancor and animus exhibited by parties and proxies during and after the 2020 presidential election was among the worst examples of it. As discussed earlier, in the hours following the announcement by national TV networks and the Associated Press that Joe Biden would serve as the forty-sixth president of the United States, President Trump, his administration, and legions of his supporters cried foul and began a campaign to overturn the election.

A target of the Stop the Steal campaign was voting machines manufactured by Dominion Voting Systems Corporation (Dominion) and Smartmatic, both privately held companies incorporated in the United States. The attacks on those companies were led in large part by former New York Mayor Rudy Giuliani, former federal prosecutor Sidney Powell, and a number of Fox News media personalities. At time of press Dominion had separately sued Giuliani, Powell, and Fox News for defamation and is threatening suits against other Trump surrogates.[24] Smartmatic has sued Giuliani, Powell, Fox News, and a number of Fox news anchors in a single suit, also alleging defamation.[25] Some of the specific details in the lawsuits differ, but in general, all allege the defendants falsely and recklessly accused Dominion and Smartmatic of fraud, election fixing, conspiracy, and bribery. Those accusations, the suits assert, provoked outrage and otherwise impugned both corporations' integrity, ethics, and honesty and damaged their financial integrity.[26]

In its thirty-page, 28,000-word complaint against Giuliani, Dominion lists a litany of false accusations leveled by him in television interviews, podcasts, radio broadcasts, and speeches, including unsubstantiated claims that "Dominion participated in a scheme to fix the 2020 presidential election by manipulating votes and the vote count" and that "Dominion is owned by or is a front for a company created in Venezuela to rig elections for Hugo Chavez."[27] The complaint specifically alleges that Giuliani falsely asserted, with no evidence, that Dominion machines flipped votes; in other words, votes cast for Trump were somehow registered as votes for Biden.[28] On top of that, Dominion includes allegations that Giuliani falsely and recklessly described Dominion machines as "calculators rather than counters" and claimed that the machines use algorithms so that every three or four votes for Biden were matched by one vote for Trump regardless of the actual votes cast.[29]

Notably, Dominion accuses Giuliani of actual malice because he knowingly or recklessly misrepresented the truth "to support his false accusations; purposefully avoiding or intentionally disregarding abundant and publicly available evidence, facts, and reliable sources rebutting and disproving his false claims." The complaint alleges that Giuliani espoused "inherently improbable accusations; forming and sticking to a false preconceived narrative in spite of the facts; relying on facially unreliable sources; and—when specifically put on notice of the truth and asked to retract—doubling down on and republishing his false accusations." Dominion concludes that Giuliani's speech and behavior was "all in furtherance of his plan to financially enrich himself, to maintain and enhance his public profile, and to ingratiate himself to Donald Trump for money and benefits he expected to receive as a result of that association, including, but not limited to, a reported $20,000 per day fee."[30]

And finally, Dominion alleges irreparable harm caused directly and consequently by Giuliani. Dominion contends it has been unfairly subjected to the hatred, contempt, and distrust of tens of millions of American voters and the elected officials who are Dominion's actual and potential customers. Dominion calculates lost profits of $200 million over the next five years and irreparable damage to its reputation and value.[31] Dominion makes similar allegations against Powell and Fox News in its lawsuits against them.

In its massive 285-page lawsuit against Giuliani, Powell, Fox News, and others, Smartmatic alleges that the defendants:

- Falsely stated and implied that Smartmatic fixed, rigged, and stole the 2020 US election for Joe Biden and Kamala Harris;
- Falsely stated and implied that Smartmatic sent votes to foreign countries for tabulation during the 2020 US election;
- Falsely stated and implied that Smartmatic's election technology and software were compromised or hacked during the 2020 US election;
- Falsely stated and implied that Smartmatic was previously banned from providing election technology and software in the United States;
- Falsely stated and implied that Smartmatic is a Venezuelan company founded and funded by corrupt dictators from socialist and communist countries; and
- Falsely stated and implied that Smartmatic's election technology and software were designed to fix, rig, and steal elections.

Like Dominion, Smartmatic alleges actual malice and irreparable harm to its reputation and corporate value. It seeks damages in the amount of 2.7 billion dollars.[32]

While both corporations allege actual malice, neither of them necessarily concede that they are public figures and that they therefore must meet that higher standard in proving their cases. However, it is possible, even likely, that both Dominion and Smartmatic will be considered public figures in the 2020 election controversy and must prove that the proclamations by the defendants defied logic or that they entertained serious doubts about The Big Lie they were promoting. The First Amendment will require the plaintiffs to work hard to prove that speech uttered about issues as central to our democracy as election integrity must be punished because the recklessness of the lies was profound and unconscionable. The plaintiffs must prove that the defendants' lies caused great harm, diminished the marketplace of ideas, and injured its patrons and participants. In response, the media defendants, Fox and its news anchors, might successfully defend their actions as part and parcel of the exercise of their own First Amendment right to report the news, including any and all controversial topics on matters of public concern.

JUST US PLAIN FOLKS

All libel plaintiffs are not equal. Public officials, public figures, and people caught up in public events have a higher bar to clear; those people must prove actual malice to recover monetary damages for injury to their reputations. The focus of attention in defamation actions brought by public officials and public figures is the public's right to know and debate. A person who is in the public eye can affect public discourse. They cannot then turn around and use the First Amendment as a shield to protect themselves from criticism. But just plain folks, private people engaged in matters of private concern, should not be subject to public discussion, particularly discussion that negatively affects their reputation.

That is, a gossip who, by mouth or by keyboard, publishes false statements about a private person (a person who is not a public official or public figure) cannot claim First Amendment protection from liability for the harm done by the defamatory statements. If the publication about a private person is false, the private injured party can sue the neighborhood gossip and collect damages. Generally, the injured party will be awarded punitive damages (money paid as punishment for having done harm) only if the publication is made with actual malice.[33] However, a gossip who is merely opining might be able to use the First Amendment as an ally. While there is no wholesale exemption from liability for a statement of opinion, the First Amendment will protect a person who makes a declaration that clearly cannot be interpreted as a statement of fact. There is an obvious caveat there. Opinions are protected by the First Amendment only if they are not used as a foil to publish defamatory factual statements. Opinions can cause as much damage to a private person's reputation, happiness, and ability to earn an income as any assertion presented as fact. It is simply too easy to proclaim, "It was only my opinion that Johnny is a liar and a cheat" and escape responsibility for the damage done to Johnny. The opinionated gossip will be just as liable for defamatory damages as the gossip who is brazen enough to declare a lie as the truth.[34]

Finally, truthful reporting by a journalist or news organization about private people concerning issues and proceedings that are not otherwise shielded from view, by a court (gag) order or legislation, is also protected, even if the reporting is demeaning or embarrassing to the subject of the article. For example, publishing the name of the victim of a sexual assault—if the information was obtained legally from public records—is constitutionally protected, albeit unethical.[35] The rationale favors the truthful reporting of information that is of public interest without burdening the reporter with ethical considerations that, while important to society, are not within the boundaries of First Amendment jurisprudence.

THE SOCIAL MEDIA DILEMMA

Remember, Section 230 of the Communications Decency Act provides that an individual who has been defamed online can only recover damages from the person or the entity that originated or perpetuated the defamation. Internet service providers (ISPs) or websites that host comments are immune from liability for their role in the publication of defamatory comments. The ISP or website is considered merely a communicative tool or vehicle. It is not an active participant in the defamation. While ISPs can claim immunity from liability for defamatory statements published on their platforms, once again, social media has the potential to upend well-established legal precedent with regard to the entities that post on the platforms.

The Supreme Court has extended the actual malice standard to apply to public figures for a limited purpose. Generally, such individuals must inject themselves voluntarily into the limelight, or be otherwise voluntarily drawn into a particular public controversy. The court has stated that sometimes, albeit rarely, private persons can find themselves thrust in the middle of affairs of public interest involuntarily, and while ensconced in that limelight, can be considered public figures for that limited occasion.[36] However, the court has been loath to impose public figure status simply because a person finds themself in the middle of a maelstrom. By way of example, in 1979 the Supreme Court refused to impose public figure status on Ilya Wolston, an individual who was wrongly identified as a Soviet agent in a book published by the *Reader's Digest Association* (*Digest*), which chronicled the Soviet Union's espionage activities following World War II. Twenty years earlier, Wolston had been convicted of contempt of court for failure to appear before a grand jury investigating suspicions of spying by his aunt and uncle. Wolston's contempt charge and conviction had at that time been the subject of newspaper accounts. However for the twenty years between his conviction and the *Digest*'s publication, Wolston had led a private life. Upon being sued by Wolston, the *Digest* tried to label Wolston a public figure for a limited purpose so that the *Digest* would not be held liable for defamation without proof of actual malice. The court rejected the attempt. Writing for the eight-justice majority in *Wolston v. Reader's Digest Assn., Inc.*, Justice Rehnquist wrote:

> Petitioner's failure to appear before the grand jury and citation for contempt no doubt were "newsworthy," but the simple fact that these events attracted media attention also is not conclusive of the public figure issue. A private individual is not automatically transformed into a public figure just by becoming involved in or associated with a matter that attracts public attention. . . . A libel defendant must show more than mere newsworthiness to justify application of the demanding burden of *New York Times* [*v. Sullivan*].[37]

Some First Amendment scholars question whether social media will blur the line between private and public persons or matters of private and public interest.[38] Social media makes publishers of us all. People post about a range of issues to a small or vast audience depending on privacy settings and number of followers. Will the constitutional principles developed in the golden age of newspapers and legacy media hold firm, or does social media have the power to transform a private matter into a matter of public interest and a private person into a public figure by virtue of its global reach and massive audience? Will a post to a large social media following morph a matter into an issue of public interest and the subject of the post into a public figure for a limited purpose so that the actual malice standard will apply in a defamation action? So far, it seems the principles enunciated by the court in *Wolston* will control. The prevailing opinion seems to be that while technology has changed the communication landscape, constitutional principles of defamation will remain firm.[39]

REVISITING BULLYING AND
THE FIRST AMENDMENT

Bullying is different than mere gossip. It is a loathsome cross between hate speech and defamation. Bullying, like hate speech, has proven to be incredibly difficult to fit within First Amendment constructs. As noted earlier, public schools can provide enhanced protection to students and faculty by asserting that the spotlighted speech caused substantial disruption to the educational environment, a standard outlined in the premier public school speech case *Tinker v. Des Moines School Dist.*[40] External to the school setting, the better approach is to assert a true threat or harassing behavior, taking the allegation outside of First Amendment protection.

WHY DO PEOPLE LIE? BECAUSE THEY CAN

The First Amendment might not protect the local gossip for damage done to the target of their venom, but the frequent or pathological liar who preens or obfuscates about their personal triumphs or failures can celebrate the power to lie. Sometimes, lies gain traction and are perpetuated, more so in this digital age than ever before. Without a compelling state interest or proof of harm, the First Amendment does not precondition speech on its truthfulness. The First Amendment avows that the most effective weapon against lies is the glare provided by open discussion and debate and the hope that enough people are willing to engage in the debate so that the lie will eventually wither in the face of truth. Such was the experience of Xavier Alvarez.

Xavier Alvarez might have desired to bathe in the glow of glory, but he had not earned the honor. Alvarez was a liar and a cheat. In 2007, at a public meeting of a California water district board, he introduced himself, saying, "I'm a retired Marine of twenty-five years. I retired in the year 2001. Back in 1987, I was awarded the Congressional Medal of Honor. I got wounded many times by the same guy."[41] None of this was true—Alvarez was not a Marine, had never been injured in combat, and had not been awarded the Medal of Honor. The Medal of Honor is awarded by the president and reserved only to a member of the military who "distinguishes himself conspicuously by gallantry and intrepidity at the risk of his life above and beyond the call of duty."[42] The award is so venerated that Congress passed the Stolen Valor Act, which criminalizes false representations of having been awarded the medal.[43]

To many, Alvarez's lie was evident, and he suffered public ridicule for it. More importantly, the meeting was recorded, and the recording was delivered to an FBI agent who then shared it with federal prosecutors. Alvarez was tried and convicted for violating the Stolen Valor Act. He was sentenced to probation for three years and a $5,000 fine.[44] In *United States v. Alvarez*,[45] the Supreme Court held, in a 6–3 decision, that his criminal conviction was unconstitutional. The lies told by Alvarez, according to a plurality of the justices, were protected. As explained by Justice Kennedy, writing for the plurality, the Stolen Valor Act criminalized speech based on content, and it failed the necessary strict scrutiny analysis. Kennedy acknowledged the compelling interest of the government to recognize and award "those who, in the course of carrying out the supreme and noble duty of contributing to the defense of the rights and honor of the nation have acted with extraordinary honor"; however, to punish falsity without any showing of "some other legally cognizable harm associated with a false statement" casts too wide a net.[46] The statute was not narrowly tailored. Justice Kennedy reiterated that, "some false statements are inevitable if there is to be an open and vigorous expression of views in public and private conversation, expression the First Amendment seeks to guarantee."[47] Alvarez could claim First Amendment protection because the Stolen Valor statute unconstitutionally criminalized speech based only on its false content. Justices Alito, Scalia, and Thomas disagreed. They argued the statute was perfectly crafted to protect a valuable and compelling government interest and was narrowly constructed so that the only speech that was punished was speech that undermined the identified government interest. The dissenting justices declared that Alvarez's lies, and the lies of others who seek to claim false honor never earned, do in fact inflict real harm on actual medal recipients and their families.

In 2013, President Obama signed a new Stolen Valor Act into law that corrected the deficits of the previous version. The new version specifically criminalized claims of military honors with the intent to procure tangible benefits.[48] It is not clear if Alvarez would have been convicted under the new version of the act, but several who have sought financial gain based upon their false claims have since found themselves behind bars.

Just to be clear, lies that are by definition criminal, or lies that promote or support crime or create civil harm, and lies that undermine government's ability to function for the benefit of the people, are not protected by the First Amendment.

HUMOR

Humor does not claim a mantle of truth, even if the truth behind the joke is the reason for the laughter that follows. The audience laughs because they are in on the game. *Saturday Night Live* (*SNL*) habitually skewers people in the public eye, portraying them as dopey, liars, sexual predators, and criminals. The routines are plainly intended to entertain, and they are steeped in satire and exaggeration, but there is no question that the humor will often include unflattering accusations with no barometer as to their truth or falsity. The 2008 *SNL* sketch "A Nonpartisan Message from Governor Sarah Palin & Senator Hillary Clinton,"[49] with Tina Fey portraying vice presidential candidate Sarah Palin and Amy Poehler portraying Hillary Clinton, is often cited as critical to the public perception of Palin as poorly prepared for the responsibilities of the office. It was an image Palin vehemently disputed. Palin might argue that *SNL* used humor as a foil to publish defamatory lies about her. However, parody and satire are protected by the First Amendment. Reverend Jerry Falwell found this out the hard way.

Reverend Falwell was a fundamentalist Baptist pastor, a televangelist, and a founder of the Moral Majority, a largely Christian conservative group that bemoaned what they characterized as the moral decay of American society. The Moral Majority opposed integration, abortion rights, and the secularization of schools. They lamented what they characterized as the deterioration of the traditional family structure, which included exclusively heterosexual coupling and parenting.

Larry Flynt was the publisher of *Hustler* magazine, which in the latter part of the twentieth century was either a symbol of sexual freedom or an example of pornographic decadence, depending on where your politics and moral center lay. He did not like the Reverend Jerry Falwell. Flynt believed Falwell was a hypocrite, a man who preached the gospel but spread messages of exclusion and hate; who sought to shackle racial, gender, and sexual minorities, and maintain the supremacy of the White Christian male. Reverend Falwell wasn't much of a fan of Larry Flynt either. To Falwell, Flynt represented everything that was wrong with America, and using his televangelist megaphone, Falwell made a point of that at every opportunity.

Flynt decided to fight back. He had his magazine, which boasted a vast audience. Campari Liqueur provided the perfect vehicle. Campari Group, the manufacturer of Campari Liqueur, placed ads for the aperitif in the pages of *Hustler*. In 1983, the Campari Group ran an ad campaign that profiled celebrities and included the tag line, "You'll never forget your first time." It was an apparent double entendre for the first time the celebrities experienced the liqueur. It was also a perfect scaffolding to poke fun at and even embarrass the Reverend Jerry Falwell. And it did.

In November 1983, *Hustler* ran a parody of the Campari Liqueur ad. On the inside of the front cover of that issue, the reader was offered the opportunity to read about Falwell's first time. Copying the form and layout of the original Campari ads, the Falwell piece was framed as an interview. The responses to the interview questions portray Falwell's mother as a drunk with whom Falwell had an incestuous rendezvous in an outhouse. There was a disclaimer at the bottom of the page, printed in a small font that read: "ad parody—not to be taken seriously."[50]

Falwell was not amused. He was livid. He claimed embarrassment and emotional injury as a result of the publication and sought monetary recompense for the pain caused by the publication of the ad parody. But the libel case never got very far. It was clear that Flynt never intended to present the interview as a true depiction of events. There was no reckless disregard of truth; there was an open and obvious acknowledgment that the interview never really happened. However, Flynt admitted the purpose of the ad was to hurt and embarrass Falwell. Could Falwell recover damages for that intentional injury? The answer: No.[51] Falwell was undeniably a public figure who affected discussion and debate about issues of public concern. Through his televised sermons and speeches, he was able to reach millions, and as measured by the voice of the Moral Majority, he was very effective. Even though Flynt intended to injure Falwell, Falwell could not recover damages of any kind unless Falwell could prove Flynt acted with actual malice—reckless disregard of falsity. As was evident in the lawsuit by the Louisiana judges against James Carothers Garrison, the actual malice standard was constructed to protect even speech that stings.

The court analogized the Campari parody to a political cartoon, which is part of political discourse. Political parody, like political cartoons, often serves as a weapon of attack and is simply part of the sometimes turbulent and intemperate nature of debate. The First Amendment shields debate—even debate that is debasing and rude.

Flynt and Falwell later became friends and often shared the debate stage, each finding in the other something good and honest. That outcome leaves the rest of us with a modicum of hope that even the First Amendment can provide a road to reconciliation, despite beliefs that divide us.

The moral of this part of the First Amendment story is that conversation and discourse are often messy. They are infused with emotion and humor; they are not dry recitations of fact. We are, by nature, storytellers, and frequently enhance our stories with exaggeration, nuance, and even half-truths. Memories are unreliable, and words are imprecise. If we are held to a standard that requires absolute fidelity to provable facts and face litigation and penalties when we fall short of that, we will be restrained, not free to speak our minds. The laws and court cases that protect defamatory speech and its close cousins—humor, satire, opinion, and salacious news—attempt to balance the right to speak freely and support an open marketplace of ideas against the right to the integrity of our reputations. The balance is difficult to strike, but the courts often yield to the essential principles upon which the First Amendment was built and will protect speech.

OBSCENITY AND THE FIRST AMENDMENT

Stories that exaggerate, offend, or embarrass might claim protection from the First Amendment, but stories, speech, visuals, and performances that are obscene can claim no such shelter. Obscene speech is part of a class of speech on which the First Amendment essentially turns its back. The Supreme Court has twisted itself into a pretzel to determine whether ordinances regulating nudity or sexually indecent messages can be regulated without running afoul of the First Amendment.

In the years before the seminal case setting forth the current test for determining what is and is not obscene, *Miller v. California*,[52] the court received hundreds of petitions seeking reversal of decisions adjudicating material as obscene. Many of the petitions included original documents—books, photos, even full-length movies—reviewed in detail by the justices and their clerks. In fact, except for Justices Black, Douglas, and Burger, the justices and the clerks enjoyed a regular set of movie days at the court where they sat in one of the larger rooms in the building as a group and watched the feature-length porn films.[53] They watched the films, perused the photos, and read the books, ostensibly to reach a consensus on the definition of **obscenity**. It almost didn't happen. It took months of debate and scores of draft opinions and memos for five of the nine justices to agree to a definition that would provide some guidance as to the constitutional confines of obscene communication.

The Supreme Court explained that depictions of sex alone are not obscene. To be obscene, the communication must appeal to prurient interest, which is variously described as appealing to sexual desire or evidencing a degrading or unhealthy interest in sex.[54] And what might be obscene in one community may be perfectly acceptable in another. States and communities can generally define obscenity by their own standards as long as statutes regulating such speech are well confined and do not restrict speech that otherwise exhibits serious literary, artistic, or scientific value.[55]

There have been tremendous shifts in societal values since *Miller*. As a general rule, we have become much more tolerant of material that might have been considered patently offensive in 1973, the year *Miller* was decided. Moreover, once again, technology has impacted the communication landscape. In the words of Geoffrey R. Stone, the Edward H.

Levi Distinguished Service Professor of Law at the University of Chicago, as he explained the ever-narrowing impact of the *Miller* decision:

> Technology had changed, society had changed, cultural values had changed and, as a result, the law had changed. By the early years of [the] twenty-first century, given the pervasiveness of sexually explicit pornography on the Internet and elsewhere in society, we had for all practical purposes reached the end of obscenity. As Robert Peters, the president of Morality in Media, a religious organization established to combat pornography, reluctantly conceded, "the war is over and we have lost."[56]

Today, most statutes regulating morality related to sex or nudity are confined to zoning restrictions—limiting establishments that trade in those products, whether they be materials or performances, to a bounded geography. The court has upheld those constraints, recognizing that communities have a compelling interest in limiting the porn industry's secondary effects: increased crime, prostitution, and decreased property values in the neighborhoods where these establishments do business.

Adult pornography that is not obscene can claim the guardianship of the First Amendment. However, child pornography is not protected speech.[57] Even the possession of child pornography is not constitutionally protected.[58]

Child pornography is the exploitation of children.

It is criminal.

Period.

14 : THE LANGUAGE OF MONEY

There is no right more basic in our democracy than
the right to participate in electing our political leaders.
—Chief Justice John Roberts[1]

It all started with a movie. All the declarations regarding the corruption of the political process and the flood of money into our elections started with a movie. A movie with the less-than-creative title, *Hillary: The Movie*. It features Hillary Clinton as the protagonist, the villain, and the symbol of the coming of the end of days. The supporting characters include leading conservative voices Newt Gingrich, Ann Coulter, David Bosse, and others.

The movie is essentially an editorialized documentary. It was released in January 2008 when Hillary Clinton was seeking the Democratic Party's nomination for president of the United States. Her chief rival was Barack Obama, who eventually won the nomination and the presidency. The movie was produced by Citizens United, a nonprofit corporation dedicated to promoting and advocating conservative political causes. The film had been released to the public in movie theaters and was also available in DVD format. As the Democratic primary approached, Citizens United wanted to increase the documentary's distribution and make it available in digital format as a video on demand. The problem was that their plan might run afoul of criminal proscriptions regarding campaign finance. Rather than face criminal prosecution, they sought a declaratory judgment from the Supreme Court. Declaratory judgments may be available to a party if there is uncertainty regarding legal rights and obligations.

THE ALPHABET SOUP OF FEDERAL AGENCIES AND POLITICAL SPEECH

After the Watergate debacle, legislatures and the courts were particularly wary of political trickery. In 1974, Congress passed an amendment to the Federal Election Campaign Act of 1971 (FECA). In doing so, it created the Federal Election Commission and enacted more stringent requirements on federal election contributions and expenditures than had been in effect prior to that time. Then, in 2002, Congress added to the alphabet soup of legislation and passed another amendment to the FECA: the Bipartisan Campaign Reform Act (BCRA). Each piece of legislation faced court challenges. The decisions were often extremely complicated, addressing tax code implications, electoral fairness, and free speech. Those pieces of legislation and the governing bodies that execute them, the Internal Revenue Service (IRS) and the Federal Election Commission (FEC), regulate contributions, expenditures, and disclosures related to political campaigning. In plain English, the IRS and FEC regulate the money that is both collected and spent in federal political campaigns. In addition, those governing bodies enforce reporting requirements pertaining to campaign activities and donors.

ISSUE ADVOCACY VS. EXPRESS ADVOCACY

Information regarding the character and positions of candidates running for elective office affect electoral outcomes. The necessity of an informed electorate is at the very core of our democracy, making First Amendment protections for electoral communication essential. However, political messaging is costly. One cannot thoroughly discuss politics and political communication without discussing the impact of money, which is infused into every part of the process.

Paid political communication runs the spectrum from messaging that directly supports or opposes a candidate to messaging that addresses public policy issues. Paid political communication that addresses public policy, referred to as **issue advocacy**, does not aim directly at affecting electoral outcomes. Instead, it aims to educate and persuade the public about broader subjects: gun control, the environment, education, and the like. Issue advocacy is generally free from contribution and expenditure limits and is subject to few disclosure requirements. From a First Amendment perspective, such political messaging deserves the highest protection. The underlying theory is that money spent on issue advocacy facilitates the exchange of ideas.[2]

In contrast, messages that are "susceptible of no reasonable interpretation other than as an appeal to vote for or against a specific candidate"[3] are characterized as **express advocacy** and are subject to various contribution, expenditure, and disclosure requirements. All ads sponsored by candidates are, by definition, express advocacy. From a First Amendment perspective, express advocacy differs from issue advocacy because express advocacy can be corrupted. For example, contributions to a single candidate or a single political party by individuals, corporations, or unions could create, or at least implicate, a quid pro quo—in other words, supporting unethical commitments of a candidate to the donor, or "dollars for political favors."[4] Even if a political supporter is restricted in the amount of money they can directly contribute to a candidate, that same supporter can end-run the restriction merely by creating their own express advocacy messages, all in consultation with the candidate. A candidate might then feel indebted to that supporter if the candidate is successful in their election bid.

Prior to 2010, corporations and unions could not participate in express advocacy messages that sought the election or defeat of any particular candidate. Corporations and unions could create separate entities called political action committees (PACs), which are organized for the purpose of raising and spending money to elect or defeat candidates. PACs could engage in express advocacy, but the funds supporting the PACs could only be collected from individual shareholders, members, and employees, which in most situations yielded far less money than what was directly available from the corporate bank account. A PAC could not (except for some administrative expenses) receive money directly from the corporation or union. The tectonic shift came in 2010, when the court decided *Citizens United v. FEC*.[5]

CONTRIBUTIONS

Citizens United had accepted donations from for-profit corporations to produce, distribute, and advertise *Hillary: The Movie*. So, if *Hillary: The Movie* was considered express political advocacy, Citizens United would run afoul of the FECA ban on spending corporate funds on express advocacy, and civil and criminal penalties could be assessed against it.

Citizens United described *Hillary: The Movie* as "a documentary film that examines certain historical events."[6] In contrast, the Supreme Court described the documentary as "a feature-length negative advertisement that urges viewers to vote against Senator Clinton for President."[7] One of the film's characters calls Clinton Machiavellian and asks the audience whether she is "the most qualified to hit the ground running if elected president."[8] The court made short shrift of Citizens United's claim that *Hillary: The Movie* was anything other than express advocacy.

What really shook the political landscape was the court's decision that while corporations and unions should not and still could not directly contribute to a candidate or political party, they should be able to directly contribute to other political organizations, all funded from enormous corporate and union treasuries, and those organizations could engage in express advocacy. Corporations and unions no longer had to depend on the necessarily smaller contributions to PACs from employees, shareholders, and members. The *Citizens United* case presaged the explosion of super PACs.

By a bare majority of five to four, the court concluded that banning a corporation or a union from directly funding speech that expressly advocated for the election or defeat of a candidate was censorship fortified by criminal penalties. It reiterated the well-known and acknowledged necessity of speech as an essential mechanism of democracy. The freedom to speak, the court said, "is a precondition to enlightened self-government and a necessary means to protect it."[9] And most importantly, the "First Amendment has its fullest and most urgent application to speech uttered during a campaign for political office."[10] The majority dismissed concerns articulated by the dissent about undue corporate influence on the political process. Rather, the court insisted that pivotal to First Amendment protection is the recognition that the speaker's identity should not determine whether or not the speech can be suppressed. To restrict speech based on the speaker's identity, wrote the majority, was too often a back door to control the content of speech. It would privilege some speech over other speech, which is an obvious transgression of First Amendment principles. Moreover, the court explained that corporations and unions, like individuals, make valuable contributions to the marketplace of ideas.[11] Citizens United would not face criminal penalties for accepting donations directly from corporations to finance the express advocacy promoted in *Hillary: The Movie*.

The court declared that the pre-2010 ban on express advocacy financed by and through a corporation was unconstitutional; however, these contributions can only be used for independent expenditures that are not coordinated with a candidate or political party. The details of this important limitation are addressed below as part of the discussion on expenditures.

The fallout from the *Citizens United* case has magnified the implications of the reams of money used to fund political messaging. It has also brought to the forefront the debate regarding whether free-flowing money in the campaign process upends the basic democratic principle of one person, one vote. The concern is that money donated in support of or in opposition to a candidate effectively makes the donor's vote more valuable to a winning candidate.

As a direct result of the *Citizens United* decision, the quantity of political speech available in the marketplace has increased exponentially as money has poured into the pockets of the most star-studded super PACs. Just the same, the effect of all that money and messaging is unclear, particularly in this digital age when it is easy to exit out of what you don't want to hear and click into what you do want to hear. The fate of the super PAC American Crossroads in the 2012 election is a legendary case in point.

American Crossroads is a super PAC behemoth that supported Republican candidates in the 2012 election to the tune of $300 million. Still, even with all that money, only 6 percent of the candidates supported by American Crossroads won their races, leading to questions about whether the change in election financing after *Citizens United* was that impactful.[12] Not to be outdone, in the 2016 race Hillary Clinton's super PACs raised $217.5 million to Donald Trump's $82.3 million, and we all know who won that race.[13]

AGGREGATE CONTRIBUTION LIMITS

Importantly, *Citizens United* did not affect caps, which are set forth by the Federal Election Commission, to contributions made by individuals to politicians or political parties. However, following *Citizens United*, the Supreme Court expanded contribution options by lifting the aggregate limit a donor could spend supporting multiple candidates. In *McCutcheon v. Federal Election Commission*[14] the court held that limiting the aggregate amount of contributions in a two-year political cycle is unconstitutional. In that case, Shaun McCutcheon donated a total of $33,088 to sixteen different federal candidates. He wanted to donate money to an additional twelve candidates, but if he did so, he would outspend aggregate contribution limits and run afoul of the FECA as amended by the BCRA. The aggregate limit, he argued, unconstitutionally restricted speech. The Supreme Court agreed and held that aggregate limits on contributions did not advance the anticorruption rationale underlying campaign finance laws. The decision did not affect base limits on contributions from individuals to candidates; those remained restricted to avoid any appearance of undue influence paid for by political contributions directly to a candidate.

Now, an individual can donate an amount up to the FEC's limits to any number of candidates running for federal office.[15] The result is that if a person wants to push the agenda of one political party, that individual can support every candidate running on that party's ticket, surely amplifying the donor's voice. In both *Citizens United* and *McCutcheon*, the court insisted that the amplification of some voices over the voices of others is constitutionally permissible. The First Amendment does not support an argument in favor of equalizing the participants' voices in political debate.

EXPENDITURES

There is an undeniable relationship between contributions and expenditures in the political sphere. Politicians, political parties, and PACs that are subject to contribution limits are not, for the most part, subject to restrictions on their express advocacy expenditures. In addition, they can coordinate their messages with one another without penalty. Super PACs, which are not subject to contribution limits, may make unlimited expenditures on express advocacy; however, those expenditures must be independent and may not be coordinated with a person running for federal office or with a political party. This is an important distinction. Super PAC speech, supported by corporate and union dollars, has the potential to drown out all other voices. While the prohibition on coordinating messaging might be little more than a convenient fiction, given the myriad of ways super PACs can follow and learn the messaging priorities of any candidate running for office, it at least provides some protection for the public and their right to know. The First Amendment implications are clear: The value of political speech is not measured by the amount of money spent or the intensity and volume of speech belonging to a single speaker; instead, it is measured by its impact on the growth and expansion of the marketplace of ideas.

DISCLOSURES

The final variable in the money-in-politics equation is disclosure: revealing the details regarding financial sources. In theory, disclosure promotes veracity. Disclosure helps voters evaluate the message, it deters corruption, and it is an essential means to collect data and monitor election violations.[16] On the other hand, the right to anonymity is a recognized corollary to the right to speak freely.[17] Without anonymity, some might be afraid to speak for fear of retribution for unpopular ideas, or some might want the ideas to stand or fail on their own merit without reference to authorship.

In this digital age, the anonymity of the internet promotes distorted messaging. Indeed, some argue the rampant fake news and planted stories of recent elections were made possible mainly because the speakers could remain hidden on social media platforms. In fact, Senators Mark Warner, Amy Klobuchar, and Lindsey Graham sponsored legislation titled the Honest Ads Act,[18] which is intended to improve the transparency of political ads in online media. The legislation is stalled in Congress. We will see if it ever makes it to a vote.

The folks who produced *Hillary: The Movie* wanted to keep their identities anonymous. The movie was controversial; they wanted the viewers to assess it on its own terms, without the filter of knowing who authored and orchestrated it. The FECA, as amended by the BCRA, required that the closing credits at the end of the proposed ads and at the end of the movie include a disclaimer identifying Citizens United as the producer. Citizens United believed the required disclaimer would not assist viewers in assessing the message; instead, they believed it would color viewer assessment. The court rejected the producers' protests. The proposed ads for the movie and the movie itself were scheduled to air and play within thirty days of the Democratic primary. Messages close to elections can have a powerful temporal impact with little time for a target to respond. Providing the audience with information regarding production and authorship is vital to assisting the audience in assessing the message. At the very least, the disclaimers avoid confusion by making clear that the messages "are not funded by a candidate or political party."[19]

In addition, the court required Citizens United to disclose the identities of its donors. The court explained that identifying the financial sources of a message should be required as a means of disclosure so "that the people will be able to evaluate the arguments to which they are being subjected." The court found that the FEC regulations regarding disclosure under these circumstances provided transparency, allowing citizens to make informed judgments as to the validity of a message, based in part on the speaker's identity. They also served as a means to keep corporate boards accountable to their shareholders, clients, and customers, to say nothing of accountability of elected officials who are the beneficiaries of corporate messaging.[20]

It turns out that while Citizens United won the war—corporations and unions could contribute unlimited money to the election landscape in the form of uncoordinated, independent expenditures—it lost the battle on disclaimers and disclosures. Citizens United was required to provide a disclaimer noting that the organization was the creator of the movie, and it was required to disclose those that had donated to its production. The bottom line: After the 2010 *Citizens United* decision, there are no upper limits on contributions to super PACs. Super PACs can engage in unlimited independent and uncoordinated messaging; however, they must register with the IRS, publicly disclose their donors, and file periodic reports of contributions and expenditures.

DARK MONEY

In fact, most political messaging entities are required to disclose their donors. There are, however, specific organizations—social welfare organizations, referred to by their IRS designation as a 501(c)(4) corporation—that can engage in political messaging and lobbying without disclosing their donors. A 501(c)(4) organization can only cloak its donors' identities as long as the organization spends the majority of its funds (51 percent) on its primary mission of social welfare.

The definition of "social welfare" is ambiguous and has been the subject of a lot of discussion, dispute, and litigation. So, too, the anonymity provided to the 501(c)(4) has been used creatively by many donors. Donors, both individual and corporate, give sums to the 501(c)(4); the 501(c)(4) then donates to a super PAC, which launches volumes of political messages; all the while, the actual donors remain anonymous, unfortunately undercutting the rationale developed by the court that supports disclosure requirements. Media and political watchdog reports about financing political messages with dark money generally refer to these organizations.

The epilogue to the chronicle about money and its relationship to political speech remains unwritten. The impact of open corporate coffers may grow or diminish in the coming elections. And the responsibility for protecting the electorate from propaganda and lies might fall to nongovernmental enterprises that, for all intents and purposes, control the world wide web.

THE PRICE OF SILENCE

As is clear from a reading of the *Citizens United* decision, the Supreme Court has acknowledged the intricate and interdependent relationship between money and speech. Individuals, corporations, and unions can purchase speech to benefit and enhance their position and power. After *Citizens United* and its progeny, the ability to purchase political speech expanded, but even before that expansion, each of those entities could pay to enhance their voices. The notable difference is that individuals garner funds from numerous sources, whereas corporate coffers are filled by corporate profits, and union coffers are filled with union dues.

Until 2018, public employees who were duly and legally represented by a union were required to pay a portion of union dues even if they opted out of union representation. Those particular funds, referred to as agency fees, were restricted and could be used only for activities related to the union's collective bargaining activities. Even after *Citizens United*, the restricted agency fees could not be used for overtly political speech. However, it is undoubtedly apparent that union collective bargaining activities are, by definition, speech. As part of its collective bargaining activities, a union speaks for the employees and negotiates terms of employment, benefits, and the like.

Mark Janus is an older man in his 60s. He introduces himself as a person who has served his community his whole life.[21] He is an Eagle Scout and credits Scouting with his commitment to public service. In 2007, after having worked in the private sector, Janus returned to public-sector work as a child-support specialist. As an employee of the state of Illinois Department of Healthcare and Family Services, he was charged with ensuring that children whose parents have divorced are being provided for as required by any legal settlement or court order. Janus was among 35,000 public employees for the state who were represented by the duly elected American Federation of State, County, and Municipal Employees, Council 31 (union). However, Janus was opposed to many of the union's positions. He believed it was in part responsible for the budget and pension crisis in Illinois. He was also opposed to many of the candidates backed by the union, believing them to be fiscally irresponsible, so he refused to join. Nonetheless, every month, $45 was deducted as a union agency fee from his paycheck to support union activities on his behalf. He challenged the agency fee's constitutionality, arguing that his compelled financial support also effectively compelled him to support views he found objectionable. In *Janus v. American Federation of State, County, and Municipal Employees, Council 31*, the Supreme Court agreed.[22] Requiring public employees to pay agency fees to a union was a violation of such employees' right to be free from compelled or coerced speech. Writing for a majority of five, Justice Alito noted that the violation of First Amendment principles was so obvious in cases of compelled speech that there had been relatively few of them compared to cases that rule on speech restrictions.[23] The justice explained that compelled speech is particularly loathsome because it requires an individual to betray their convictions.[24] Justice Elena Kagan, joined by Justices Ruth Bader Ginsburg, Stephen Breyer, and Sonia Sotomayor, offered a fiery dissent. She labeled the union speech on behalf of those it represents as "managerial," accomplishing tasks such as "negotiating and administering a collective-bargaining agreement and representing the interests of employees in settling disputes and processing grievances."[25] She concluded that the First Amendment should not be weaponized against union protections.[26]

Of course, in reality, this is not quite a David-and-Goliath tale. Janus' lawsuit was funded by the National Right To Work Legal Defense Fund, a politically conservative nonprofit antiunion group associated with a 501(c)(4) lobbying arm and the Liberty Justice Center, a public litigation center that supports conservative political causes. Those groups are funded by industrialists and conservative activists Richard Uihlein and the Koch brothers.[27] Subsequent to his successful lawsuit, Janus left public service and is now employed by the Liberty Justice Center and travels the United States speaking in favor of right-to-work issues. He continued his legal battle against the union and sued them for repayment of back dues, but was unsuccessful in that quest.[28]

The Janus decision was uniquely focused on the rights and obligations of public unions and public employees. However, the First Amendment's role in protecting against compelled speech is working its way to the forefront of First Amendment contests. Political hot-button issues such as LGBTQ civil rights is a case in point and will be addressed further in the next chapter.

GOVERNMENT SPEECH

The government might be financed by your tax dollars, but it is assigned its own identity and can claim its own First Amendment right to opine and advocate when it speaks. The Constitution only constricts the government's ability to circumscribe the rights of the citizenry. In contrast, like any individual and any corporate entity, the government can exercise its own right to access and add to the marketplace of ideas. For instance, speeches by elected officials on matters of public policy, reports by executive agencies, and taxpayer-subsidized public service announcements are all examples of government speech. In fact, government expression would seem to be a necessary element to the robust debate that fuels our democracy. To put it succinctly: "To govern, government has to say something."[29]

COMMERCIAL SPEECH

The primary purpose of a corporation is to make a profit, so it can be assumed that any public communication created by a corporation is motivated by economic reward. Without doubt, the political speech of corporations is financially driven. Corporations donate to super PACs that craft messages and take positions that will positively affect their bottom line. While corporations can boast broad First Amendment rights, there are boundaries to the freedom of corporations to engage in political speech. Corporations, like individuals can engage in unlimited issue advocacy. But, if a corporation seeks to promote the election or defeat of a candidate, in other words, if the corporation seeks to engage in express advocacy, the speech must be independent from and not coordinated with a politician or political party. Commercial speech (corporate or not), too, enjoys First Amendment protection.

In the middle part of the last century, the Supreme Court embraced the concept that commercial messages play an essential part in our lives. While, of course, the speaker of a commercial message seeks to persuade the audience to purchase the suggested product or service, from a First Amendment perspective, commercial messages provide information to consumers. As such, commercial speech is valuable in both the economic marketplace and the marketplace of ideas. However, constitutional protection is withdrawn if the speech is illegal or fraudulent. Commercial speech can also be constrained if the government has a compelling interest that is accomplished by speech restrictions that are narrowly tailored to support that interest.[30] Part of the Rhode Island laws that regulated the sale of liquor failed that test.

In 1956, the Rhode Island legislature passed a law that prohibited vendors from advertising the price of any alcoholic beverages. 44 Liquormart was a licensed vendor in Rhode Island. In 1991, its owners devised a decidedly creative method of avoiding the statutory prohibition. They placed an ad in a Rhode Island newspaper that promoted the mixers and snacks it sold at low prices and included pictures of liquor bottles next to the word "wow," in caps. The ad included a disclaimer that said, "State law prohibits advertising liquor prices."[31] In spite of the disclaimer, the meaning was unambiguous. Without mentioning the actual price, 44 Liquormart was advertising its liquor's low cost, in violation of the statute. The Rhode Island Liquor Control Administrator was unimpressed and assessed 44 Liquormart a fine. Asserting that the advertising ban violated the liquor store's right to free speech, 44 Liquormart paid the fine and then went to court, seeking a declaration that the statute was unconstitutional. The case eventually made it to the Supreme Court.

In defending the advertising ban, the State of Rhode Island asserted an interest in promoting temperance and reducing its citizens' alcohol consumption. The state argued that banning advertising would reduce collusive competition and keep alcohol prices high, thereby reducing consumption. While it might be an admirable goal to reduce alcohol consumption, the Supreme Court found that banning commercial speech, which served the purpose of educating citizens about the price of alcohol, was an intemperate method. Moreover, the ads in question were not misleading, and as long as a person was above the minimum legal drinking age, alcohol consumption was not unlawful in Rhode Island. A far better method of effectuating the temperance goal would be to increase the state's liquor tax. The Supreme Court reiterated the proposition that purchased speech or speech directed at making a profit retains its essential constitutional characteristics. It provides information to the audience and adds to the marketplace of ideas.

A corollary to the right to speak is the audience's right to know. While the government is interested in protecting its citizens, censorship of commercial speech may, in reality, undermine public safety. A democratic government oversteps when it seeks to hide information from the public for its own good. The public has a right to know about the value and benefits of goods and services in the economic marketplace, even if that knowledge can only be obtained by communication packaged in promises and hype. However, commercial speech loses its First Amendment protection if it is false or misleading or otherwise targeted at unlawful activity.[32]

In the political sphere, speech restrictions include contribution, expenditure, and disclosure requirements. In the commercial sphere, speech restrictions require that the activity promoted is legal, and that the promotion itself is generally true and accurate. In both spheres, the right to speak freely maintains primacy.

15 : WHEN SPEECH AND FAITH COLLIDE

[T]here is room for play in the joints.
—Justice Ruth Bader Ginsburg[1]

As James Madison crafted the Bill of Rights, he had an astute vision of the value of free speech to the nascent democracy's health. He also understood the significance of faith to the populace. If its placement in a sentence can measure the importance of a concept, religion beats speech. There are two religion clauses in the First Amendment; both of them precede the Free Speech Clause. A short jaunt through some history might help clarify the complex dynamic, the push and the pull, between these three clauses of the First Amendment.

Many of us can repeat the mantra that the Constitution requires a wall of separation between church and state. The religion clauses of the First Amendment read: "Congress shall make no law respecting an establishment of religion, or prohibiting the free exercise thereof." Notice, there is no language of walls or separation. That concept of a separating wall was developed by Thomas Jefferson, one of the Founding Fathers and the third president of the United States. Today, most experts interpret the two constitutional prohibitions regarding religion, the Establishment Clause and the Free Exercise Clause, as requiring the government to insulate government and faith institutions from one another. What that means in practice is open to interpretation depending on how you feel about the role religion should play in the public sphere.

THE ESTABLISHMENT CLAUSE
The government may make no law respecting
an establishment of religion.

The intended purpose of the Establishment Clause was to ensure that the government remains neutral in matters of faith. The government should not, in appearance or reality, support one faith over another. Religion should remain a private matter between a person and their God or no God at all, and should be free from government interference.[2]

The Supreme Court has evidenced a head-spinning inconsistency concerning the Establishment Clause. The decisions are frequently dependent on context, making it difficult to discern a general rule of application.

In 1973, the city of Pawtucket, Rhode Island, included a nativity scene as part of its yearly holiday display. In *Lynch v. Donnelly*, the court found that the display was constitutional.[3] The court explained that while the Establishment Clause prohibits hostility toward any particular religion, it also requires tolerance of all religions. However, in 2005, the court found a display of the Ten Commandments placed six years earlier in the county courts in McCreary and Pulaski Counties, Kentucky, unconstitutional. In *McCreary County v. American Civil Liberties Union of Ky.*, the court found that the displays violated the Establishment Clause.[4] The backstory to the displays demonstrated that they were installed to invoke biblical concepts of morality and law, including the commandments that require fealty to God and an admonition to remember the Sabbath and keep it holy. To be fair, while the court found the displays unconstitutional, it went to great lengths to say that this decision was fact-specific and could not be generalized to other displays of the Ten Commandments on public property. The late Justice Antonin Scalia posted a scathing dissent in *McCreary*, arguing the display of the Ten Commandments as evidence of support for monotheistic faiths is constitutional.

Then, in *Van Orden v. Perry*, argued and decided the same day as *McCreary*, the court held that even though the Ten Commandments are an acknowledged religious symbol, their display at the Texas State Capitol was just fine![5] The court explained that religion has always been part of our history. Many of our government institutions presuppose a supreme being. The court noted that our monetary currency claims "In God we Trust" and that we pledge allegiance to our country as "one country under God." Context again prevailed. The display in this case was part of a larger display invoking the role faith plays in providing moral guidance to our government. Justice Scalia was thrilled, but he chastised the court for its inconsistencies.[6]

There are even financial implications to the Establishment Clause. The court faced questions regarding whether tax dollars could constitutionally be used to support programs and opportunities hosted by religious institutions. Especially concerning nonsecular (religious) primary and secondary schools, K–12, the court has ruled favorably on any indirect financial support. For example, using tax dollars to reimburse private schools, including parochial Catholic schools, for students' transportation costs to and from school is constitutional.[7] In addition, the court has favorably ruled on the constitutionality of a school voucher program that provided tuition assistance to low-income students enrolled in public or private schools of the parents' choosing.[8]

However, the court has found that programs that foster an excessive entanglement with religion cross the line of constitutional acceptability. The court struck down a program that in part provided taxpayer-supported funding for parochial schools, that included full or supplemental funding for teachers' salaries, textbooks, and instructional materials for secular (nonreligious) subjects.[9]

The court has been more consistent in finding Establishment Clause violations relating to internal school operations. It has evidenced sensitivity to the dangers of coercion in a school setting, focusing on the nature of the educational enterprise and the students' youth. In *Engel v. Vitale*, the court held that public school teachers could not lead students in voluntary, nondenominational prayer during the school day as part of the school curriculum.[10] In *Lee v. Weisman*, the court found a violation of the Establishment Clause when the school included prayers offered by a clergy member at official public school ceremonies—in this case, graduation from middle school.[11] The court acknowledged that recognition and appreciation for divine guidance in education might have deep meaning for many students and parents; however, such a prayer represents "an identification of governmental power with religious practice, endorses religion, and violates the Establishment Clause."[12] The court rejected the argument put forth by the school that attendance at graduation was not compulsory and that students could have opted out of the event or refused to stand, thus indicating protest. Giving constitutional recognition to the power of peer pressure, especially in school, the court noted that the options available to a young student, while they exist in theory, are impractical and unfair and place the student in a "conflict of conscience"[13] whereby they are "induced to conform."[14] The court went on to cite social science data in support of its position: "Research in psychology supports the common assumption that adolescents are often susceptible to pressure from their peers towards conformity, and that the influence is strongest in matters of social convention."[15]

Some of the Supreme Court's most incendiary and thought-provoking decisions involve curriculum issues, specifically whether or not to teach creationism or its modern equivalent, intelligent design, in the science curriculum along with evolution. The court has consistently ruled that creationism may not be taught in science class. In 1982, the State of Louisiana passed the Balanced Treatment for Creation-Science and Evolution-Science in Public School Instruction Act (Creationism Act), which required that if the origins of life are taught in science class, both creationism and evolution must be included in the curriculum. It is well settled that states and local school boards have wide discretion in developing school curriculum, but the scope of that discretion ends at the perimeters of the Constitution. The Supreme Court found a clear religious purpose to the statute, which was "to advance the religious viewpoint that a supernatural being created humankind."[16] And because the purpose of the Creationism Act was to endorse a religious doctrine, the act sought to entangle the government, through the public schools, in a religious purpose, which violates the Establishment Clause of the First Amendment.

THE FREE EXERCISE CLAUSE
The government may make no law prohibiting the free exercise of religion.

Unlike the Establishment Clause, there seems to be some level of consistency in the Supreme Court's application of the Free Exercise Clause. The freedom to exercise one's faith is vast, as long as there is no other competing governmental interest that is compelling. However, in the face of such compelling state interests, any incidental effects to religious beliefs or practices are constitutionally acceptable.

Abraham Braunfeld was an Orthodox Jew. According to his religious practice, he could not work as a clothing and furniture salesman on Saturdays, the Jewish Sabbath. His business was located in Pennsylvania. In 1959, the Pennsylvania legislature passed a criminal blue law statute that prohibited most retail sales on Sunday, including clothing and furniture. Mr. Braunfeld objected to the blue law, arguing that it would cause him significant financial loss since he was required by his faith to close his store on Saturday and then required by the law to shutter his store on Sunday. He argued that the blue law was an infringement of his right to the free exercise of religion since it placed him in the position of working Saturday and having to abandon his religious principles or working on Sunday and facing criminal prosecution. The Supreme Court disagreed, stating that the law was secular and not directed at any particular religious practice or belief. The law did not criminalize any religious belief or opinion, and it did not force anyone to embrace any religious belief or practice that conflicted with religious tenets. They found the law was neutral in intent and application and therefore constitutional, even in the face of an incidental impact on Braunfeld's faith. The court found the law was properly within government rights and responsibilities. Without explaining why Sunday, the Christian Sabbath, was the chosen day of the week, the court interpreted the law as aimed at providing the citizens of Pennsylvania "a weekly respite from all labor and at the same time to set one day of the week apart from the others as a day of rest, repose, recreation and tranquility."[17]

Conversely, the court held in *Wisconsin v. Yoder* that when government policy has the effect of interfering with legitimate religious practices, it may do so only if the policy is supported by an interest "of sufficient magnitude to override the interest claiming protection under the Free Exercise Clause."[18] The Old Order Amish religion and the Conservative Amish Mennonite Church were successful in their challenge to the Wisconsin compulsory education law that required, under criminal penalty, that children remain in school until the age of sixteen. The Amish instead desired to remove their children from the school system after completing the eighth grade. They would then continue to educate their children consistent with the pastoral and religious dictates of their faith. The faith groups successfully argued that sending their children to high school would endanger their salvation, preclude them from participating in community life at a crucial time in their intellectual and emotional development, and create "a serious barrier to the integration of the Amish child into the Amish religious community."[19] The court recognized the State's important responsibility to protect and promote education of its citizens; however, compelling education beyond the eighth grade unduly burdened the groups' free exercise of their faiths. The Supreme Court found that the Wisconsin law served as an unconstitutional imposition on the Amish and Mennonite communities' religious practices. Perhaps one can better understand the Supreme Court's differing decisions in the *Braunfield* and *Yoder* cases by examining context. Braunfield grounded his argument on the economic effects of the blue law; Yoder grounded his argument on the domestic impacts of the compulsory education law. Considerations of parental control over childrearing might have garnered greater compassion from the justices.

The Free Exercise Clause also protects people who reject religion or the concept of the divine. Roy R. Torasco was an atheist and an activist. He respected others' religious views, but he bristled at what he interpreted as government attempts to impose those beliefs upon him. Torasco worked as a bookkeeper for a construction firm in Bethesda, Maryland. The business frequently required the signature of a notary public, and Torasco's boss requested that Torasco apply for an appointment by the governor. It seemed innocent enough; however, Torasco was denied the commission because he objected to the legislative requirement that he declare his belief in God as part of the qualification for the office. Torasco argued that the oath was an impermissible burden on his right to profess his disbelief in God. The Supreme Court agreed.[20]

The power of the Free Exercise Clause even extends to practices that, while not criminal, are socially unacceptable. To most in the United States, ritual animal sacrifice is immoral and cruel, but to those that practice the Santeria religion, it is a standard practice of their faith. A conflict arose between the Church of the Lukumi Babalu Aye and the city council in Hialeah, Florida, when the church announced plans to construct a house of worship in that city. Upon learning of the church's plans, the city council went to work and quickly passed a series of ordinances that prohibited ritual animal slaughter. The church responded by suing the city and the city council, alleging a violation of their constitutional right to the free exercise of their faith. The Supreme Court found that the Florida city's ordinances were discriminatory and unconstitutional. The court explained that the ordinances would fall in the face of the free exercise protections unless the ordinances were justified by a compelling interest and were narrowly tailored to advance that interest. The court found that the ordinances were not narrowly tailored given the fact that they prohibited Santeria sacrifices even when the sacrifices did not threaten the city's public health. Considerations of cruelty and method of slaughter were also overly broad and distinctly directed at the Santeria rituals. The court made it clear that "religious beliefs need not be acceptable, logical, consistent, or comprehensible to others in order to merit First Amendment protection."[21]

THE PLAY IN THE JOINTS

As indicated by the epigraph for this chapter, Justice Ruth Bader Ginsburg highlighted the problem of the play in the joints between the Establishment Clause and the Free Exercise Clause. Sometimes, when the government seeks to abide by one prohibition, not to establish a religion, it runs afoul of the right to the free exercise of one's faith. No case better illustrates the problem than *Locke v. Davey*.[22]

In recognition of those students who earned high grades in high school but could not qualify for financial aid and did not have the economic means to attend college, the State of Washington created the Promise Scholarship Program. The program provided eligible students a scholarship for college educational expenses. Tax dollars support the scholarships. There were some financial restrictions for eligibility, and the award was applied only to degrees acquired from eligible institutions. In addition, scholarship recipients were prohibited from using the money to pursue a degree in theology.

Joshua Davey applied for and was awarded a Promise Scholarship. He enrolled in a properly accredited and eligible institution, Northwest College, a private Christian college. Davey planned to double major in business management and pastoral studies with the ultimate goal of becoming a Christian minister. When he requested the awarded funds, he was asked to certify that he was not seeking a devotional degree. He refused. In response, the state withdrew the scholarship award. Davey sued the state, alleging the scholarship program's requirements violated his right to the free exercise of his religion. Additionally, he alleged the program evidenced a hostility toward religion in violation of the Establishment Clause.

The Supreme Court disagreed.

To avoid the Establishment–Free Exercise conflict, the court characterized the scholarship restrictions as merely a choice by the government not to fund a distinct category of instruction that prepares the recipient for the ministry. The court found that refusal to support a religious degree did not evidence hostility toward religion. Furthermore, the court found that the scholarship, which by its own terms could be used to pay for tuition or educational expenses, did not prohibit the recipient from enrolling in theology courses and therefore did not require students to choose between their religious beliefs and receiving a government benefit. Predictably, Justice Scalia was fit to be tied and eviscerated the court's description of the play between the joints. He characterized the scholarship program as discriminatory and evidencing a "trendy disdain for deep religious conviction."[23]

THE MASTERPIECE CAKESHOP CASE

The recitation of the cases above provides a backdrop for the *Masterpiece Cakeshop* case.[24] This case, which arose out of a dispute over a wedding cake, was closely watched by religious and civil rights groups regarding the civic and theological conflicts engendered by constitutional recognition of marriage equality.

Jack Phillips is a man of profound faith. He embraces a conservative interpretation of the Bible, and he lives by it. He operates his business, a bakery, by the dictates he perceives as conforming to his Christian beliefs: "He is not open on Sundays, he pays his employees a higher-than-average wage, and he loans them money in times of need. Phillips also refuses to bake cakes containing alcohol, cakes with racist or homophobic messages, cakes criticizing God, and cakes celebrating Halloween, even though Halloween is one of the most lucrative seasons for bakeries."[25] Phillips asserts, as guided by his faith, that marriage should be consecrated only between one man and one woman.

Phillips considers himself an artist, hence the name of his business: Masterpiece Cakeshop. His logo includes an artist's paint palette and brush, along with a baker's whisk. His website contains pictures of him and a container of brushes of varying sizes as he studiously paints a design on a wedding cake. He designs cakes for every occasion, but this discussion focuses on his wedding cake designs. He describes his method of creating each such cake as an individualized process. He begins with a sketch on paper and then works with the couple to choose a color scheme. He proceeds to sculpt and decorate the cake to reflect the significance of their moment.

While Phillips insists that he serves all people regardless of race, ethnicity, or sexual orientation, he refused to sell Charlie Craig and David Mullins a wedding cake as part of the planned celebration of their union. In fact, Phillips specifically explained to the couple that he would sell them any other product he created—his only exclusion: a wedding cake. Craig and Mullins were understandably offended by Phillips' refusal, and they filed a complaint with the Colorado Civil Rights Commission. The commission is responsible for monitoring violations of the Colorado Anti-Discrimination Act, which in part prohibits discrimination based on sexual orientation by a business engaged in sales to the public.

Craig and Mullins argued that Phillips could not use his faith as a weapon to protect him from liability resulting from his illegal behavior. His constitutional right to the free exercise of his faith was not violated by demanding that he comply with a law that prohibited discrimination based on sexual orientation. The commission ruled in favor of the couple and ordered Phillips and Masterpiece Cakeshop to cease and desist from discriminating against same-sex couples. The commission also ordered additional remedial measures, including staff training regarding discrimination and the preparation of quarterly compliance reports for two years. Phillips appealed the commission's decision, and the case ultimately ended up on the Supreme Court docket.

Craig and Mullins were married in 2012. At that time, the State of Colorado did not recognize the legality of same-sex marriage, so the couple was married in Massachusetts, which did recognize same-sex marriage. The men held the wedding reception later in their home state. In 2015, the Supreme Court decided *Obergefell v. Hodges*, which recognized the right to marry as a fundamental liberty protected by the Fourteenth Amendment's Due Process Clause.[26] As such, it recognized the constitutional viability of marriage equality. Even though the dispute between Craig, Mullins, and Phillips occurred prior to the *Obergefell* decision, their case was decided by the Supreme Court after *Obergefell*. The *Masterpiece Cakeshop* case presented a problem that had been forecast by Justice Thomas in his dissenting opinion in *Obergefell*: "I warned that the Court's decision would inevitabl[y] . . . come into conflict with religious liberty, as individuals . . . are confronted with demands to participate in and endorse civil marriages between same-sex couples. This case proves that the conflict has already emerged."[27]

There was no Establishment Clause issue in the *Masterpiece Cakeshop* case. Phillips was charged with violating an antidiscrimination statute, and there was no reasonable argument that the statute violated the Establishment Clause. However, Phillips did have a cognizable Free Exercise claim. Phillips briefly argued that requiring him to provide a wedding cake for Craig and Mullins, like the Amish parents in *Yoder*, unconstitutionally forced him to behave in a manner that was contrary to his religious belief system. But despite the ability to ground his argument on the right to religious freedom, Phillips chose instead to argue primarily that the Colorado Civil Rights Commission violated his right to freely express his political views.

Phillips explained that a wedding cake is a piece of symbolic, expressive art. His wedding cakes express approval of the marital union of the two people who are purchasing the cake. He disputed the assertion that he, as an artist, is merely an instrument of the purchaser, and a wedding cake is only a cake, a product with little or no speech elements baked into it. Phillips claimed that requiring him to make a wedding cake for a same-sex couple, whether he refused for political or religious reasons, amounted to compelled speech, which is unconstitutional. Phillips argued he had a First Amendment right to refuse to bake Craig and Mullins a cake for any reason. It did not matter if he refused to speak (through his cake designs) in support of Craig and Mullen's marriage because he objected to expanding civil rights to LGBTQ couples, or if he refused to speak in support Craig and Mullen's marriage because he believed it to be morally indefensible according to religious doctrine. Phillips analogized his situation to one faced decades before by the South Boston Allied War Veterans Council.

In 1947, the city of Boston authorized the South Boston Allied War Veterans Council (Veterans Council) to organize and conduct the St. Patrick's Day parade. Each year the Veterans Council applied for and received a permit for the parade. There were no other applicants.[28] In 1992, a group of openly gay, lesbian, and bisexual descendants of Irish immigrants formed the Irish-American Gay, Lesbian and Bisexual Group of Boston (GLIB) for the singular purpose of marching in the parade to express pride in their Irish heritage and to demonstrate their solidarity with the LGBTQ community. The Veterans Council denied their application. In response, GLIB obtained a court order requiring the council to admit the group, and so GLIB marched in the parade after all, without incident. GLIB made the same application to the Veterans Council in 1993, and they were denied again. This time, they sued the Veterans Council and the city, asserting that GLIB was the subject of unconstitutional discrimination. Ultimately, the Supreme Court agreed to hear the case.

At the outset, the Supreme Court recognized the expressive elements of a parade:

> If there were no reason for a group of people to march from here to there except to reach a destination, they could make the trip without expressing any message beyond the fact of the march itself. Some people might call such a procession a parade, but it would not be much of one. Real parades are public dramas of social relations, and in them performers define who can be a social actor and what subjects and ideas are available for communication and consideration.[29]

The court also recognized the communicative nature of GLIB's inclusion in the parade and stressed that the Veterans Council did not deny any LGBTQ individual the opportunity to march in the parade; rather the Veterans Council limited its denial to GLIB as a group whose purpose in entering the parade was to carry its own banner and promote GLIB's message. The court held that the Veterans Council had a First Amendment right to refuse to accommodate GLIB's message as part of the parade. Requiring the Veterans Council to include GLIB would be tantamount to the Veterans Council endorsing GLIB's message, to which

the Veterans Council objected. The court stated, "one important mani-
festation of the principle of free speech is that one who chooses to speak
may also decide what not to say. . . . [W]hatever the reason, it boils down
to the choice of a speaker not to propound a particular point of view,
and that choice is presumed to lie beyond the government's power to
control."[30]

Like the Veterans Council in Boston, Phillips argued that he, as a busi-
nessperson and artist, was protected from being compelled to speak in
a manner that did not represent his beliefs. He argued that the Colorado
Civil Rights Commission's decision, forcing him to provide a wedding
cake to Craig and Mullins, violated his First Amendment rights. As it
turned out, Phillips would not be required to create a cake for Craig and
Mullins, but the court left the question regarding the interplay of the
Free Exercise and Free Speech clauses of the First Amendment for another time. In other words, the court punted. It did not decide whether
the First Amendment safeguarded his silence based on either religious
or political justification.

Justice Kennedy wrote the decision for the court. His opinion spoke
for a seven-person majority of the justices. Apparently, the Colorado
Civil Rights Commission was offended by Phillips' refusal and treated
his claims with derision. The court, in turn, was offended by the commission's treatment of Phillips. The Supreme Court found that the commission failed to treat Phillips' objections and religious affirmations
with the appropriate neutrality and respect that was constitutionally
required. In fact, transcripts of the hearing reveal one of the commissioners referencing Phillips' reliance upon his religious beliefs to deny
Craig and Mullins his baking services as "despicable."[31] In an interesting twist, while the court did not decide whether Phillips' refusal to bake
the cake was discriminatory, the court did find the commission's treatment of Phillips discriminatory. Justice Kennedy soundly chastised the
commission and rebuked it for its "clear and impermissible hostility"
toward Phillips and his religious beliefs. The commission's order was
set aside.[32]

The concurring and dissenting justices were bolder in their assertions
regarding the relationship between the Free Exercise Clause and the

Free Speech Clause. In his concurring opinion, Justice Thomas, joined by Justice Neil Gorsuch, unequivocally asserted that a wedding cake created and designed in the manner in which Phillips creates and designs his cakes is symbolic speech deserving of full First Amendment protection. Then, in his own concurring opinion, Justice Gorsuch, joined by Justice Alito, argued that an objection to speak grounded in faith is no different than an objection to speak based on nonreligious moral principles. Both objections are protected by the First Amendment. Justice Ginsburg characteristically dissented in *Masterpiece* and was joined by Justice Sotomayor. She rejected the assertion that a wedding cake is a piece of expressive art. It is a cake. If it expresses anything, the expression belongs to the celebrants, not to the baker. But alas, the writings of the concurring and dissenting justices, while interesting, have no far-reaching or precedential effect. Concurring opinions merely elaborate on the views of the justice writing the opinion, and those who join the writer; they do not serve as justification for the majority decision. Dissenting opinions voice disagreement, and so also merely represent the opinions of the individual justices and not the majority decision of the court.

Whether the Supreme Court's failure to directly address the internal First Amendment conflict (between the Free Exercise and Free Speech clauses of the First Amendment) has served as a blessing or a curse for Jack Phillips is up for debate. LGBTQ groups have certainly targeted him. In fact, he reports that on the same day the Supreme Court agreed to hear the *Masterpiece Cake* case, he was contacted by a local attorney, Autumn Scardina, to bake a pink and blue cake celebrating her gender transition. When Phillips refused, Scardina filed a complaint with the commission that was ultimately dismissed, but Scardina followed it with a civil suit seeking $100,000 in damages.[33] Other members of the LGBTQ community have also continued to make requests of and filed complaints against Phillips. On the other hand, the case has provided Phillips a platform and a book deal. *The Cost of My Faith: How a Decision in My Cake Shop Took Me to the Supreme Court* is currently available for purchase on Amazon.

The conflict between the Establishment and Free Exercise clauses continues to present challenges for the Supreme Court, as does the relationship between the Free Exercise Clause and the general right of the freedom to speak or not to speak. Presently, there does not appear to be a clear path forward. The only certain thing is that at some time, likely in the near future, the Supreme Court will have to address this issue head-on.

We have anarchists, socialists, religious zealots, and civil rights activists, among many others, to thank for their contributions to our understanding of the boundaries and the boundlessness of our First Amendment right to speak freely.

If First Amendment inquiry has a starting point, it must be: What exactly is the speech it protects? For starters, the First Amendment completely ignores speech that is by definition criminal; for example, perjury, blackmail, and criminal conspiracies. Speaking, language, words, and documents are inherent to all of these crimes and some others, but the First Amendment remains utterly inaccessible to them. A criminal defendant cannot claim they were exercising their First Amendment right in the furtherance of a crime. However, once it is clear that as a threshold matter the First Amendment protections are implicated, the First Amendment's magnetism[1] is so strong that the likelihood that the speech in question enjoys constitutional protection is high. So once the First Amendment shows up, often the inquiry shifts to the strength and scope of its power in any particular context. The First Amendment embraces messaging communicated through an ever-expanding list of mediums, including digital spaces, clothing, and even silence. It embraces speech spoken in anger, for laughs, to celebrate, or to insult.

Tolerance for discord is built into the very fabric of the First Amendment. That said, some argue that the boundaries of protected speech are too broad and otherwise infringe on the rights of the rest of us to pursue liberty and happiness. Others question whether increasingly targeted threats, some of which have latent and deadly consequences, can be adequately constrained under current First Amendment judicial proscriptions. Presently, First Amendment jurisprudence acknowledges that a clash of views might create anxiety and disharmony but accepts those as part of the character of democratic discourse. Vigor and force, emotion, is often essential to get the message heard above the din. The release of anger and frustration through words instead of violence has value, and the protective mantle of the First Amendment provides the speaker with ample room.

While the First Amendment's language regarding our right to the freedom of speech—and the legions of judicial decisions interpreting that right—provide a roadmap for constitutional protections, they do not necessarily encourage civility, morality, and ethics. Undeniably, the court decisions adjudicating our constitutional right seem to ripen from uncivil, immoral, and unethical speech.

In the words of Circuit Judge Frank H. Easterbrook in *American Booksellers Assn., Inc. v. Hudnut*:[2]

> The ideas of the Klan may be propagated. Communists may speak freely and run for office. The Nazi Party may march through a city with a large Jewish population. People may criticize the President by misrepresenting his positions, and they have a right to post their misrepresentations on public property. People may teach religions that others despise. People may seek to repeal laws guaranteeing equal opportunity in employment or to revoke the constitutional amendments granting the vote to blacks and women. They may do this because above all else, the First Amendment means that government has no power to restrict expression because of its message or its ideas.

As a civil society, it is up to us to infuse the First Amendment with morality. Using the First Amendment as a weapon to inflict pain, to insult, to heckle, or to embarrass dishonors its purpose. It is our responsibility as citizens of a democratic collective and as human beings to honor the First Amendment's intentions by speaking to one another and communicating in a manner that respects the value of the other.

44 Liquormart Inc. v. Rhode Island, 517 U.S. 484, 492 (1996)

Abrams v. United States, 250 U.S. 616 (1919)

Ashcroft v. American Civil Liberties Union, 542 U.S. 656 (2004)

Axson-Flynn v. Johnson, 356 F.3d 1277 (10th Cir. 2004)

Bethel School Dist. No 403 v. Fraser, 478 U.S. 675 (1986)

Bible Believers v. Wayne County, 805 F.3d 228 (6th Cir. 2015)

B.L. v. Mahanoy Area School Dist., 964 F.3d 170, 175–176 (3d Cir. 2020)

Brandenburg v. Ohio, 395 U.S. 444 (1969)

Braunfeld v. Brown, 366 U.S. 599 (1961)

Brown v. Louisiana, 383 U.S. 131 (1966)

Brown v. Board of Education, 347 U.S. 483 (1954)

Buckley v. Valeo, 424 U.S. 1 (1976)

Chaplinsky v. New Hampshire, 315 U.S. 568 (1942)

Church of the Lukumi Babalu Aye, Inc. v. Hialeah, 508 U.S. 520 (1993)

Citizens United v. Federal Election Commission, 558 U.S. 310 (2010)

Cohen v. California, 403 U.S. 15 (1971)

Cox v. New Hampshire, 312 U.S. 569 (1941)

Cutter v. Wilkinson, 544 U.S. 709 (2005)

Edwards v. Aguillard, 482 U.S. 578 (1987)

Elonis v. United States, 135 S. Ct. 2001 (2015)

Engel v. Vitale, 370 U.S. 421 (1962)

Everson v. Board of Education, 330 U.S. 1 (1947)

FCC v. Pacifica Foundation, 438 U.S. 726 (1978)

FEC v. National Conservative Political Action Committee, 470 U.S. 480 (1985)

Fields v. Twitter, Inc., 200 F. Supp. 3d 964 (N.D. Ca. 2016)

Florida Star v. B.J.F., 491 U.S. 524 (1989)

Food Employees v. Logan Valley Plaza, Inc., 391 U.S. 308 (1968)

Forsyth County, Georgia v. Nationalist Movement, 505 U.S. 123 (1992)

Garrison v. Louisiana, 379 U.S. 64 (1964)

Gertz v. Robert Welch, Inc., 418 U.S. 323 (1974)

Ginzberg v. United States, 383 U.S. 463 (1966)

Gitlow v. New York, 268 U.S. 652 (1925)

Greenbelt Co-Operative Publishing Assn., Inc. v. Bresler, 398 U.S. 6 (1970)

Greer v. Spock, 424 U.S. 828 (1976)

Harte-Hanks Communications, Inc. v. Connaughton, 491 U.S. 657 (1989)

Hill v. Colorado, 530 U.S. 703 (2000)

Hurley v. Irish American Gay, Lesbian and Bisexual Group of Boston, Inc.,
    515 U.S. 557 (1995)

Hustler Magazine, Inc. v. Falwell, 485 U.S. 46, 51 (1988)

Janus v. American Federation of State, County, and Municipal Employees, Council 31, 138 S. Ct. 2448; 201 L. Ed. 2d 924 (2018)

Johnson v. Campbell, 332 F.3d 199 (3d Cir. 2003)

Justice for All v. Faulkner, 410 F.3d 760 (5th Cir. 2005)

Knight First Amendment Institute v. Trump, 928 F.3d 226 (2d Cir. 2019)

Kowalski v. Berkeley County Schools, 652 F.3d 565 (4th Cir. 2011), cert. denied, 132 S. Ct. 1095 (2012)

Lee v. Weisman, 505 U.S. 577 (1992)

Lemon v. Kurtzman, 403 U.S. 602 (1971)

Locke v. Davey, 540 U.S. 712 (2004)

Lynch v. Donnelly, 465 U.S. 668 (1984)

Mahanoy Area School Dist. v. B.L., No. 20-255, slip op. (Sup. Ct. June 23, 2021)

Masterpiece Cakeshop, Ltd. v. Colorado Civil Rights Commission, 138 S. Ct. 1719 (2018)

McCutcheon v. FEC, 572 U.S. 185, (2014)

McCreary County v. American Civil Liberties Union of Ky., 545 U.S. 844 (2005)

McCullen v. Coakley, 573 U.S. 464 (2014)

McDonald v. Chicago, 561 U.S. 742 (2010)

McIntyre v. Ohio Elections Commission, 514 U.S. 334 (1995)

Miami Herald Publishing Co. v. Tornillo, 418 U.S. 241 (1974)

Milkovich v. Lorain Journal Co., 497 U.S. 1 (1990)

Miller v. California, 413 U.S. 15, 24 (1973)

Morse v. Frederick, 551 U.S. 393 (2007)

NAACP v. Claiborne Hardware Co., 458 U.S. 886 (1982)

New York Times Co. v. U.S., 403 U.S. 713 (1971)

New York Times Co. v. Sullivan, 376 U.S. 254 (1964)

New York v. Ferber, 458 U.S. 747 (1982)

Obergefell v. Hodges, 576 U.S. 644 (2015)

Osborne v. Ohio, 495 U.S. 103 (1990)

Packingham v. North Carolina, 582 U.S., 137 S. Ct. 1730, 198 L. Ed. 2d 273 (2017)

Palko v. Connecticut, 302 U.S. 319 (1937)

Pickering v. Board of Education, 391 U.S. 563 (1968)

Pleasant Grove City v. Summum, 555 U.S. 460 (2009)

Red Lion Broadcasting Co. v. FCC, 395 U.S. 367 (1969)

Reno v. ACLU, 521 U.S. 844 (1997)

Roe v. Wade, 410 U.S. 113 (1973)

Schenck v. United States, 249 U.S. 47 (1919)

Shuttlesworth v. City of Birmingham, 180 So. 2d 114 (Ala. Crim. App. 1965)

Shuttlesworth v. City of Birmingham, 394 U.S. 147 (1969)

Skinner v. Railway Lab. Execs. Assn., 489 U.S. 602 (1989)

Snyder v. Phelps, 533 F. Supp. 2d 567 (D. Md. 2008)

Actual Malice Proof of actual malice requires evidence that the false statement was made with knowledge that it was false or with reckless disregard of whether it was false or not.

Amicus Curiae Brief A brief filed by a party who is not a litigant in the case, but who might be affected by the outcome of the case and files structured legal arguments in support of their position.

***Brandenburg* Incitement Test** According to the *Brandenburg* test, three criteria must be met to criminalize speech for inciting unlawful action by the audience: (1) There must be a determination that the speaker intended to incite violence or crime in the moment, not conditioned on a secondary event or passage of time; (2) The expressions and vocabulary used by the speaker must reveal that their purpose was to produce violence or crime. In other words, there must be an immediate call to action, either explicitly or implied; (3) There must be an objective likelihood that the speech would cause the audience to engage in violence or crime, directly and currently, taking no opportunity for rational reflection—so that there must be an explosive or combustible aspect to the situation. The *Brandenburg* test ensures that punishment will be levied only against speech that shows immediacy, gravity, and a high probability of agitating or provoking an audience to break the law.

Briefs Structured legal arguments written by attorneys in support of their client's position.

Clear and Present Danger A test used to identify speech that purportedly had a natural or probable effect of inciting illegal activity; this speech was then stripped of First Amendment protection. The test was largely replaced by the *Brandenburg* incitement test in 1969.

Compelling State Interest A substantial or important matter relating to the polity or government function that is within governmental powers to control.

Concurring Opinion A concurring opinion is written by a lower court judge or Supreme Court justice who agrees with the outcome of the case, but offers further commentary, or an alternate justification for the decision. Judges or justices may join in each other's concurring opinions.

Content Based A statute that is targeted at messaging is considered content based. In order for a content-based statute to withstand the withering glare of the First Amendment, it must satisfy the "strict scrutiny" test.

Content Neutral A content-neutral statute or regulation is one that is not directed at speech. A First Amendment content-neutral analysis proceeds along three lines of inquiry: (1) Is the statute directed at behavior that is important to a government function and unrelated to the suppression of speech? (2) Is the statute calibrated to that government interest so that it is not overly broad? (3) Even if the statute has a collateral effect on speech, are other means of communicating the message still available? (See: Content Based)

Constitutional Precedent Prior judicial decisions.

Criminal Syndicalism Laws Modeled after the Espionage Act of 1917, they were state laws that criminalized certain types of advocacy directed at political, industrial, or social change. Most such laws have been repealed.

Defamation: libel (written) or slander (oral) Defamatory statements must be false and must include three additional elements: (1) a statement by the defendant, the person alleged to have done the speaking or writing; (2) a statement of and concerning the plaintiff, the person complaining of the injury to reputation; and (3) publication, meaning communication, to at least one person.

Dissenting Opinion A dissenting opinion is written by a lower court judge or Supreme Court justice that disagrees with the majority opinion. Judges or justices may join in each other's dissenting opinions, or a judge or justice may write their own dissenting opinion, particularly when they dissent for different reasons.

Fairness Doctrine Until 1987, under Federal Communications Commission rules, licensed broadcast producers were obligated to follow the Fairness Doctrine, which required that they dedicate airtime to all sides of a controversial issue to allow for a balanced discussion of opposing views.

Enjoin Legal term: to forbid or prohibit. The court will enjoin an activity by issuing an injunction.

Express Advocacy Messages that are susceptible of no reasonable interpretation other than as an appeal to vote for or against a specific candidate are characterized as express advocacy and are subject to various contribution, expenditure, and disclosure requirements. All ads sponsored by candidates are, by definition, express advocacy.

Fighting Words Fighting words are words that by their very utterance, inflict injury or tend to incite an immediate breach of the peace. Essentially, fighting words can be analogized to assaultive speech. Fighting words provoke a reaction from the target, often toward the speaker. The words are inflammatory; they are calculated to bait the target into action and, for that reason, according to the Supreme Court, deserve no constitutional protection.

First Amendment Jurisprudence Court decisions and legal philosophy.

Hypodermic Needle Theory This communication theory analogizes communication to vaccinations—all recipients have the same response to the inoculation, or in this case, the communication. (See also: Magic Bullet Theory, Limited Effects Theory)

Injunction A court order prohibiting (enjoining) a particular activity. (See: Temporary Restraining Order)

Issue Advocacy Paid political communication that addresses public policy. It does not aim directly at affecting electoral outcomes. Instead, it aims to educate and persuade the public about broader subjects: gun control, the environment, education, and the like. Issue advocacy is generally free from contribution and expenditure limits and is subject to few disclosure requirements. From a First Amendment perspective, such political messaging deserves the highest protection. The underlying theory is that money spent on issue advocacy facilitates the exchange of ideas.

Limited Effects Theory A communication theory that recognizes that audiences are composed of individuals who listen to a message for different reasons, with different levels of attentiveness that elicit different kinds of responses. Further, individuals have the ability to process and understand messages based on intellect, culture, and education.

Litigants Parties to a lawsuit.

Magic Bullet Theory A communication theory that imagines the audience as monolithic, uncritical, and easily manipulated. It follows then that an easily manipulated audience, one that can be influenced by a magic bullet of words, is dangerous to the public welfare. (See: Hypodermic Needle Theory, Limited Effects Theory)

Political Speech Political speech is not merely communication transmitted during campaigns or among politicians, legislators, lobbyists, and activists. Any person expressing an opinion or engaging in debate on a matter of public concern, whether that be matters of policy, morality, economics, or the like, is engaging in political speech.

Prior Restraint An action that silences communication before the messenger has an opportunity to express their opinion or release information.

Narrow Tailoring Statutory analysis. A statute or regulation is narrowly tailored if it affects only as much speech as necessary to accomplish the statute's stated purpose. (See: Overbroad, Compelling State Interest)

Negligence Negligence is defined by the Cornell Law School Legal Information Institute as "A failure to behave with the level of care that someone of ordinary prudence would have exercised under the same circumstances. The behavior usually consists of actions, but can also consist of omissions when there is some duty to act."

Obscenity To be obscene, the communication must appeal to prurient interest, which is variously described as appealing to sexual desire or evidencing a degrading or unhealthy interest in sex. And what might be obscene in one community may be perfectly acceptable in another. States and communities can generally define obscenity by their own standards as long as statutes regulating such speech are well confined and do not restrict speech that otherwise exhibits serious literary, artistic, or scientific value.

Overbroad Statutory analysis. A statute or regulation is overbroad if it affects more speech than necessary to accomplish the statute's stated purpose. (See: Narrow Tailoring, Compelling State Interest)

Overturn or Overrule A decision that is overturned by the Supreme Court is no longer good law and cannot serve as controlling precedent.

Public Figure A person who has achieved general fame or notoriety or a celebrity who engages the public's attention in the community in which that individual lives, works, or plays.

Public Forum Public forums include streets and parks and public facilities. Public forums are generally open to speech and debate such that content-based restrictions directed at their use will be subject to a strict scrutiny analysis. They are, in essence, held in trust for public use. However, that use is not absolute and can be subject to meaningful content-neutral limitations regarding time of day, location, and even means of expression.

Right to Know A corollary to the right to speak, belonging to the audience experiencing the communication. Philosophy espoused by Justice Louis Brandeis and Justice Hugo Black. They each asserted that speaking freely and hearing uncensored views are inseparable elements of the whole and, as such, must be protected in all but the most extreme circumstances.

Safe Harbor Rule The Safe Harbor Rule demarcates the time during which indecent speech may be legally (safely) broadcast. According to the Federal Communications Commission's Safe Harbor Rule, programming and advertising in legacy broadcast media that is inappropriate for children and families can only be broadcast between 10:00 p.m. and 6:00 a.m.

Scarcity Rationale The rationale employed by the government to impose regulations upon legacy broadcast media. The rationale is based on the limited availability of radio waves and electromagnetic signals. There are only a finite number of radio waves and electromagnetic signals from which legacy broadcast radio and television stations can operate. The purpose of the guidelines is to preserve the marketplace of ideas and encourage a diversity of viewpoints, as well as to enhance educational programming and protect children from indecent content. (See: Fairness Doctrine)

Strict Scrutiny The strict scrutiny test requires that a statute targeted at speech must be designed to protect a compelling government interest. Further, the statute must be so narrowly tailored it employs the least intrusive means of restricting speech to achieve the government objective. (See: Compelling State Interest, Narrow Tailoring)

Symbolic Speech Ideas communicated in a medium other than the spoken word or words printed on a page.

Temporary Restraining Order A short-term injunction to prevent irreparable harm until a court hearing can be held on the merits of the case.

True Threat A true threat induces a sense of dread in the victim such that they fear violence or death. The unconstitutional nature of a true threat focuses on the language used and the terror it induces, even if the action threatened is never commenced and even if there was never any real intent by the speaker to actuate the threat.

Viewpoint Discrimination From a First Amendment perspective, viewpoint discrimination is the worst kind of content-based restriction, because it targets only one side of the debate. The disfavored side is muted, but the favored side is allowed full expression.

Writ of Certiorari A petition addressed to an appellate court or to the Supreme Court asking it to review the decision of a lower court. Certiorari is the common method for cases to be heard before the U.S. Supreme Court.

1. A HISTORY LESSON

1. Mark E. Peterson, *Woodrow Wilson Quotes*, Woodrow Wilson Presidential Library and Museum, https://www.woodrowwilson.org/blog/2019/1/21/woodrow-wilson-quotes (last visited Apr. 30, 2020).

2. "The Founding Fathers: Virginia," *National Archives—America's Founding Documents*, https://www.archives.gov/founding-docs/founding-fathers-virginia (last visited Aug. 2, 2020).

3. Cecelia M. Kenyon, "The Papers of George Mason," *New York Times*, July 5, 1970, at 137–38.

4. Jeff Broadwater, *George Mason: Forgotten Founder* (Chapel Hill: University of North Carolina Press, 2006), 184.

5. Letter from George Mason to George Mason Jr., May 20, 1787, Online Library of Liberty (1977), available at https://oll.libertyfund.org/.

6. "Discontent with the Articles of Confederation," Lehrman Institute, *History—Founders*, https://lehrmaninstitute.org/history/constitution-revised.html (last visited Aug. 3, 2020) (citing *The Records of the Federal Convention of 1787*, ed. Max Farrand [New Haven, CT: Yale University Press, 1911], 94–95, see https://lehrmaninstitute.org/history/constitution-revised.html#discontent.

7. Ibid., 43 (citing Gordon S. Wood, *The Creation of the American Republic, 1776–1787* [Chapel Hill: University of North Carolina Press and Omohundro Institute, 1969], 467.

8. "Constitution of the United States—A History," *National Archives—America's Founding Documents*, https://www.archives.gov/founding-docs/more-perfect-union (last visited Aug. 1, 2020).

9. Robert K. Wright Jr., and Morris J. MacGregor Jr., *Soldier-Statesmen of the Constitution* (Totnes, Devon, UK: University Press of the Pacific, 2004), 79–81, 154–55, available at https://history.army.mil/books/RevWar/ss/ss-fm.htm.

10. Lillian Cunningham, "Constitutional Podcast is Here! Episode 1: 'Framed,'" *Washington Post*, July 24, 2017, https://www.washingtonpost.com/news/on-leadership/wp/2017/07/24/constitutional-podcast-is-here-episode-01-framed/.

11. Reference to letter from George Washington to James Madison, "Constitution of the United States—A History."

12. "Constitution of the United States—A History."

13. "Discontent with the Articles of Confederation" (citing Fritz Hirschfeld, *George Washington and Slavery: A Documentary Portrayal* [Columbia: University of Missouri Press, 1997], 171.

14. Max Farrand, *The Fathers of the Constitution: A Chronicle of the Establishment of the Union* (London: Forgotten Books, 2018; orig. 1921), 109.

15. "Discontent with the Articles of Confederation" (citing Jack N. Rakove, *Original Meanings: Politics and Ideas in the Making of the Constitution* [New York: Knopf Doubleday, 1997], 58–59).

16. "The Rising Sun Armchair (George Washington's Chair)," https://www .ushistory.org/more/sun.htm (last visited Aug. 4, 2020).

17. Farrand, *The Fathers of the Constitution*, 109.

18. "Discontent with the Articles of Confederation" (citing Forrest McDonald, *E Pluribus Unum: The Formation of the American Republic, 1776–1790*, [New York: Houghton Mifflin, 1965], 319–20).

19. *James Madison*, WhiteHouse.gov, https://www.whitehouse.gov/about-the -white-house/presidents/james-madison (last visited August 3, 2020).

20. "Discontent with the Articles of Confederation."

21. Ibid. (citing Max Farrand, *The Fathers of the Constitution*, 89), available at https://www.gutenberg.org/files/3032/3032-h/3032-h.htm.

22. "Constitution of the United States—A History."

23. "Constitution Questions and Answers," *National Archives, America's Founding Documents*, https://www.archives.gov/founding-docs/constitution -q-and-a (last visited Aug. 2, 2020).

24. "George Mason: The Reluctant Founder," *Center for Civic Education*, https://civiced.org/lesson-plans/mason (last visited on Aug. 2, 2020).

25. Broadwater, *George Mason*, 195.

26. *History—Essays, Bill of Rights*, Lehrman Institute, https://lehrmaninstitute .org/history/BillofRights.html (citing Richard Brookhiser, *James Madison* [New York: Basic Books, 2011] 70 (last visited Aug. 4, 2020).

27. *The Federalist*, No. 84 (Alexander Hamilton).

28. "Constitution of the United States—A History."

29. *History—Founders*, "The Election of 1800–1801," Lehrman Institute (citing letter from Thomas Jefferson to John Adams, Nov. 13, 1787), https:// lehrmaninstitute.org/history/constitution-revised.html, n. 343 (last visited August 3, 2020).

30. *History—Essays*, "Bill of Rights," Lehrman Institute, https:// lehrmaninstitute.org/history/BillofRights.html#Madison.

31. *History—Founders*, "The Election of 1800–1801," (citing Richard Labunski, "James Madison and the Struggle for the Bill of Rights," n. 201 [2006]).

32. U.S. Constitution, Amendments I–X.

33. Vincent Blasi, *The Checking Value in First Amendment Theory*, 3 *American Bar Foundation Research Journal* 521, 524 (1977).

2. FOUNDATIONS AND BUILDING BLOCKS

1. Nomination of Robert H. Bork to Be Associate Justice of The Supreme Court of The United States, Before the S. Comm. on the Judiciary, 100th Cong. (1987), https://www.c-span.org/search/basic/?query=bork+nomination.

2. Ethan Bonner, "A Conservative Whose Supreme Court Bid Set the Senate Afire," *New York Times*, December 19, 2012, https://www.nytimes.com/2012/12/20/us/robert-h-bork-conservative-jurist-dies-at-85.html.

3. Jane Coaston, "Borking, Explained: Why a Failed Supreme Court Nomination in 1987 Matters," *Vox*, September 27, 2018, https://www.vox.com/2018/9/26/17896126/bork-kavanaugh-supreme-court-conservatives-republicans.

4. Bonner, "A Conservative Whose Supreme Court Bid Set the Senate Afire."

5. Kenneth B. Noble, "New Views Emerge of Bork's Role in Watergate Dismissals," *New York Times*, July 26, 1987, 23.

6. "Robert H. Bork, 47," *Indiana Law Journal* 1 (1971): 27–28.

7. Ibid.

8. Ibid.

9. Manuel Miranda, "The Original Borking," *OpinionJournal*, August 24, 2005, https://web.archive.org/web/20051028035123/http:/www.opinionjournal.com/nextjustice/?id=110007149.

10. Linda Greenhouse, "Bork's Nomination Is Rejected, 58–42: Reagan 'Saddened,'" *New York Times*, October 24, 1987.

11. Miranda, "The Original Borking."

12. "Borking," Merriam-Webster, https://www.merriam-webster.com/dictionary/borking.

13. Lillian Cunningham, "Episode 15 of the Constitutional Podcast: 'Privacy,'" *Washington Post*, January 15, 2018, https://www.washingtonpost.com/news/on-leadership/wp/2018/01/15/episode-15-of-the-constitutional-podcast-privacy/.

14. James M. Landis, "Mr. Justice Brandeis and the Harvard Law," *Harvard Law Review* 55 (1941): 184.

15. *Whitney v. California*, 274 U.S. 357, 375 (1927) (Brandeis, J., concurring).

16. Thomas I. Emerson, "Toward a General Theory of the First Amendment," *Yale Law Journal* 72 (1966): 879, https://digitalcommons.law.yale.edu/cgi/viewcontent.cgi?article=3769&context=fss_papers.

17. William A. Carroll, "Natural Law and Freedom of Communication Under the Fourteenth Amendment," *Notre Dame Law Review* 42 (1967): 219, 230–31.

18. This specific metaphor was first used by Justice William O. Douglas in *United States v. Rumely*, 345 U.S. 41, 56 (1953).

19. 250 U.S. 616, 630 (1919).

3. THE ROAD TO THE SUPREME COURT

1. *Palko v. Connecticut*, 302 U.S. 319, 327 (1937).

2. *Roe v. Wade*, 410 U.S. 113 (1973).

3. David Harris et al., "Legal Abortion 1970–1971—The New York City Experience," *American Journal of Public Health* 63 (1973): 409, 410.

4. Shira Schoenberg, "Anti-Abortion Plaintiff Eleanor McCullen Says Clinic Protests Are About 'Surrounding Women With Love,'" *MassLive*, January 7, 2019, https://www.masslive.com/politics/2014/06/anti-abortion_plaintiff_eleano.html.

5. *McCullen v. Coakley*, 573 U.S. 464, 469 (2014).

6. *Gitlow v. New York*, 268 U.S. 652 (1925).

7. *McDonald v. Chicago*, 561 U.S. 742, 754 (2010).

4. SYMBOLICALLY SPEAKING

1. *Cohen v. California*, 403 U.S. 15, 25 (1971).

2. Military Selective Service Act, 50 U.S.C. para. 3801 et seq. (formerly 50 U.S.C.A. para. 451 et seq.).

3. See Michael S. Foley, "Confronting the War Machine: Draft Resistance During the Vietnam War" (Spring 1999) (unpublished PhD dissertation, University of New Hampshire), https://scholars.unh.edu/dissertation/2068.

4. Ibid., 42.

5. "Draft Card Burners Beaten up in Boston," *Transcript* (North Adams, MA), March 31, 1966, 1.

6. Richard Gross, "Draft Card Burner Shocked by Ruling," *Sun* (Lowell, MA), May 28, 1968, 8.

7. Foley, "Confronting the War Machine," 86.

8. "Draft Card Burner Changes His Mind," *Daily Reporter* (Wellsville, NY), November 16, 1968, 5.

9. *Tinker v. Des Moines Independent Community School Dist.*, 393 U.S. 503 (1969).

10. *Brown v. Louisiana*, 383 U.S. 131 (1966).

11. *United States v. Grace*, 461 U.S. 171 (1983); *Food Employees v. Logan Valley Plaza, Inc.*, 391 U.S. 308 (1968).

12. *NAACP v. Claiborne Hardware Co.*, 458 U.S. 886 (1982).

13. *United States v. O'Brien*, 391 U.S. 367, 376 (1968).

14. Ibid., 376.

15. "Draft Card Burner Changes His Mind."

16. Randall P. Bezanson, "Story One: The Jacket" (*Cohen v. California*), in *Speech Stories: How Free Can Speech Be?* 7 (1998): 7–35.

17. Daniel A. Farber, "Civilizing Public Discourse: An Essay on Professor Bickel, Justice Harlan, and the Enduring Significance of *Cohen v. California*," *Duke University Law Journal* (1980): 283, 286.

18. *Cohen v. California*, 403 U.S. 15, 17 (1971).

19. Farber, "Civilizing Public Discourse," 303 n.114.

20. *Cohen v. California*, 403 U.S. 26.

21. Ibid., 22.

22. Eugene Volokh, "Opinion: What Ever Happened to Cohen, of *Cohen v. California*," *Washington Post*, May 4, 2016, https://www.washingtonpost.com/news/volokh-conspiracy/wp/2016/05/04/what-ever-happened-to-cohen-of-cohen-v-california/.

23. Franklyn S. Haiman, "Nonverbal Communication and the First Amendment: The Rhetoric of the Streets Revisited?" *Quarterly Journal of Speech* 68 (1982): 371, 382.

24. *Cohen v. California*, 403 U.S. 25–26.

25. See David P. O'Brien, "The Development of Propositional Reasoning from the Perspective of a System of Inference Rules" (Spring 1999) (unpublished PhD dissertation, Order No. 8210538, Temple University, 1981), Ann Arbor ProQuest LLC, March 21, 2021.

26. David B. Green, "This Day in Jewish History | 1971: Court Finds for Jacket in 'Fuck the Draft' Case," *Haaratz*, June 7, 2016, updated: April 10, 2018, https://www.haaretz.com/jewish/.premium-1971-court-finds-for-jacket-in-fuck-the-draft-case-1.5392245.

27. "Campaign '84; NEWLN: Convention Miscellany," *United Press International*, August 8, 1984, https://www.upi.com/Archives/1984/08/08/Campaign-84NEWLNConvention-miscellany/4704460785600/.

28. "Dallas Fire Department Planning for Republican National Convention Security, 1984," City of Dallas, https://dallascityhall.com/government/citysecretary/archives/Pages/Archives_2014-004.aspx (last visited Aug. 7, 2020).

29. Jane Perlez, "Liberal Democrat from Queens," *New York Times*, July 13, 1984, A1.

30. Ralph Blumenthal, "When the Press Vetted Geraldine Ferraro," *New York Times*, "City Room," September 4, 2008, https://cityroom.blogs.nytimes.com/2008/09/04/when-the-press-vetted-geraldine-ferraro/.

31. Wayne King, "Dallas Is Girding Delegates and Demonstrations," *New York Times*, August 13, 1984, A10.

32. *Texas v. Johnson*, 491 U.S. 397, 400 (1989).

33. "99 Arrested in Dallas Protest," *New York Times*, August 23, 1984, A26.

34. "Man Given Year in Jail for Burning U.S. Flag," *New York Times*, December 15, 1984, 8.

35. *Texas v. Johnson*, 491 U.S. 399.

36. Ibid.

37. Ibid.

38. Ibid., 400.

39. Ibid., 406 (citations omitted).

40. "Man Given Year in Jail for Burning U.S. Flag."

41. Linda Greenhouse, "Justices to Rule Whether Burning the Flag Is Legal," *New York Times*, October 18, 1988, A27.

42. *Texas v. Johnson*, 491 U.S. 403.

43. Ibid.

44. Ibid., 408.

45. Ibid.

46. Ibid.

47. Ibid., 429.

48. Ibid., 422.

49. Ibid., 432.

50. Ibid., 414 (citations and internal quotes omitted).

51. "4 Are Held in Burning of 3 Flags to Test Law," *New York Times*, October 31, 1989, A25.

52. *United States v. Haggerty*, F. Supp. 415 (W.D. Wash. 1990).

53. 496 U.S. 310 (1990).

54. Neil A. Lewis, "Arguments on Flag Burning Heard," *New York Times*, May 15, 1990, A16.

55. Nicholas Bogel-Burroughs, "Cleveland Is Paying $225,000 to a Man Who Burned the American Flag," *New York Times*, June 14, 2019, https://www.nytimes.com/2019/06/14/us/flag-burning-cleveland.html.

56. *United States v. Eichman*, 496 U.S. 310 (1990).

57. "Two Centuries of Burning Flags, a Few Years of Blowing Smoke," *New York Times*, December 17, 1995, 7.

5. THE TROUBLING SOUND OF SILENCE

1. *Ginzberg v. United States*, 383 U.S. 463, 498 (1966).

2. News Release, Dept. of Defense, "Name of Technical Sergeant Richard B. Fitzgibbon to Be Added to the Vietnam Veterans Memorial" (November 6, 1998), https://www.archives.gov/research/military/vietnam-war/casualty-statistics (last visited Nov. 17, 2019).

3. See "Vietnam War U.S. Military Fatal Casualty Statistics," National Archives, https://www.archives.gov/research/military/vietnam-war/casualty-statistics (last visited Nov. 17, 2019).

4. Jake Kobrick, "The Pentagon Papers in the Federal Courts" (2d ed. 2019), 28, https://www.fjc.gov/history/cases/famous-federal-trials/us-v-new-york-times-pentagon-papers.

5. Ibid., 29.

6. Ibid.

7. Floyd Abrams, "The Pentagon Papers a Decade Later," *New York Times Magazine*, June 7, 1981, 22.

8. Ibid.

9. Ibid.

10. Ibid.

11. Kobrick, "The Pentagon Papers in the Federal Courts," 4.

12. Ibid., 8.

13. Ibid., 30–31.

14. Melville B. Nimmer, "National Secrets v. Free Speech: The Issues Left Undecided in the Ellsberg Case," *Stanford Law Review* 26 (1974): 311, 312–13.

15. Douglas O. Linder, "The Pentagon Papers (Daniel Ellsberg) Trial: An Account," *Famous Trials*, https://www.famous-trials.com/ellsberg/273-home (last visited Aug. 20, 2020).

16. Ibid.

17. Ibid.

18. Malcolm Gladwell, "Daniel Ellsberg, Edward Snowden, and the Modern Whistle-Blower," *New Yorker*, December 11, 2016, https://www.newyorker.com/magazine/2016/12/19/daniel-ellsberg-edward-snowden-and-the-modern-whistle-blower.

19. Lindner, "The Pentagon Papers (Daniel Ellsberg) Trial."

20. Kobrick, "The Pentagon Papers in the Federal Courts," 35.

21. Ben Bradlee Jr., "The Deceit and Conflict Behind the Leak of the Pentagon Papers," *New Yorker*, April 8, 2021, https://www.newyorker.com/news/american-chronicles/the-deceit-and-conflict-behind-the-leak-of-the-pentagon-papers.

22. Lindner, "The Pentagon Papers (Daniel Ellsberg) Trial."

23. Janny Scott, "Now It Can Be Told: How Neil Sheehan Got the Pentagon Papers," *New York Times*, January 7, 2021, https://www.nytimes.com/2021/01/07/us/pentagon-papers-neil-sheehan.html.

24. Ibid.

25. Abrams, "The Pentagon Papers a Decade Later."

26. Nancy Wartik, "The Pentagon Papers Team Tells How the Times Defied Censorship," *New York Times*, January 20, 2018, https://www.nytimes.com/2018/01/20/reader-center/history-of-pentagon-papers.html.

27. See Betsy Wade, "Herstory," http://herstory.rjionline.org/032.html (last visited Aug. 20, 2020).

28. Wartik, "The Pentagon Papers Team Tells How the Times Defied Censorship."

29. Abrams, "The Pentagon Papers a Decade Later."

30. Kobrick, "The Pentagon Papers in the Federal Courts," 31.

31. Pat Peterson, "The Truth about Tonkin," *Naval History* 22 (2008), https://www.usni.org/magazines/naval-history-magazine/2008/february/truth-about-tonkin.

32. Scott, "Now It Can Be Told."

33. Kobrick, "The Pentagon Papers in the Federal Courts," 96–105.

34. Neil Sheehan, "Vietnam Archive: Pentagon Study Traces 3 Decades of Growing U.S. Involvement," *New York Times*, June 13, 1971, 1.

35. David W. Dunlap, "Supreme Court Allows Publication of Pentagon Papers," *New York Times*, June 30, 2016, https://www.nytimes.com/2016/06/30/insider/1971-supreme-court-allows-publication-of-pentagon-papers.html.

36. See Hedrick Smith, "Mitchell Seeks to Halt Series on Vietnam, but *Times* Refuses," *New York Times* on the Web, June 15, 1971, https://archive.nytimes.com/www.nytimes.com/books/97/04/13/reviews/papers-mitchell.html.

37. Max Frankel, "Court Step Likely: Return of Documents Asked in Telegram to Publisher," *New York Times*, June 14, 1971, 1.

38. *Frontline*, "Washington's Culture of Secret Sources and Leaks," https://www.pbs.org/wgbh/pages/frontline/newswar/part1/frankel.html.

39. Kevin Casey, "Till Death Do Us Part: Prepublication Review in the Intelligence Community," *Columbia Law Review*, 115:2 (2015): 417–60.

40. Kobrick, "The Pentagon Papers in the Federal Courts," 5.

41. "The Vietnam Papers," *New York Times*, June 21, 1971, 28.

42. Abrams, "The Pentagon Papers a Decade Later."

43. Ibid., 34–35.

44. 403 U.S. 713, 714 (1971).

45. Abrams, "The Pentagon Papers a Decade Later."

46. Ibid.

47. Ibid.

48. *New York Times Co. v. United States*, 403 U.S. 713, 717 (1971).

49. Ibid., 715.

50. Ibid., 725, 729 (Brennan, J., Stewart, P., concurring).

51. Ibid., 753 (Harlan, J., dissenting).

52. Ibid., 750 (Burger, J., dissenting).

53. Abrams, "The Pentagon Papers a Decade Later."

54. National Archives, "Pentagon Papers," https://www.archives.gov/research/pentagon-papers (last visited Dec. 25, 2019).

55. Charlie Savage, "Manning Is Acquitted of Aiding the Enemy," *New York Times*, July 20, 2013, https://www.nytimes.com/2013/07/31/us/bradley-manning-verdict.html.

56. Steve Fishman, "Bradley Manning's Army of One," *New Yorker*, July 1, 2011, https://nymag.com/news/features/bradley-manning-2011-7/.

57. David E. Pozen, "The Leaky Leviathan: Why the Government Condemns and Condones Unlawful Disclosures of Information," *Harvard Law Review* 127 (2013): 512.

58. Ibid., 513.

59. Lindner, "The Pentagon Papers (Daniel Ellsberg) Trial."

60. Ibid.

61. Ibid.

62. Egil Krogh, "The Break-In That History Forgot," *New York Times*, June 30, 2007, https://www.nytimes.com/2007/06/30/opinion/30krogh.html.

63. Kobrick, "The Pentagon Papers in the Federal Courts," 108; "Text of Ruling by Judge in Ellsberg Case," *New York Times*, May 12, 1973, 14.

64. Lida Maxwell, "Whistleblower, Traitor, Soldier, Queer?" *Yale Review*, January 2018 https://yalereview.yale.edu/whistleblower-traitor-soldier-queer (last visited Aug. 22, 2020).

65. "Bradley Manning's Army of One."

66. "The Chelsea Manning Case: A Timeline," ACLU, May 9, 2017, https://www.aclu.org/blog/free-speech/employee-speech-and-whistleblowers/chelsea-manning-case-timeline.

67. Maxwell, "Whistleblower, Traitor, Soldier, Queer?"

68. Charlie Savage and Emmarie Huetteman, "Manning Sentenced to 35 Years for a Pivotal Leak of U.S. Files," *New York Times*, August 21, 2013, https://www.nytimes.com/2013/08/22/us/manning-sentenced-for-leaking-government-secrets.html.

69. Charlie Savage, "Chelsea Manning to Be Released Early as Obama Commutes Sentence," *New York Times*, January 17, 2017, https://www.nytimes.com/2017/01/17/us/politics/obama-commutes-bulk-of-chelsea-mannings-sentence.html.

70. Maxwell, "Whistleblower, Traitor, Soldier, Queer?"

71. Jacy Fortin, "Chelsea Manning Ordered Back to Jail for Refusal to Testify in WikiLeaks Inquiry," *New York Times*, May 16, 2019, https://www.nytimes.com/2019/05/16/us/chelsea-manning-jail.html.

72. Matthew Barakat, "Judge Orders Chelsea Manning Be Freed from Jail," NBC Boston, March 12, 2020, https://www.nbcboston.com/news/national-international/judge-orders-chelsea-manning-released-from-jail/2090134/.

73. https://wikileaks.org/What-is-WikiLeaks.html.

74. Janet Reitman, "Snowden and Greenwald: The Men Who Leaked the Secrets," *Rolling Stone*, December 4, 2013, https://www.rollingstone.com/culture/culture-news/snowden-and-greenwald-the-men-who-leaked-the-secrets-104970/.

75. See Criminal Complaint at 1, *United States v. Snowden*, 806 F.3d 1030 (10th Cir. 2015) (No. 15-1107).

6. POLITICALLY SPEAKING

1. "A Testament of Hope: The Essential Writings and Speeches of Martin Luther King, Jr, *Tennessee Tribune*, February 4, 2008.

2. John Blake, "'Most-Hated,' Anti-Gay Preacher Once Fought for Civil Rights," CNN, May 14, 2010, http://www.cnn.com/2010/US/05/05/hate.preacher/index.html.

3. Dan Gardner, "Phelps and the Value of Hate Speech," https://www.dangardner.ca/article/fred-phelps-and-the-value-of-hate-speech (last visited Aug. 15, 2020).

4. *Brown v. Board of Education*, 347 U.S. 483 (1954).

5. Theodore A. Hiff, "Linda Brown: A Symbol Lost in the Crowd," *Hutchinson News*, May 12, 1974, 85.

6. Napp Nazworth, "Before Fred Phelps Preached Hate, He Was a Civil Rights Hero," *Christian Post*, March 20, 2014, https://www.christianpost.com/news/before-fred-phelps-preached-hate-he-was-a-civil-rights-hero.html.

7. Steven Petrow, "Fred Phelps Preached Hate, But His Death Is No Reason to Celebrate," *Washington Post*, March 20, 2014, https://www.washingtonpost.com/lifestyle/style/fred-phelps-preached-hate-but-his-death-is-no-reason-to-celebrate/2014/03/20/0fd06408-b050-11e3-95e8-39bef8e9a48b_story.html.

8. Fred Mann, "2006: What Led Westboro's Fred Phelps to His Beliefs and Actions?" *Wichita Eagle*, December 18, 2012, https://www.kansas.com/latest-news/article1104966.html.

9. Michael Paulson, "For Antigay Church, Losing Its Cause Before Its Founder," *New York Times*, March 22, 2014, https://www.nytimes.com/2014/03/23/us/for-antigay-church-losing-its-cause-before-its-founder-fred-phelps.html.

10. "Salisbury Temperature History March 2006," https://weatherspark.com/h/m/22683/2006/3/Historical-Weather-in-March-2006-in-Salisbury-Maryland-United-States#Figures-Temperature.

11. *Snyder v. Phelps*, 533 F. Supp. 2d 567, 572 (Md. 2008).

12. Ibid., 573.

13. *Snyder v. Phelps*, 562 U.S. 443 (2011).

14. Ibid., 448–49, 451 (citations and internal quotation marks omitted).

15. Ibid., 455 (citations omitted).

16. Ibid., 475.

17. See generally *New York Times Co. v. United States*, 403 U.S. 713, 713 (1971).

18. See generally *Brandenburg v. Ohio*, 395 U.S. 444 (1969).

19. See generally *Cohen v. California*, 403 U.S. 15 (1971).

20. See generally *Hustler Magazine, Inc. v. Falwell*, 485 U.S. 46 (1988).

21. Romain Patterson, Opinion, "Let Westboro Baptist Have Their Hate Speech. We'll Smother it with Peace," *Washington Post*, March 3, 2011, https://www.washingtonpost.com/opinions/let-westboro-baptist-have-their-hate-speech-well-smother-it-with-peace/2011/03/03/ABXcNoN_story.html.

22. Katherine A. Ritts, "The Constitutionality of 'Let Them Rest in Peace' Bills: Can Government Say 'Not Today, Fred' to Demonstrations at Funeral Ceremonies?" *Syracuse Law Review* 58 (2007): 137, 145

7. WARNING! DANGEROUS SPEECH AHEAD

1. "The Churchill Spirit in His Own Words," *New York Times*, August 2, 1964, https://timesmachine.nytimes.com/timesmachine/1964/08/02/109567478.html?pageNumber=1.

2. Office of the Historian, "U.S. Entry into World War I, 1917," https://history.state.gov/milestones/1914-1920/wwi (last visited Aug. 29, 2020).

3. Ibid.

4. Caryn E. Neumann, "Committee on Public Information," Middle Tennessee State University Free Speech Center (2009), https://www.mtsu.edu /first-amendment/article/1179/committee-on-public-information.

5. Michael Duffy, "Primary Documents—U.S. Espionage Act, 15 June 1917," Firstworldwar.com (August 22, 2009), http://www.firstworldwar.com/source /espionageact.htm.

6. Pub.L. 65–150, 40 Stat. 553 (originally enacted as of May 16, 1918, repealed 1921).

7. Joseph Russomanno, "Cause and Effect: The Free Speech Transformation as Scientific Revolution," *Communication Law and Policy* 20 (2015): 213, 223.

8. Michael R. Levinson, "Clear and Present Danger During World War I," *Litigation* 35:4 (Summer 2009): 47.

9. Russomanno, "Cause and Effect," 223.

10. *Schenck v. United States*, 249 U.S. 47, 51 (1919).

11. Levinson, "Clear and Present Danger During World War I," 48.

12. Thomas Healy, *The Great Dissent: How Oliver Wendell Holmes Changed His Mind—and Changed the History of Free Speech in America* (New York: Holt, Metropolitan Books, 2013), 82.

13. Levinson, "Clear and Present Danger During World War I," 49.

14. Healy, *The Great Dissent*, 16.

15. *Schenck v. United States*, 249 U.S. 47, 52 (1919).

16. Emily Bazelon, "Better Judgment," *New York Times*, June 17, 2015, https:// www.nytimes.com/2015/06/21/magazine/better-judgment.html.

17. Russomanno, "Cause and Effect," 218.

18. See generally Zosa Szajkowski, "Double Jeopardy: The Abrams Case of 1919," *American Jewish Archives* 23 (1971): 6.

19. Melvin I. Urofsky, "The Case of the Gentle Anarchist: *Abrams v. United States (1919)*," in *Supreme Decisions: Great Constitutional Cases and Their Impact* (New York: Routledge, 2012), Vol. 2: 209.

20. Richard Polenberg, "Jacob Abrams," in Melvin I. Urofsky, ed., *100 Americans Making Constitutional History: A Biographical History* (Thousand Oaks, CA: Sage, CQ Press, 2004), 1.

21. Ibid.

22. Paul Avrich, "Mollie Steimer: An Anarchist Life," in *Anarchist Portraits* (Princeton, NJ: Princeton University Press, 1988), 214.

23. *Abrams v. United States*, 250 U.S. 616 (1919) (internal quotation marks omitted).

24. Avrich, "Mollie Steimer," 214–19.

25. Ibid.

26. "The Case of Mollie Steimer, Jacob Abrams, Hyman Lachowsky and Samuel Lipman," Libcom.org (Mar. 11, 2008), https://libcom.org/forums/history /case-mollie-steimer-jacob-abrams-hyman-lachowsky-samuel-lipman-11032008.

27. Richard Polenberg, "Progressivism and Anarchism: Judge Henry D. Clayton and the Abrams Trial," *Law and History Review* 3 (1985): 397, 404.

28. Ibid., 407.

29. *Abrams v. United States*, 250 U.S. 616 (1919).

30. Polenberg, "Progressivism and Anarchism," 1–3.

31. Ibid.

32. Anthony Lewis, "Abroad and at Home: Freedom to Disagree," *New York Times*, December 31, 1987, A27.

33. *Abrams v. United States*, 250 U.S. 624 (Holmes, J., dissenting).

34. Ibid., 630.

35. Healy, *The Great Dissent*, 14–15.

36. Russomanno, "Cause and Effect," 243.

37. Ibid., 236–23.

38. Ibid., 237–42.

39. *Abrams v. United States*, 250 U.S. 630

40. Vincent Blasi, "The First Amendment and the Ideal of Civic Courage: The Brandeis Opinion in *Whitney v. California*," *William and Mary Law Review* 29 (1988): 653, 655.

41. Repealed by California Stats. 1991, c. 186 (A.B. 436).

42. Peter G. Renstrom, "Charlotte Anita Whitney," in Urofsky, ed., *100 Americans Making Constitutional History*, 205–07.

43. Ibid.

44. Ibid.

45. *Whitney v. California*, 274 U.S. 357, 363 (1927).

46. Ibid., 360.

47. Renstrom, "Charlotte Anita Whitney," 205–07.

48. Ronald K. L. Collins and David M. Skover, "Curious Concurrence: Justice Brandeis's Vote in *Whitney v. California*," *Supreme Court Review* (2005): 333, 349.

49. Ibid., 363.

50. Renstrom, "Charlotte Anita Whitney," 205–7.

51. *Whitney*, 274 U.S. 371 (citations omitted).

52. Ibid., 379.

53. Russomanno, "Cause and Effect," 245–50.

54. *Whitney*, 274 U.S. 375.

55. Ibid., 377.

56. Russomanno, "Cause and Effect," 255.

57. Collins and Skover, "Curious Concurrence," 334.

8. ADVOCACY VS. INCITEMENT?

1. "Read Trump's Jan. 6 Speech, A Key Part of Impeachment Trial," NPR.org, February 10, 2021, https://www.npr.org/2021/02/10/966396848/read-trumps-jan-6-speech-a-key-part-of-impeachment-trial.

2. "Kukluxer Sentenced," Morgantown, WV, *Dominion News*, January 6, 1967, 2.

3. *Brandenburg v. Ohio*, 395 U.S. 444, 446 n.1 (1969).

4. Ibid., 446.

5. "Accused Klan Chief Bound Over," Middletown, OH, *Journal Newspaper*, August 14, 1964, 2.

6. "Conviction of Klansman Upheld," Marysville, CA, *Appeal Democrat*, January 25, 1968, 26.

7. "Ohio Law Target of Klan Appeal," Middletown, OH, *Journal Newspaper*, February 28, 1969, 9.

8. *Brandenburg v. Ohio*, 395 U.S. 447.

9. *Gitlow v. New York*, 268 U.S. 652, 673 (1925).

10. *NAACP v. Claiborne Hardware Co.*, 458 U.S. 886, 899 (1982).

11. Emilye Crosby, *A Little Taste of Freedom: The Black Freedom Struggle in Claiborne County, Mississippi* (Chapel Hill: University of North Carolina Press, 2005), 130.

12. *NAACP v. Claiborne Hardware Co.*, 458 U.S. 902.

13. Crosby, *A Little Taste of Freedom*, 139 (citations omitted).

14. 458 U.S. 886 (1982).

15. Stuart Taylor, "Port Gibson, Miss., Awaits Ruling on 60's Boycott," *New York Times*, December 7, 1981, B16.

16. Crosby, *A Little Taste of Freedom*, 130 (citations omitted).

17. *NAACP v. Claiborne Hardware Co.*, 458 U.S. 927–28.

18. Ibid., 910 (1982).

19. Ibid., 929.

20. Dustin Volz, "Officials Say 2020 Election is Most Secure in History, but Plead for Patience," *Wall Street Journal*, November 3, 2020, https://www.wsj.com /livecoverage/trump-biden-election-day-2020/card/Cp6Qn4nfW4MfEBymCHgK.

21. Daniel Funk, "Here's How We Know Trump's Repeated Claim of a Landslide Victory is Wrong," *Politifact*, January 6, 2021, https://www.politifact .com/factchecks/2021/jan/07/donald-trump/trump-clings-fantasy-landslide -victory-egging-supp/.

22. Daniel Dale, "Fact Check: Trump Delivers the Most Dishonest Speech of His Presidency as Biden Closes in on Victory," CNN, November 6, 2020, https:// www.cnn.com/2020/11/05/politics/fact-check-trump-speech-thursday-election -rigged-stolen/index.html.

23. Jim Rutenberg, et al., "77 Days: Trump's Campaign to Subvert the Election," *New York Times*, January 31, 2021, https://www.nytimes .com/2021/01/31/us/trump-election-lie.html.

24. Aaron Blake, "Trump's 'Big Lie' Was Bigger than Just a Stolen Election," *Washington Post*, February 12, 2021, https://www.washingtonpost.com /politics/2021/02/12/trumps-big-lie-was-bigger-than-just-stolen-election/.

25. Ryan Goodman, Mari Dugas, and Nicholas Tonckens, "Incitement

Timeline: Year of Trump's Actions Leading to the Attack on the Capitol," Just Security, January 11, 2020, https://www.justsecurity.org/74138/incitement-timeline-year-of-trumps-actions-leading-to-the-attack-on-the-capitol/.

26. William Cummings, Joey Garrison, and Jim Sergent, "By the Numbers: President Donald Trump's Failed Efforts to Overturn the Election," *USA Today*, January 6, 2020, https://www.usatoday.com/in-depth/news/politics/elections/2021/01/06/trumps-failed-efforts-overturn-election-numbers/4130307001/.

27. Goodman, et al., "Incitement Timeline."

28. Public Gathering Permit #21-0278, United States Department of Interior (January 5, 2021), on file with author.

29. Philip Bump, "The Central Flaw in Trump's Impeachment Defense: Without Trump's Advocacy and Falsehoods, There's Almost Certainly No Violence at the Capitol on Jan. 6," *Washington Post*, February 8, 2021, https://www.washingtonpost.com/politics/2021/02/08/central-flaw-trumps-impeachment-defense/.

30. Ibid.

31. Spencer S. Hsu, et al., "Self-styled Militia Members Planned on Storming the U.S. Capitol Days in Advance of Jan. 6 Attack, Court Documents Say," *Washington Post*, January 19, 2021, https://www.washingtonpost.com/local/legal-issues/conspiracy-oath-keeper-arrest-capitol-riot/2021/01/19/fb84877a-5a4f-11eb-8bcf-3877871c819d_story.html.

32. "Read Trump's Jan. 6 Speech, A Key Part of Impeachment Trial."

33. Ibid.

34. James Crowley, "Twitter Confirms It Halted 'Hang Mike Pence' as a Trending Topic," *Newsweek*, January 9, 2021, https://www.newsweek.com/twitter-stops-hang-mike-pence-trending-1560253.

35. "In re Impeachment of President Donald J. Trump. Trial Memorandum of the United States House of Representatives in the Impeachment Trial of President Donald J. Trump," 45–48, https://judiciary.house.gov/search/?q=Trial+Memorandum+of+the+United+States+House+of+Representatives+in+the+Impeachment+Trial+of+President+Donald+J.+Trump (last visited Feb. 15, 2021), internal citations omitted.

36. Ibid., 8.

37. Ibid., 7–10.

38. Rosalind S. Hilderman, et al., "On Cusp of Impeachment Trial, Court Documents Point to How Trump's Rhetoric Fueled Rioters who Attacked Capitol," *Washington Post*, February 7, 2021, https://www.washingtonpost.com/politics/trump-impeachment-incitement-rioters/2021/02/07/7a6f0c64-6701-11eb-8c64-9595888caa15_story.html.

39. Courtney Subramanian, "A Minute-by-Minute Timeline of Trump's Day as the Capitol Siege Unfolded on Jan. 6," *USA Today*, February 11, 2021, https://

www.usatoday.com/story/news/politics/2021/02/11/trump-impeachment-trial
-timeline-trump-actions-during-capitol-riot/6720727002/.

40. "McConnell on Impeachment: 'Disgraceful Dereliction' Cannot
Lead Senate to 'Defy Our Own Constitutional Guardrails,'" https://www
.republicanleader.senate.gov/newsroom/remarks/mcconnell-on-impeachment
-disgraceful-dereliction-cannot-lead-senate-to-defy-our-own-constitutional
-guardrails (last visited February 15, 2021).

9. STICKS AND STONES AND WORDS THAT HARM

1. Janine Anderson, "Westminster Group Discuss Fight Against Racism,"
Orange County (CA) *Register*, August 2, 1988, 15.

2. Greg Zoraya, "Ruling Could Affect Penalty for Convicted Cross-Burner,"
ibid., April 7, 1989, 33.

3. *United States v. Skillman*, 922 F.2d 1370, 1378 (9th Cir. 1991).

4. *Virginia v. Black.*

5. Ibid., 538 U.S. 343, 350.

6. Ibid.

7. Ibid., 352.

8. Ibid., 357.

9. Ibid., 391 (citing Brief for Petitioner at 26, *Virginia v. Black*, 538 U.S. 343
[2002]).

10. Ibid., 357.

11. *Chaplinsky v. New Hampshire*, 315 U.S. 568, 589 (1942).

12. Shawn F. Peters, "Re-hearing 'Fighting Words': *Chaplinsky v. New
Hampshire* in Retrospect," *Journal of Supreme Court History* 24 (1999): 282, 284.

13. Ibid., 286.

14. Ibid.

15. Ibid., 289.

16. Ibid.

17. *Chaplinsky v. New Hampshire*, 315 U.S. 568, 589 (1942).

18. Peters, "Re-hearing 'Fighting Words,'" 289.

19. Ibid., 292.

20. *Chaplinsky v. New Hampshire*, 315 U.S. 589.

21. Ibid., 572.

22. Ibid.

23. Shawn F. Peters, "Walter Chaplinsky," in Melvin I. Urofsky, ed., *100
Americans Making Constitutional History: A Biographical History* (Thousand Oaks,
CA: Sage, CQ Press, 2004), 34.

24. Clay Calvert, "Fighting Words in the Era of Texts, IMS and E-Mails: Can a
Disparaged Doctrine Be Resuscitated to Punish Cyber Bullies?" *DePaul Journal of
Art, Technology & Intellectual Property Law* 21 (2010): 1, 3.

25. See *Johnson v. Campbell*, 332 F.3d 199, 212 (3d Cir. 2003) and the cases cited therein.

26. *State v. Riley*, No. 2017AP97-CR, 2017 Wisc. App. LEXIS 890, at *1 (Wis. Ct. App. Nov. 16, 2017).

27. *Bible Believers v. Wayne County*, 805 F.3d 228 (6th Cir. 2015).

28. Ibid., 235.

29. Ibid., 238

30. Samuel Smith, "'Stoned' Street Preachers' Freedom of Speech Case to Be Reviewed by US Appeals Court," *Christian Post*, October 30, 2014, https://www .christianpost.com/news/stoned-street-preachers-freedom-of-speech-case-to-be -reviewed-by-us-appeals-court.html.

31. *Bible Believers v. Wayne County*, 805 F.3d 238.

32. Ibid., 244, 245, 246.

33. Ibid., 249.

34. *Chaplinsky v. New Hampshire*, 315 U.S. 568, 572 (1942).

35. *Wisconsin v. Mitchell*, 508 U.S. 476, 480 (1993).

36. David Margolick, "Test of a 'Hate Crime' Law Reaches Center Stage," *New York Times on the Web*, April 20, 1993, https://archive.nytimes.com/www.nytimes .com/library/national/race/042093race-ra.html.

37. Linda P. Campbell, "Lawyers Seek Line Separating Hate-Based Crimes, Free Speech," *Chicago Tribune*, April 19, 1993, https://www.chicagotribune.com /news/ct-xpm-1993-04-19-9304190107-story.html.

38. *Wisconsin v. Mitchell*, 480.

39. Ibid., 487.

40. Margolick, "Test of a 'Hate Crime' Law Reaches Center Stage."

41. See *State v. Drahota*, 788 N.W.2d 796, 804 (Neb. 2010).

42. *Elonis v. United States*, 135 S. Ct. 2001, 2006 (2015).

43. Ibid., 2008.

44. Ibid., 2011.

45. Ibid., 2001.

46. Abraham J. Rein, et al., "Elonis Facebook Case Has Life Beyond 2015 SCOTUS Decision," June 27, 2017, https://www.postschell.com/insights/elonis -facebook-case-life-beyond-scotus-decision.

47. "Anthony Elonis is Back in Jail on Federal Violation," *Lehigh Valley Regional News*, May 30, 2015, https://www.wfmz.com/news/area/lehighvalley/ anthony-elonis-is-back-in-jail-on-federal-violation/article_bc758b7c-03e0-5bf8 -a5de-35c8b1859d39.html.

10. WHAT THE #@*%! SCHOOL SPEECH, CAMPUS CODES, AND CANCEL CULTURE

1. *Skinner v. Railway Lab. Execs. Assn.*, 489 U.S. 602, 635 (1989).

2. *Cohen v. California*, 403 U.S. 15 (1971).

3. *Mahanoy Area School Dist. v. B.L.*, No. 20-255, slip op. (Sup. Ct. June 23, 2021), https://www.oyez.org/cases/2020/20-255 (last visited May 17, 2021).

4. *Tinker v. Des Moines Independent Community School Dist.*, 393 U.S. 503 (1969).

5. Ibid., 513.

6. Ibid., 508–509.

7. Ibid., 512.

8. *Bethel School Dist. No 403 v. Fraser*, 478 U.S. 675, 687 (1986).

9. 551 U.S. 393 (2007).

10. Ibid., 397.

11. *B.L. v. Mahanoy Area School Dist.*, 964 F.3d 170, 175–176 (3d Cir. 2020).

12. Ibid.

13. Brief for the Respondent, 4, *B.L. v. Mahanoy Area School Dist.*, 964 F.3d 170, 175–176 (3d Cir. 2020) No. 20-255 (https://www.scotusblog.com/case-files/cases /mahanoy-area-school-district-v-b-l/).

14. *Mahanoy Area School Dist. v. B.L.*

15. Brief for the Petitioner, 7, *B., Oyez Project*, https://www.scotusblog.com /2021/05/now-available-on-oyez-april-may-oral-argument-audio-aligned-with -the-transcripts/

16. *B.L. v. Mahanoy Area School Dist.*, 964 F.3d 190.

17. Brief for the Petitioner, *B.L. v. Mahanoy Area School Dist.*

18. *Mahanoy Area School District v. B.L.*

19. Ibid.

20. Ibid., 7.

21. Ibid.

22. Ibid., 9.

23. Ibid.

24. John E. Usalis, "Former Mahanoy Area Cheerleader has 'No Regrets' as Free Speech Battle Reaches US Supreme Court," *Republican & Herald* (Pottsville, PA), April 25, 2021, https://sports.yahoo.com/former-mahanoy-area-cheerleader -no-224900191.html.

25. Denisa R. Superville, "US. Supreme Court Rules for Cheerleader Who Posted Vulgar Snap," *EducationWeek*, June 23, 2021, https://www.edweek.org/ policy-politics/u-s-supreme-court-rules-for-student-on-regulation-of-off-campus -speech/2021/06.

26. Thomas L. McAllister, "Rules and Rights Colliding: Speech Codes and the First Amendment on College Campuses," *Tennessee Law Review* 59 (1992): 409, 410.

27. 721 F. Supp. 852 (E.D. Mich. 1989).

28. Ibid., 854–55.

29. Ibid., 856.

30. Ibid., 852 (internal quotes omitted).

31. See "Free Speech 101: The Assault on the First Amendment on College

Campuses: Before the S. Comm. on the Judiciary," 115th Congress (2017) (statement of Sen. Charles Grassley, Chairman of Senate Committee on the Judiciary), https://www.judiciary.senate.gov/meetings/free-speech-101-the -assault-on-the-first-amendment-on-college-campuses.

32. Kelly Sarabyn, "Free Speech at Private Universities," *Journal of Law and Education* 39 (2010):145, 159–60.

33. Clay Calvert, "College Campuses as First Amendment Combat Zones and Free-Speech Theatres of the Absurd: The High Price of Protecting Extremist Speakers for Shouting Matches and Insults," *First Amendment Law Review* 16 (2018): 454, 458.

34. Southern Poverty Law Center, "Richard Bertrand Spencer," https://www .splcenter.org/fighting-hate/extremist-files/individual/richard-bertrand-spencer -0 (last visited Sept. 13, 2020).

35. Anemona Hartocollis, "University of Florida Braces for Richard Spencer," *New York Times*, October 17, 2017, https://www.nytimes.com/2017/10/17/us /florida-richard-spencer.html.

36. Joe Heim, et al., "'Go Home, Spencer!' Protesters Disrupt White Nationalist's Speech at the University of Florida," *Washington Post*, October 18, 2017, https://www.washingtonpost.com/news/grade-point/wp/2017/10/18/uf/.

37. Calvert, "College Campuses as First Amendment Combat Zones and Free-Speech Theatres of the Absurd," 457.

38. *Pickering v. Board of Education*, 391 U.S. 563, 574 (1968).

11. PUBLIC SPACES

1. 394 U.S. 147, 152 (1969).

2. Harrison E. Salisbury, "Fear and Hatred Grip Birmingham," *New York Times*, April 12, 1960, 1.

3. Randall Kennedy, "*Walker v. City of Birmingham* Revisited," *Supreme Court Review* (2017): 313, 314.

4. Salisbury, "Fear and Hatred Grip Birmingham."

5. Ibid.

6. See "Birmingham Manifesto," in *Southern Christian Leadership Council Newsletter* 10 (July 1963), 2.

7. *Shuttlesworth v. City of Birmingham*, 394 U.S. 147, 149 (1969).

8. Salisbury, "Fear and Hatred Grip Birmingham."

9. Deborah Ann Roy, "The 1963 Good Friday Parade in Birmingham, Alabama: *Walker v. City of Birmingham* (1967) and *Shuttlesworth v. City of Birmingham* (1969)," *Journal of Supreme Court History* 38 (2013): 413, 415.

10. *Boyton v. Virginia*, 364 US 454 (1960); *Morgan v. Virginia*, 328 U.S. 373 (1946).

11. Melvin I. Urofsky, "*New York Times Co. v. Sullivan* as a Civil Rights Case," *Communication Law and Policy* 19 (2014): 157, 160.

12. William A. Nunnelly, *Bull Connor* (Tuscaloosa: University of Alabama Press, 1990), 164.

13. Martin Luther King Jr., "Letter from Birmingham Jail" (Stanford, CA: The Martin Luther King, Jr. Research and Education Institute, 1963), https://kinginstitute.stanford.edu/encyclopedia/letter-birmingham-jail.

14. Ibid.

15. Roy, "The 1963 Good Friday Parade in Birmingham, Alabama," 416.

16. Ibid., 418.

17. Jon Nordheimer, "Rev. Fred L. Shuttlesworth, an Elder Statesman for Civil Rights, Dies at 89," *New York Times*, October 5, 2011, https://www.nytimes.com/2011/10/06/us/rev-fred-l-shuttlesworth-civil-rights-leader-dies-at-89.html.

18. Ibid.

19. Ibid.

20. *Shuttlesworth v. City of Birmingham*, 394 U.S. 147, 150 (1969).

21. Roy, "The 1963 Good Friday Parade in Birmingham, Alabama," 421.

22. *Shuttlesworth v. City of Birmingham*, 180 So. 2d 114 (Ala. Crim. App. 1965).

23. *Shuttlesworth v. City of Birmingham*, 394 U.S. 164–65 n.1–2.

24. See *Hague v. C.I.O.*, 307 U.S. 496 (1939).

25. See *Cox v. New Hampshire*, 312 U.S. 569 (1941).

26. *Hill v. Colorado*, 530 U.S. 703, 710 n.7 (2000) (citations and internal quotes marks omitted).

27. Ibid.

28. Ibid., 788–89.

29. Ibid., 763–64.

30. Shira Schoenberg, "Anti-Abortion Plaintiff Eleanor McCullen Says Clinic Protests Are About 'Surrounding Women With Love,'" *MassLive*, January 7, 2019, https://www.masslive.com/politics/2014/06/anti-abortion_plaintiff_eleano.html.

31. Morris S. Thompson, "Marchers Descend on County that Progress Forgot," *Washington Post*, January 24, 1987, https://www.washingtonpost.com/archive/politics/1987/01/24/marchers-descend-on-county-that-progress-forgot/09cd8e25-984a-4182-8ef4-2e7b5129d67c/.

32. Dudley Clendinen, "Thousands in Civil Rights March Jeered by Crowd in Georgia Town," *New York Times*, January 25, 1987, 1.

33. *Forsyth County, Georgia v. Nationalist Movement*, 505 U.S. 123, 125 (1992).

34. Ibid., 126.

35. Ibid., 128.

36. Ibid., 136.

37. *Greer v. Spock*, 424 U.S. 828 (1976).

38. *Southeastern Promotions, Ltd. v. Conrad*, 420 U.S. 546 (1975).

39. Ibid., 549, n.4.

40. Ibid., 549.

41. Ibid., 555.

42. Ibid., 559 (citations omitted).

43. Andrew Cohen, "The Man Arrested for Praising Jesus," *The Marshall Project*, February 20, 2017, https://www.themarshallproject.org/2017/02/20/the-man-arrested-for-praising-jesus.

44. *Packingham v. North Carolina*, 137 S. Ct. 1730, 1733 (2017).

45. "Leading Cases, Constitutional Law: First Amendment—Freedom of Speech—Public Forum Doctrine—*Packingham v. North Carolina*," *Harvard Law Review* 131 (2017): 233.

46. Cohen, "The Man Arrested for Praising Jesus."

47. *Packingham v. North Carolina*, 137 S. Ct. 1737.

48. *Knight First Amendment Institute v. Trump*, 928 F.3d 226 (2d Cir. 2019).

49. Ibid., 231.

50. Ibid., 230.

51. *Widmar v. Vincent*, 454 U.S. 263 (1981).

52. *Justice for All v. Faulkner*, 410 F.3d 760 (2005).

53. *Widmar v. Vincent*, 454 U.S. 267 n.5.

54. *Axson-Flynn v. Johnson*, 356 F.3d 1277 (10th Cir. 2004).

55. *Wooley v. Maynard*, 430 U.S. 705 (1977).

56. *Axson-Flynn v. Johnson*, 356 F.3d 1285.

57. Ibid., 1290.

12. THE MESSAGE AND THE MEDIUM

1. John Culkin, "A Schoolman's Guide to Marshall McLuhan," *The Saturday Review*, March 18, 1967, available at https://www.unz.com/print/SaturdayRev-1967mar18-00051.

2. "The Rise and Fall of Pat Tornillo," *The Ledger*, August 30, 2003.

3. *Miami Herald Publishing Co. v. Tornillo*, 418 U.S. 241, 258 n.1 (1974).

4. Ibid., 251.

5. Ibid., 258.

6. Ibid., 260.

7. "The Rise and Fall of Pat Tornillo."

8. Ibid.

9. Vaishali Honawar, "Disgraced Union Leader Pat Tornillo Dies," *Education Week*, June 27, 2007, https://www.edweek.org/teaching-learning/disgraced-union-leader-pat-tornillo-dies/2007/06.

10. Ibid.

11. 395 U.S. 367 (1969).

12. *Miami Herald Publishing Co. v. Tornillo*, 418 U.S. 258.

13. *Red Lion Broadcasting Co., Inc. v. FCC*, 395 U.S. 367, 387 (1969).

14. Jennifer Graham, "No, Donald Trump Probably Won't Replace Rush Limbaugh. But Here's Who Might," *Deseret News* (Utah), March 8, 2021, https://www.deseret.com/indepth/2021/3/8/22298060/no-donald-trump

-probably-wont-replace-rush-limbaugh-but-heres-who-might-sean-hannity
-ben-shapiro.

15. John K. Wilson, *The Most Dangerous Man in America: Rush Limbaugh's Assault on Reason* (New York: MacMillan, 2011).

16. Jason Silverstein, "Rush Limbaugh Now Has a Presidential Medal of Freedom. Here Are Just 20 of the Outrageous Things He's Said," *CBS News*, February 6, 2020, https://www.cbsnews.com/news/rush-limbaugh-presidential-medal-of-freedom-state-of-the-union-outrageous-quotes/.

17. 47 U.S.C. para. 315.

18. Ibid., para. 312.

19. *FCC v. Pacifica Foundation*, 438 U.S. 726 (1978).

20. *Miller v. California*, 413 U.S. 15, 21 (1973).

21. *FCC v. Pacifica Foundation*, 438 U.S. 726.

22. "Industry Guidance on the Commission's Case Law Interpreting 18 U.S.C. para.1464 and Enforcement Policies Regarding Broadcast Indecency," para. 4, ibid., 730. See also chrome-extension: https://www.fcc.gov/document/industry-guidance-commissions-case-law-interpreting-18-usc.

23. *FCC v. Pacifica Foundation*, 438 U.S. 730.

24. Ibid., 748.

25. Ibid., 749.

26. *Turner Broadcasting System, Inc. v. FCC*, 512 U.S. 622, 637 (1994).

27. Sarah Warburg-Johnson, "Democracy in the Digital Age: Why the Equal Time Rule Should Be Abandoned," *N.Y.U. Annual Survey of American Law* 72 (2018): 275, 300–301.

28. *Reno v. ACLU*, 521 U.S. 844 (1997).

29. *Ashcroft v. ACLU*, 542 U.S. 656 (2004).

30. *Fields v. Twitter, Inc.*, 200 F. Supp. 3d 964 (N.D. Cal. 2016).

31. Ibid., 966.

32. Ibid., 967.

13. WHEN SPEECH OFFENDS

1. *485 U.S. 46, 51* (1988).

2. James E. Clayton, "Battle Over New Orleans Vice Arrays Stubborn DA Against Stubborn Judge: Orleans Feud Pits Stubborn Judge," *Washington Post and Times Herald*, February 10, 1963, A1.

3. Alecia P. Long, "The Garrison Tactics," *64 Parishes*, https://64parishes.org/the-garrison-tactics (last visited May 8, 2020).

4. James Savage, "Born on Bourbon Street: Jim Garrison's French Quarter Fracas and the Shady Origins of a First Amendment Milestone, 1962–1964," *Louisiana History* 44 (2008): 136.

5. Clayton, "Battle Over New Orleans Vice Arrays Stubborn DA Against Stubborn Judge."

6. James E. Clayton, "District Attorney Convicted of Libel Takes Case Against Jurists to Public," *Washington Post and Times Herald*, February 11, 1963, A1.

7. Ibid.

8. Savage, "Born on Bourbon Street."

9. Ibid., 157–58.

10. Ibid., 159.

11. 376 U.S. 254 (1964).

12. *Garrison v. Louisiana*, 379 U.S. 64 (1964).

13. *New York Times v. Sullivan*, 376 U.S. 257–58 (internal quotes omitted).

14. Ibid.

15. Ibid., 266.

16. Ibid., 270.

17. Ibid., 268.

18. Ibid., 269.

19. https://www.law.cornell.edu/wex/negligence.

20. *St. Amant v. Thompson*, 390 U.S. 727, 731 (1968).

21. *Greenbelt Co-Operative Publishing Assn., Inc. v. Bresler*, 398 U.S. 6 (1970).

22. *Harte-Hanks Communications, Inc. v. Connaughton*, 491 U.S. 657 (1989).

23. Savage, "Born on Bourbon Street," 160.

24. Complaint, *US Dominion, Inc. v. Giuliani*, 2021 WL 242155 (D.C. Cir. Jan. 25, 2021) (No. 1:21-cv-00213); Complaint, *US Dominion, Inc. v. Powell*, 2021 WL 73903 (D.C. Cir. Jan. 8, 2021) (No. 1:21-cv-000040-CJN).

25. *Smartmatic USA Corp. v. Fox Corporation et al.*, https://www.smartmatic .com/us/media/article/smartmatic-files-27-billion-defamation-lawsuit-against -fox-corporation/. Supreme Court of the State of New York, County of New York (last visited Feb.18, 2021).

26. *US Dominion Inc. v Giuliani*, 106 para. 84.

27. Ibid., 76 para. 178 (a).

28. Ibid.

29. Ibid., 92 para. 178 (cc).

30. Ibid., 105 para. 182.

31. Ibid., 56 para. 135.

32. *Smartmatic USA Corp. v Fox Corporation et al.*

33. See *Gertz v. Robert Welch, Inc.*, 418 U.S. 323 (1974).

34. *Milkovich v. Lorain Journal Co.*, 497 U.S. 1 (1990).

35. *Florida Star v. B.J.F.*, 491 U.S. 109 (1989).

36. *Gertz v. Robert Welch, Inc.*, 418 U.S. 323, 345 (1974).

37. *Wolston v. Reader's Digest Assn., Inc.*, 443 U.S. 157, 167–168 (1979).

38. Rebecca Phillips, "Comment: Constitutional Protection for Nonmedia Defendants: Should There be a Distinction Between You and Larry King?" *Campbell Law Review* 33 (2010): 173.

39. Joshua Azriel and Charles Mayo, "Fifty Years after *New York Times Co. v. Sullivan* and Forty Years after *Gertz v. Welch*: How these Twentieth-Century

Supreme Court Rulings Impact Twenty-First Century Online Social Media Libel Claims," *Boston University Journal of Science & Technology Law* 20 (2014): 191.

40. 93 U.S. 503 (1969).

41. *United States v. Alvarez*, 567 U.S. 709, 714 (2012).

42. 32 C.F.R. para. 578.4(a) (2002).

43. 18 U.S.C. para. 704(b) (2006).

44. *United States Courts*, "Facts and Case Summary—*U.S. v. Alvarez*," https://www.uscourts.gov/educational-resources/educational-activities/facts-and-case-summary-us-v-alvarez (last visited Oct. 4, 2020).

45. 567 U.S. 709 (2012).

46. *United States v. Alvarez*, 567 U.S. 716, 719.

47. Ibid., 718.

48. 18 U.S.C. para. 704 (Supp. I).

49. See *Saturday Night Live*, "Sarah Palin and Hillary Address the Nation—SNL," YouTube, September 13, 2013, https://www.youtube.com/watch?v=vSOLz1YBFG0.

50. See "Jerry Falwell Talks About His First Time," *Hustler*, https://i2.wp.com/boingboing.net/images/falwell-hustler-first-time.jpg (last visited May 8, 2020).

51. *Hustler Magazine Inc. v. Falwell*, 485 U.S. 46 (1988).

52. 413 U.S. 15 (1973).

53. Bob Woodward and Scott Armstrong, *The Brethren: Inside the Supreme Court* (New York: Simon and Schuster, 1979), 239.

54. *Miller v. California*, 413 U.S. 15 (1973).

55. Ibid., 24.

56. Geoffrey R. Stone, "Sex and the First Amendment: The Long and Winding History of Obscenity Law," *First Amendment Law Review* 17 (2008): 134 (internal citations omitted).

57. *New York v. Ferber*, 458 U.S. 747 (1982).

58. *Osborne v. Ohio*, 495 U.S. 103 (1990).

14. THE LANGUAGE OF MONEY

1. *McCutcheon v. FEC*, 572 U.S. 185, 185 (2014).

2. *Buckley v. Valeo*, 424 U.S. 1 (1976).

3. *Citizens United v. FEC*, 558 U.S. 310, 325 (2010).

4. *FEC v. National Conservative Political Action Committee*, 470 U.S. 480, 497 (1985).

5. *Citizens United v. FEC*, 558 U.S. 310.

6. Ibid., 325.

7. Ibid., 317–18.

8. Ibid., 325.

9. Ibid., 323.

10. Ibid.

11. Ibid., 326.

12. Karen Tumulty, "Karl Rove and His Super PAC Vow to Press On," *Washington Post*, November 10, 2012, https://www.washingtonpost.com/politics /karl-rove-and-his-super-pac-vow-to-press-on/2012/11/10/19ed28ea-2a96-11e2 -b4e0-346287b7e56c_story.html.

13. Bill Allison et al., "Tracking the 2016 Presidential Money Race," *Bloomberg*, December 9, 2016, https://www.bloomberg.com/politics/graphics/2016 -presidential-campaign-fundraising/.

14. *McCutcheon v. FEC*, 572 U.S. 185.

15. Contribution limits for 2019–2020, FEC (Feb. 7, 2019), https://www.fec .gov/updates/contribution-limits-2019-2020/.

16. *Buckley v. Valeo*, 424 U.S. 65 (citing *United States v. O'Brien*, 391 U.S. 367, 377 n.76 [1968]).

17. *McIntyre v. Ohio Elections Commission*, 514 U.S. 334 (1995).

18. S. Res. 1989, 115th Cong. (2017–2018) (enacted), https://www.warner .senate.gov/public/index.cfm/the-honest-ads-act.

19. *Citizens United v. FEC*, 558 U.S. 310, 353 (citations and internal quotation marks omitted).

20. Ibid., at 355 (citations and internal quotation marks omitted).

21. *Stand With Workers*, "Who is Mark Janus?" https://standwithworkers.org/ mark-janus.

22. 138 S. Ct. 2448 (2018).

23. Ibid., 2463.

24. Ibid., 2464.

25. Ibid., 2488.

26. Ibid., 2492.

27. Elizabeth Bruenig, Opinion, "Workers Are Free at Last—to Sink," *Washington Post*, June 28, 2008, https://www.washingtonpost.com/opinions/ workers-are-free-at-last--to-sink/2018/06/28/fec6a558-7a37-11e8-aeee -4d04c8ac6158_story.html.

28. Sarah Mansur, "SCOTUS Declines to Hear Janus' Lawsuit Seeking Union Dues Reimbursement," *The State-Journal Register* (Springfield, IL), January 27, 2021, https://www.sj-r.com/story/news/2021/01/27/scotus-declines-hear-janus -lawsuit-seeking-union-dues-reimbursement/4277024001/.

29. *Pleasant Grove City v. Summum*, 555 U.S. 460, 468 (2009).

30. *Central Hudson Gas and Electric Corp. v. Public Service Commission of New York*, 447 U.S. 557 (1980).

31. *44 Liquormart Inc. v. Rhode Island*, 517 U.S. 484, 492 (1996).

32. *Virginia State Board of Pharmacy v. Virginia Citizens Consumer Council, Inc.*, 425 U.S. 748, 765 (1976).

15. WHEN SPEECH AND FAITH COLLIDE

1. *Cutter v. Wilkinson*, 544 U.S. 709, 710 (2005).
2. *Everson v. Board of Education*, 330 U.S. 1 (1947).
3. *Lynch v. Donnelly*, 465 U.S. 668, 678 (1984).
4. *Van Orden v. Perry*, 545 U.S. 677 (2005).
5. *McCreary County v. American Civil Liberties Union of Ky.*, 545 U.S. 844.
6. *McCreary County v. American Civil Liberties Union of Ky.*, 545 U.S. 885–912.
7. *Everson v. Board of Education*, 330 U.S. 1.
8. *Zelman v Simmons-Harris*, 536 U.S. 639 (2002).
9. *Lemon v. Kurtzman*, 403 U.S. 602 (1971).
10. *Engel v. Vitale*, 370 U.S. 421 (1962).
11. *Lee v. Weisman*, 505 U.S. 577 (1992).
12. Ibid., 585.
13. Ibid., 596.
14. Ibid., 599.
15. Ibid., 593.
16. *Edwards v. Aguillard*, 482 U.S. 578, 588 (1987).
17. *Braunfeld v. Brown*, 366 U.S. 599, 607 (1961).
18. *Wisconsin v. Yoder*, 406 U.S. 205 (1972).
19. Ibid., 211.
20. *Torcaso v. Watkins*, 367 U.S. 488 (1961).
21. *Church of the Lukumi Babalu Aye, Inc. v. Hialeah*, 508 U.S. 520, 531 (1993).
22. *Locke v. Davey*, 540 U.S. 712 (2004).
23. Ibid., 733.
24. *Masterpiece Cakeshop, Ltd. v. Colorado Civil Rights Commission*, 138 S. Ct. 1719 (2018).
25. Ibid., 1745 (Thomas, J., concurring).
26. *Obergefell v. Hodges*, 576 U.S. 644 (2015).
27. *Masterpiece Cakeshop, Ltd. v. Colorado Civil Rights Commission*, 138 S. Ct. 1747–48 (Thomas, J., concurring) (citations and internal quotation marks omitted).
28. *Hurley v. Irish American Gay, Lesbian and Bisexual Group of Boston, Inc.*, 515 U.S. 557, 560 (1995).
29. Ibid., 568–69 (citations and quotation marks omitted).
30. Ibid., 573 (internal quotes and citations omitted).
31. *Masterpiece Cakeshop, Ltd. v. Colorado Civil Rights Commission*, 138 S. Ct. 1729.
32. Ibid.
33. David Harsanyi, "Why Jack Phillips Matters," *National Review*, April 15, 2020, https://www.nationalreview.com/2020/04/why-jack-phillips-matters/.

CONCLUSION

1. Frederick Schauer, "The Boundaries of the First Amendment: A Preliminary Exploration of Constitutional Salience," *Harvard Law Review* 117 (2004): 1765, 1787.

2. *American Booksellers Assn. v. Hudnut*, 771F.2d 323, 328 (7th Cir. 1985) *summarily affirmed*, 475 U.S. 1001 (1986) (citations and internal quotation marks omitted).

SUGGESTIONS FOR FURTHER READING

Abrams, Floyd. *The Soul of the First Amendment.* New Haven, CT: Yale University Press, 2017.

———. *Speaking Freely: Trials of the First Amendment.* New York: Penguin Books, 2006.

Broadwater, Jeff. *George Mason: Forgotten Founder.* Chapel Hill: University of North Carolina Press, 2006.

Fish, Stanley. *The First: How to Think About Hate Speech, Campus Speech, Religious Speech, Fake News, Post-Truth, and Donald Trump.* New York: Atria/One Signal 2020.

———. *There's No Such Thing as Free Speech: And It's a Good Thing, Too.* Oxford: Oxford University Press, 1994.

Lewis, Anthony. *Freedom for the Thought That We Hate: A Biography of the First Amendment.* New York: Basic Books, 2008.

———. *Make No Law: The Sullivan Case and the First Amendment.* New York: Vintage Books, 1992.

Parker, Richard, ed. *Free Speech on Trial: Communication Perspectives on Landmark Supreme Court Decisions.* Birmingham: University of Alabama Press, 2003.

Strossen, Nadine. *HATE: Why We Should Resist it With Free Speech, Not Censorship.* Oxford: Oxford University Press, 2018.

Brandeis Series in Law and Society

ROSALIND KABRHEL, J.D. AND DANIEL BREEN, J.D., EDITORS

Justice Louis D. Brandeis once said that "if we desire respect for the law, we must first make the law respectable." For Justice Brandeis, making the law "respectable" meant making it work in the interests of humankind, as a help rather than a hindrance in the manifold struggles of persons of all backgrounds to achieve justice. In that spirit, the Law and Society Series publishes works that take interdisciplinary approaches to law, drawing richly from the social sciences, and humanities, with a view towards shedding critical light upon the variety of ways in which legal rules, and the institutions that enforce them, affect our lives. Intended for practitioners, academics, students, and the interested general public, this series will feature titles that contribute robustly to contemporary debates about law and legal reform, all with a view towards adding to efforts of all sorts to make the law "respectable."

For a complete list of books that are available in the series,
visit brandeisuniversitypress.com

Pain and Shock in America: Politics, Advocacy, and the
   Controversial Treatment of People with Disabilities
   Jan A. Nisbet

When Freedom Speaks:
   The Boundaries and the Boundlessness of Our First Amendment Right
   Lynn Greenky

Education Behind the Wall: Why and How We Teach College in Prison
   Mneesha Gellman